Depression
and Narrative

Depression and Narrative

Telling the Dark

Edited by
Hilary Clark

Published by State University of New York Press, Albany

Printed in the United States of America

For information, contact State University of New York Press, Albany, NY
www.sunypress.edu

Production by Diane Ganeles
Marketing by Michael Campochiaro

Library of Congress Cataloging-in-Publication Data

Depression and narrative : telling the dark / [edited by] Hilary Clark.
        p. cm.
    Includes bibliographical references and index.
    ISBN: 978-0-7914-7569-0 (hardcover : alk. paper)
    ISBN: 978-0-7914-7570-6 (pbk. : alk. paper)   1. Melancholy in literature.
2. Depression, Mental, in literature.   3. Mental illness in literature   I. Clark, Hilary
Anne, 1955–

PN56.M4D47   2008
889'.933561—dc22

                                                                    · 2007047994

                            10 9 8 7 6 5 4 3 2 1

Contents

I. *Negotiating Illness Identity and Stigma*

II. Gender and Depression

III. Depression across the Media

IV. Literary Therapies

V. Depression and the Limits of Narrative

Illustrations

Acknowledgments

The idea for this book began in the experience of teaching Women, Depression, and Writing, a Women's and Gender Studies course at the University of Saskatchewan. I would like to thank the students in successive versions of this course for their feedback and ideas, and the Women's and Gender Studies Department for continuing to support the course, despite chronically limited resources.

I thank all the contributors for their wonderful work: their essays show that the concept of depression and narrative can be imagined and realized in many ways and many different contexts. Finally, my thanks to Henry Sussman for initially encouraging me to bring the project to State University of New York Press, and to James Peltz for welcoming me on board once again.

Introduction

Depression and Narrative

Hilary Clark

"I did not think such anguish possible," William Styron writes of the depression that almost killed him.[1] It is likely each sufferer has had some version of this thought. Worldwide, at any time, millions upon millions are enduring depression.[2] From the contours of private anguish to psychiatric, cultural, and epidemiological accounts, there is an urge to give an account(ing) of depression. As a "cultural reference point," especially with the surge in memoirs since the 1990s,[3] depression is as ubiquitous an object of lay and professional interest now as melancholy was over the centuries.[4] However, even with depression frequently in the media and with new books and memoirs on the subject appearing all the time,[5] it is still associated with stigma—an anguish added to anguish.

Why another book on depression? I would say that there can never be enough visibility for this illness[6] or condition whose stigma causes the sufferer to dissemble and "pass," forgoing needed treatment, or to withdraw from others in shame—a condition misrepresented by myths and stereotypes that inevitably color, and cover, our understanding. Why, then, depression and *narrative*? Certainly poets such as John Keats and Jane Kenyon have addressed melancholy in lyric, seeking to understand "the bile of desolation" that darkened their lives.[7] As well, innumerable papers on depression and bipolar disorder appear each year in the psychiatric and psychopharmacological fields, discourses their authors would be loath to describe as narratives. So what does narrative add to the conversation—to our knowledge—about depression?

For some, this question does not need to be asked. Across a number of disciplines today, narrative is seen as central in the constitution of

1

identity and culture. Oliver Sacks has written that "each of us constructs and lives a 'narrative' and . . . this narrative is us, our identities."[8] According to this argument for the centrality of narrative in identity formation, one can know oneself as a self only within the context of a (life) narrative. A person who has had an episode of depression might construct the following story of himself or herself: I was a happy child, but as a teenager I began suffering from anxiety attacks and long periods of sadness, and then I had my first episode of clinical depression as a young adult. Or a chronic sufferer might tell this story: I was abused as a child and my mother died when I was twelve, and soon afterward I had my first breakdown, and depression has plagued me since then. The narrative of the self is a (re)telling or plotting—establishing relations, causes and effects—of events that, in reality, simply happen one after another.[9] One cannot feel well one day, numb and oppressed the next, suicidal after a few months have elapsed, hyperenergetic and driven to talk and flirt and drive up one's credit card after a few more months, then "normal" again one day, without seeking a narrative explanation—the cycle of bipolar disorder, for instance, or the Christian narrative of sin, repentance, and redemption—in order to make sense of it all, to trace a single self through all these changes.

Jerome Bruner argues that the self is a story, "a product of our telling and not some essence"; stories "impose a structure, a compelling reality on what we experience."[10] Narratives mend the "breach in . . . ordinariness" (the latter itself involving stories of what can be expected, day after day), the breach that occurs, say, when one falls seriously ill or loses a family member to suicide; according to Bruner, narratives help one "to cope with it, . . . get things back on a familiar track."[11] In this view, narratives stitch up the wounds resulting from traumatic events or simply unexpected change. Such views on the omnipresence of narratives, shaping our experience and our sense of who we are, can be found across a number of disciplines today.[12] Families and cultures, too, are seen as products of stories told and retold—stories sometimes generative, sometimes stultifying or even destructive.

For some, however, the question "Why narrative?" *does* need to be asked. Philosopher Galen Strawson has recently questioned what he terms the "narrativist orthodoxy." He suggests that while there are many people "who are indeed intensely narrative . . . in their sense of life and self," there are others, "non-narrators," whose lives develop more like poems, who are not given to "storying"; and there are "mixed cases" in between.[13] This dissenting position has been acknowledged by James Phelan, editor of the journal *Narrative*, who concedes that such dissent offers a corrective to "narrative imperialism," addressing the "blind spots" of those who make "unsustainable extravagant claims" of the centrality of narrative in understanding identity.[14]

This debate between supporters of and dissenters against the narrative identity model might seem tangential to the concerns of a volume bearing the title *Depression and Narrative*. But it is an important context, I think, inasmuch as any reflection on depression and narrative—on narratives of depression, depression as a narrative—must engage with scholarship on life writing and particularly autopathography. Here, there is largely agreement on the centrality of narrative in (re)constructing a self and a life within or after illness. Writers such as Arthur Frank, David Karp, G. Thomas Couser, Anne Hunsaker Hawkins, Kathryn Montgomery, Arthur Kleinman, Hilde Lindemann Nelson[15]—working in and across the fields of sociology, social psychology, literary studies, medical humanities, anthropology, philosophy—all, in various ways, emphasize the preeminence of narratives (cultural, autobiographical) in shaping both the experience of illness and discourse about illness, indeed shaping professional understanding, medical knowledge itself. The same holds in the fields of disability studies and trauma studies, which, like illness studies, have burgeoned in the last twenty years or so[16]—all within a general trend in scholarship toward accepting the validity of personal narrative, both written and oral, as a source of knowledge. One can now read scholarship incorporating—indeed, building on—the author's personal narrative of illness: for instance, Arthur Frank's *At the Will of the Body* and David Karp's *Speaking of Sadness* are exemplary scholarly works taking personal experience as a foundation for analyzing the narratives associated with cancer and depression, respectively. What is notable about the scholarship on narrative and illness up until now, however, is that it has largely addressed physical illnesses like cancer and AIDS;[17] Karp and others who have written on mental illness, culture, and narrative are arguably in the minority,[18] and this volume seeks to contribute to the redressing of this imbalance.

It is argued, then, that we should listen to personal narratives of illness and disability—really attending to them on their own merits, as opposed to using them in order to come to diagnoses and impose regimes of treatment—because such narratives give voice to the ill, the traumatized, and the disabled, those trying to make sense of catastrophic interruptions or shifts in their lives, and help them navigate the bewildering, impersonal context of medical diagnosis and treatment. As Hawkins puts it, the pathography "restores the person ignored or canceled out in the medical enterprise . . . places that person at the very center. . . . [and] gives that ill person a voice."[19]

From the perspective of the ill, disabled, and/or traumatized subject, then, taking up narrative is seen by many to be empowering, as it can be for cultures at traumatic junctures such as wars and natural disasters. However, there is an obverse side to this linking of narrative and identity: while telling one's story, bearing witness, can be linked with enhanced agency, it is also the case that the stories one tells are never entirely one's own. The poststructuralist view that identity and knowledge are socially constructed by dominant narratives can lead to the more skeptical conclusion that personal narratives—even the most heartfelt personal narratives of depression posted anonymously online—are always already ideological, shaped by myths and metaphors that, while they may vary from culture to culture and over time, have remarkable sticking power. Susan Sontag made this point about metaphorical constructions of tuberculosis, cancer and AIDS, arguing that these support "the excommunicating and stigmatizing of the ill"; in her view these constructions can and should be resisted, the ideal being "to detach [illness] from these meanings."[20] Not so easy, however: in telling the story of cancer (in obituaries, for instance), one slips inevitably into battle mode, and every reader will understand. If one avoids the valiant battle, the story is no longer so readable or reassuring.

In telling the story of depression, other myths and metaphors prevail. Except in cases of suicide, depression is not fatal or only indirectly so: thus the teller will often draw on the quest or journey narrative, which organizes the real experience of depression (as it does that of other illnesses) into a story of trials, helpers, ogres, or sorcerers (often psychiatrists offering meds), and a return as a subdued but wiser person. These shaping myths are just about impossible to escape: as Fee puts it, "discourse is appropriated and lived out at intimate levels, [and] the deepest realms of somatic sensation and psychological suffering are intertwined with the technologies, knowledges, and stories of culture."[21] More than healing the self or bearing witness, these stories reproduce a dominant order that emphasizes certain identities (healthy, or physically ill) and marginalizes others (mentally ill). The experience of depression will be formulated by means of these stories unless the teller consciously "struggle[s] for rhetorical ownership of the illness."[22] It is doubtful whether this struggle can be won. In this view of narrative and illness identity, then, narratives can mystify; rather than empowering the self, they offer only the illusion of agency.

Another way of approaching narrative is to emphasize its limits—even its failure—in truly conveying suffering, especially that associated with personal and historical trauma. Here Strawson's skepticism is helpful: not all experience can be formulated in narrative form. Further, at traumatic extremes experience can be narrated only through a kind of aesthetic violation. "Transforming is what art does," Susan Sontag asserts of photography conveying the horrors of war,[23] and narrative also involves the aesthetic transformation of suffering. Claude Lanzmann has suggested that the drive to tell and make sense of the Shoah is in itself a form of traumatic violation.[24] That narrative has limits—should have limits—is an ethical issue, one that must be acknowledged, I think, in any book addressing the subject of depression and narrative.[25]

There is also a limit to what the reader will take in. What Sontag says of war photographs can be said, as well, of mental illness and trauma narratives: the audience may be overwhelmed and turn away: "Compassion is an unstable emotion. . . . The question is what to do with the feelings that have been aroused, the knowledge that has been communicated."[26] Some narratives are almost unreadable: they risk repelling the reader, who fears, via a process of emotional contagion, going under in turn.[27]

Despite these limits, the authors in this volume are very much concerned with the possibilities and the problems of narrative—its kinds, contexts, motives, strategies, effects—in representing and interpreting depression (or bipolar disorder, or "madness"). Like those who work on physical illness and narrative, the authors in this volume work within (and often across) a range of disciplines, including social work, education, psychology, cultural and media studies, gender studies, literary studies, rhetoric, and philosophy. Particular issues recur in the essays, issues that come up generally in discussions of depression: its contested causes; its gendering; the shifts, ruptures, and adjustments in identity that it entails; the problems of communication and representation, the associated stigma and shame. The essays in this volume are grouped around some of these issues, and draw variously upon the perspectives on narrative identified in the first part of this introduction.

The five chapters in the first part, "Negotiating Illness Identity and Stigma," in different ways address the fact that a diagnosis of depression confers a particular identity, one that is stigmatized to a greater or lesser degree. These essays look at some ways in which sufferers construct their identities and lives (past, present, and future) so as to defend themselves against stigma and shame. In "My Symptoms, Myself," Jennifer Radden looks at two ways in which narrators of first-person illness memoirs construct the relation between personal identity and disorienting symptoms (such as delusions). These strategies she terms "symptom alienating" and "symptom integrating": in the former, symptoms "are depicted as emanating from alien, sometimes diabolical, sources of agency outside the self," whereas in the latter, "narrators 'identify with' their symptoms," accepting them as part of their identity. Radden traces these two models, and the philosophical issues they raise, through a range of (Western) mental illness narratives from the fifteenth century to the present. In "The Language of Madness," Debra Beilke, like Radden, focuses on the manner in which the sufferer interprets disturbing symptoms that threaten the integrity of the self. Beilke identifies strategies similar to Radden's, but she draws different conclusions about them. Focusing on recent memoirs by Kay Redfield Jamison and Kate Millett, Beilke suggests that Jamison distinguishes between her symptoms and her core self, seeing her symptoms as an "outside force" alien to this core, and so is able to live with the diagnosis of manic depression. On the other hand, Millett makes no such distinction between symptoms and self; thus she must refuse to accept the diagnosis of manic depression, because to do so would be to see her self as "inherently flawed."

In "Winter Tales," Brenda Dyer looks more directly at depression narratives as such, focusing on the myths by means of which one recounts depression and constructs an identity as a depressed person. Drawing on Northrop Frye's categorization, in *Anatomy of Criticism*, of archetypal story-types—comedy, tragedy, romance, and satire/irony—Dyer explores the particular attraction that comic (recovery) and romance (quest) plots have for writers of recent depression memoirs. While the comic plot allows one to imagine a self restored to health, a "happy ending" without further symptoms, the romance plot is more realistic for those with chronic depression who must find ways of acknowledging and living with their condition.

Picking up on this issue of the narrative and interpretive strategies by which one constructs a mental illness identity, Frederick White and I examine further how sufferers manage the shame and stigma associated with such an identity. In "'Repenting Prodigal,'" I look at poet William Cowper's eighteenth-century memoir of madness, particularly his use of a "comic" conversion plot that interprets his experience of delusions and suicidal despair as a necessary stage in a return to God. As Radden would say, he alienates his symptoms, seeing them as visited on him by Satan and God. In this way he seeks to flee the shame of madness. Similarly, White traces the interpretive strategies by which, in his early diaries of the 1890s, the Russian writer Leonid Andreev tries to make sense of his ongoing struggle with depression. Looking outward to failed romances and the meaninglessness of life, and inward to a flawed self, he constructs versions of his experience that serve as the basis for his literary works.

This issue of how one interprets and constructs mental illness identities in narrative is taken up, in one form or another, in most of the essays in this volume. However, the chapters in the second part, "Gender and Depression," focus more on the uses of narrative for depressed women, and particularly the ways in which certain gendered narratives shape the therapeutic culture. In "Storying Sadness," Suzanne England, Carol Ganzer, and Carol Tosone suggest that one must examine women's own accounts of depression if one is to see beyond "the grand medical-psychiatric narrative" and recognize the sufferer's experience. The authors focus on common issues in women's depression—body image, the father-and-daughter relationship, the imbalance of power in marriage—in the work of poets Sylvia Plath and Louise Glück, and memoirist Tracy Thompson. The authors assume, rightly I think, that a poetic oeuvre traces a life narrative as much as a memoir does.

Women's depression and addiction have different cultural meanings, argues Joanne Muzak in her essay "'Addiction got me what I needed'": the female addict is taken more seriously, is seen as having a "real" and treatable disease, whereas the depressed woman "occupies a more ambiguous position." In the memoirs of Elizabeth Wurtzel, Muzak shows how addiction comes to "subsume" depression, presumably because addiction allows her to interpret and present her chronic suffering as a "real" problem. Wurtzel's personal narratives, like many others, demonstrate the impact of conflicting cultural narratives. Kimberly Emmons shows this conflict, too, in "Narrating the Emotional Woman," arguing that the gendered commonplace of the "emotional woman" shapes not only official discourse on depression but also the stories women offer to each other in exploring their common suffering. In mental health pamphlets on women and depression, Emmons traces the commonplace of feminine emotional excess and instability; and listening to depressed women, she concludes that such ideas are taken up by women in interpreting their own experiences of depression. In "Fact Sheets as Gendered Narratives of Depression," Linda McMullen does a similar exercise in a Canadian context, analyzing online "fact sheets" on postpartum depression and indicating the narratives of individual responsibility (that is, maternal blame) that underwrite the "facts." Looking in turn at personal narratives by women, McMullen concludes that, left to themselves, women see their suffering as brought about by social factors such as the isolation of new mothers and lack of family support. Interestingly, while Emmons sees women's personal narratives as ultimately incorporating cultural ones, McMullen sees the former as (at least potentially) resisting and correcting the latter.

What happens when narratives of depression fill internet blogs and discussion boards, and draw audiences to Hollywood movies and to TV? The authors in the third part, "Depression across the Media," look at what the different media bring to these stories. In "A Dark Web," Kiki Benzon suggests that internet publication can convey "the cognitive shifts and fissures" of depressive and manic thinking in a way that print publication cannot. On the internet, everyone can be an author; while the narratives vary wildly in quality, the "multitudinous narrative of depression" that goes on from day to day is an organic "cultural narrative" that, while it incorporates official constructions of causes, therapies, and so on, is much more than these. In a similar manner, in her essay "A Meditation on Depression, Time, and Narrative Peregrination in the Film *The Hours*," Diane Wiener sees the particular medium of film—with its possibilities for cutting and layering and interweaving different stories—as realizing the special temporality of depression, whose narrative is not linear but interrupted and wandering. The film *The Hours*, Wiener argues, offers a layered narrative of three women's experiences of depression that "complicates" linear narratives of cure and the regaining of one's former life.

In "Therapy Culture and TV," Deborah Staines takes on the depressed mobster Tony Soprano, showing how the serial medium of the TV drama, in *The Sopranos*, can convey the seriality of psychiatric therapy itself, a complex "episodic narrative—a story about the experience of depression—over time." After Freud, therapy has become so much a part of the Western cultural narrative that audiences watching *The Sopranos* are already, in their "psychologized and medicalized" existence, attuned to Tony Soprano's serial depression and therapy.

In part 4, "Literary Therapies," Andrew Schonebaum and Mark Clark take up the issue of therapeutic effect touched upon by earlier essays, here particularly focusing on therapy for the reader. In "For the Relief of Melancholy," Schonebaum explains how the early Chinese novel presented itself as preventing melancholy in the reader, or mitigating symptoms, by representing melancholy characters, particularly frail young women, as models of an emotional excess to be avoided. As with any medicine, the dose has to be just right: ingesting too much of this literary antidepressant could make the reader even more ill; yet to be capable of healing, the novel must be potentially contagious. In Clark's "Manic-Depressive Narration," Coleridge's *The Rime of the Ancient Mariner* is likewise presented as a kind of medicine for the reader—a devastating medicine. Clark argues that when the Wedding Guest is forced to listen to the Mariner's tale, he is caught up in the dynamics of manic-depressive thinking; through this process he sees his own world, its social hierarchies and rituals, from the Mariner's scorching perspective. Further, like the Wedding Guest, the reader of Coleridge's poem cannot remain detached but is manipulated into a "deeply empathic" understanding of the perspective of the manic other.

This volume comes to a close, in part 5, "Depression and the Limits of Narrative," with two chapters that treat the connection between trauma and depression, and how these manifest themselves in narrative symptoms of fragmentation, ambiguous perspective and temporality, altered syntax, and so on. In Geoffrey Hartman's view, figurative language itself exemplifies the "perpetual troping of [a traumatic event] by the bypassed or severely split (dissociated) psyche."[28] It seems that there is a limit to what narrative can tell—or tell via conventional means—about traumatized suffering. Yet the need to tell persists. In "Writing Self/Delusion," Sophie Blanch looks at Emily Holmes Coleman's *The Shutter of Snow*, her fictionalized memoir of postpartum depression, as an example of "scriptotherapy":[29] an attempt to write herself free of the horrors of her hospitalization for postpartum depression. However, the wounds do not heal so much as insist in the form and language of the narrative. This insistence of suffering in narrative form itself is also the subject of the final chapter, Eluned Summers-Bremner's "Depressing Books," on W. G. Sebald's haunting novels, particularly *The Rings of Saturn*. The author shows how its "circular, accretive structure"—

accompanying a mood of deep melancholy without an obvious or single cause—suggests the insistence of a traumatic past, a suffering both personal and historical. Like Clark on the reader of Coleridge's *Rime*, Summers-Bremner argues that the reader of Sebald comes to "inhabit" the narrator's melancholy perspective and gains new insight into the "defect in the human program," the trauma at the heart of human subjectivity and history. Narrative can convey this wound—indirectly, and marked by the strain—but it cannot heal it. Ethically, in the context of human suffering, narrative is most authentic as it approaches, or reaches, its limits.

Notes

1. Styron, *Darkness Visible*, 63. Styron died of old age in November 2006.

2. See World Health Organization, *Investing in Mental Health* (2003): "Today, about 450 million people suffer from a mental or behavioural disorder. According to WHO's Global Burden of Disease 2001, 33% of the years lived with disability (YLD) are due to neuropsychiatric disorders. . . . Unipolar depressive disorders alone lead to 12.15% of years lived with disability, and rank as the third leading contributor to the global burden of diseases. Four of the six leading causes of years lived with disability are due to neuropsychiatric disorders (depression, alcohol-use disorders, schizophrenia and bipolar disorder)" (8). The Executive Summary points out that "those suffering from mental illnesses are also victims of human rights violations, stigma and discrimination, both inside and outside psychiatric institutions" (4).

3. Fee, "The Broken Dialogue," in *Pathology and the Postmodern*, 12–13.

4. See Roy Porter, *Social History of Madness* (London: Weidenfeld and Nicolson, 1987).

5. On July 22, 2006, a quick check at Amazon.com (under "mental depression," to exclude economic depression) yielded 8,182 results; ten months later, on May 17, 2007, a similar check yielded 9,157 results. The majority of these books appear to be self-help volumes (offering help in "wrestling with," "beating," "overcoming," and "conquering" depression), the rest being memoirs and professional volumes. One can even find a *Depression for Dummies* (2003) and a *Postpartum Depression for Dummies* (2007).

6. For the most part, contributors to this volume assume there *is* such a thing as mental illness, that people experience mental illnesses just as they experience physical illnesses, and that they try to make sense of their experience and their suffering. It is also assumed that illness is not the same as disease. In *The Illness Narratives*, Arthur Kleinman defines illness as the "innately human experience of symptoms and suffering." This experience is at the core of our understanding of illness, which is "always culturally shaped." Disease is what the medical profession sees, "the problem from the practitioner's perspective . . . an alteration in biological structure or functioning" (3–6).

7. Jane Kenyon, "Having It Out with Melancholy" (1993), line 5. See also John Keats's "Ode to Melancholy" and "Ode to a Nightingale" (1819), and Charles Baudelaire's "Spleen" (1857).

8. Sacks, *The Man Who Mistook His Wife for a Hat*, 121.

9. This recalls the narratological distinction between story and plot, where the story is the events as they occurred, and the plot is the (re)arrangement of these events.

10. Bruner, *Making Stories*, 85, 89.

11. Ibid., 89.

12. Galen Strawson notes in his review "Tales of the Unexpected" the dominance of this narrative perspective in the humanities and social sciences, in "psychology, anthropology, philosophy, sociology, political theory, literary studies, religious studies and psychotherapy."

13. Strawson, "Tales of the Unexpected."

14. Phelan, "Editor's Column," 210.

15. See Frank, *The Wounded Storyteller*; Karp, *Speaking of Sadness*; Couser, *Recovering Bodies*; Hawkins, *Reconstructing Illness*; Montgomery, *Doctors' Stories*; Kleinman, *The Illness Narratives*; Nelson, *Damaged Identities, Narrative Repair*.

16. See Caruth, *Trauma*, and also Dori Laub and Shoshana Felman, *Testimony: Crises of Witnessing in Literature, Psychoanalysis, and History* (New York: Routledge, 1992). On disability and narrative, see Sharon L. Snyder et al., *Disability Studies: Enabling the Humanities* (New York: Modern Language Association, 2002).

17. Of course, the boundary between physical and mental is contested: the body and mind are interrelated in health, disease, and the experience of illness. However, for convenience I am using the common distinction between diseases such as cancer and AIDS, which affect the body and its systems (though often accompanied by psychological suffering), and conditions such as depression and bipolar disorder, not to mention schizophrenia, which affect moods and cognition (though often accompanied by physical suffering).

18. See also Dwight Fee, *Pathology and the Postmodern*; Ann Hudson Jones, "Literature and Medicine: Narratives of Mental Illness," *Lancet* 350.9074 (1997): 359–61; Roland Littlewood, *Pathologies of the West: An Anthropology of Mental Illness in Europe and America* (Ithaca: Cornell University Press, 2002); Arthur Kleinman and Byron Good, eds., *Culture and Depression* (Berkeley: University of California Press, 1985). David Morris writes on culture and depression in *Illness and Culture in the Postmodern Age* (Berkeley: University of California Press, 1998); Emily Martin writes on culture, depression and bipolar disorder in *Bipolar Expeditions: Mania and Depression in American Culture* (Princeton: Princeton University Press, 2007).

19. Hawkins, 12.

20. Sontag, *Illness as Metaphor*, 182.

21. Fee, 2.

22. Sontag, *Illness as Metaphor*, 181.

23. Sontag, *Regarding the Pain of Others*, 76.

24. Lanzmann, "The Obscenity of Understanding."

25. However, some authors in this volume might disagree with me on this point.

26. Sontag, *Regarding the Pain of Others*, 101.

27. See Hatfield, Cacioppo, and Rapson, *Emotional Contagion*, for a discussion of the phenomenon of emotional contagion in general. In teaching a course on women, depression, and writing, I have found depression narratives to be very

contagious: usually one or two students will become depressed enough to seek or reenter therapy. The instructor is not always immune, either. Two depression narratives that I have found to be particularly unreadable (in the sense of contagious) are John Bentley Mays's *In the Jaws of the Black Dogs: A Memoir of Depression* (Toronto: Penguin, 1995) and Marie Cardinal's *The Words to Say It*, trans. Pat Goodheart (Cambridge, MA: Van Vactor & Goodheart, 1983).

     28. Hartman, "On Traumatic Knowledge and Literary Studies," 537.

     29. "Scriptotherapy" is a term Suzette Henke uses in her book on women's trauma narratives, *Shattered Subjects: Trauma and Testimony in Women's Life-Writing* (New York: St. Martin's Press, 1998).

Bibliography

Bruner, Jerome. *Making Stories: Law, Literature, Life.* New York: Farrar, Straus and Giroux, 2002.

Caruth, Cathy, ed. *Trauma: Explorations in Memory.* Baltimore: Johns Hopkins University Press, 1995.

Couser, G. Thomas. *Recovering Bodies: Illness, Disability, and Life-Writing.* Madison: University of Wisconsin Press, 1997.

Fee, Dwight, ed. *Pathology and the Postmodern: Mental Illness as Discourse and Experience.* London: Sage, 2000.

Frank, Arthur W. *At the Will of the Body: Reflections on Illness.* Boston: Houghton Mifflin, 1991.

———. *The Wounded Storyteller: Body, Illness, and Ethics.* Chicago: University of Chicago Press, 1995.

Hartman, Geoffrey. "On Traumatic Knowledge and Literary Studies." *New Literary History* 26, no. 3 (1995): 537–63.

Hatfield, Elaine, John T. Cacioppo, and Richard L. Rapson. *Emotional Contagion.* Cambridge, UK: Cambridge University Press, 1994.

Hawkins, Anne Hunsaker. *Reconstructing Illness: Studies in Pathography.* 2nd ed. West Lafayette, IN: Purdue University Press, 1999.

Karp, David. *Speaking of Sadness: Depression, Disconnection, and the Meanings of Illness.* New York: Oxford University Press, 1996.

Kenyon, Jane. "Having It Out with Melancholy." In *A Hundred White Daffodils: Essays, Interviews.* Saint Paul, MN: Graywolf Press, 1999.

Kleinman, Arthur. *The Illness Narratives: Suffering, Healing, and the Human Condition.* New York: Basic Books, 1988.

Lanzmann, Claude. "The Obscenity of Understanding." Interview in Caruth, ed., *Trauma,* 200–20.

Montgomery (Hunter), Kathryn. *Doctors' Stories: The Narrative Structure of Medical Knowledge.* Princeton, NJ: Princeton University Press, 1991.

Nelson, Hilde Lindemann. *Damaged Identities, Narrative Repair.* Ithaca: Cornell University Press, 2001.

Phelan, James. "Editor's Column: Who's Here? Thoughts on Narrative Identity and Narrative Imperialism." *Narrative* 13, no. 3 (2005): 205–10.

Sacks, Oliver. *The Man Who Mistook His Wife for a Hat: And Other Clinical Tales.* 1985. New York: Touchstone, 1998.

Sontag, Susan. *Illness as Metaphor and AIDS and Its Metaphors.* New York: Anchor Books, 1989.

———. *Regarding the Pain of Others.* New York: Farrar, Straus and Giroux, 2003.

Strawson, Galen. "Tales of the Unexpected." Review of *Making Stories*, by Jerome Bruner. *Guardian Unlimited Books*, January 10, 2004. http://books.guardian.co.uk/review/story/0,12084,1118942,00.html (accessed January 21, 2008).

Styron, William. *Darkness Visible: A Memoir of Madness.* New York: Random House, 1990.

World Health Organization. *Investing in Mental Health.* 2003. http://www.who.int/mental_health/media/investing_mnh.pdf (accessed January 21, 2008).

I

Negotiating Illness Identity and Stigma

Chapter 1

My Symptoms, Myself

Reading Mental Illness Memoirs for Identity Assumptions

Jennifer Radden

Introduction

Portrayals of the relationship between self and psychological symptoms[1] in first-person narratives about psychiatric illness and recovery are conspicuously varied. Much of this variation will obviously be attributable to the symptoms themselves, not only their degree of disabling severity, but their nature more generally. Some of these states and traits are more abhorrent and painful than others, for example, and some affect moods, capabilities, and responses more central to self and self-identity than others.

An additional source of these variations is the beliefs and assumptions such narratives reveal about the symptoms of disorder and their relation to personal or self-identity. In some narratives, for example, the narrators' symptoms are depicted as emanating from alien, sometimes diabolical, sources of agency outside the self, while in others, narrators "identify with" their symptoms as closely as they do their other experiential states.

Taking more and less explicit form, and acknowledged in varying degrees, such variations can be discerned in many mental illness memoirs including those from today's mental health care consumers' movements. These movements have changed the landscape of mental health care in recent years. They reflect burgeoning participation by the users of mental health services in their care, treatment, and self-definition. They acknowledge the importance of the voices of "survivors" and those who are in "recovery," the efforts of "mad pride" movements modeled on other liberation movements, and an alignment with other disabilities.

They offer and emphasize new, positive models of recovery for those with psychiatric illness.

Drawing on these recent narratives and on earlier writing, I here illustrate some assumptions people have held about the relation between self and symptoms, while showing the epistemological complexity of such an inquiry. I then note implicit models and analogies found in the recent narratives and explore some of their theoretical implications. And I point to particular aspects of depression, and hence depression narratives, as they intersect with these ideas.

The term "symptoms" here refers to the manifestations in psychological states and behavioral dispositions of what to observers appears to be psychopathology.[2] Although the term is primarily a medical one, and forms part of a disease model in which symptoms (like signs) are the causal by-products of an underlying disease process, "symptom" is also used in more theoretically innocent ways, and occurs in some mental illness memoirs that explicitly reject further medical presuppositions. This simpler use will be employed here until otherwise stated.

Illness Narratives: Some Variations

The approach I am employing here sets apart the symptoms and episodes described in these accounts from their framing presuppositions and assumptions, explicit and implicit. This is not always an easy contrast to maintain, we shall see, but two premodern narratives will provide an initial illustration. The fifteenth-century *Book of Margery Kempe* is an account dictated by a troubled, pious woman whose life was interrupted by episodes when she believed herself touched by divine intervention and others when, in her words, she entirely lost her reason. Written in the eighteenth century, George Trosse's memoir is the spiritual autobiography of a Nonconformist minister looking back from middle age on his youthful experience with visions, voices, and suicidal thoughts.

Beliefs about spiritual intervention and causation frame the experiences described in these two narratives, and the person subject to those experiences is in each case conveyed as a relatively—or entirely—passive victim of nonearthly interference. Control, and at least to that extent "ownership," of symptoms is attributed to an agency external to the self.

Prolonged, uncontrolled wailing, tears, and shouting were Margery Kempe's characteristic traits throughout her life—although whether many of these were a divine blessing or symptoms of disorder was contested. At least during one twelve-day episode of what she seems to accept as an "affliction," however, she represents herself as the recipient of unbidden thoughts sent by the devil. During this time, she reports, "The devil deluded her, dallying with her with accursed thoughts. . . . And . . .

she could not say no, and *she had to do his bidding,* and yet she would not have done it for all the world. . . . Wherever she went or whatever she did, these accursed thoughts remained with her. When she would see the sacrament, say her prayers, or do any other good deed, such abomination was always *put into her mind.*"[3]

In a description apparently sharing some of the same assumptions, Trosse describes how during great inner turmoil he heard a voice bid him to cut off his hair, to which, he says, he replied: "I have no Scissors." "*It was then hinted,*" he goes on, "that a Knife would do it; but I answer'd, I have none. Had I had one, I verily believe, this Voice would have gone from my Hair to my Throat, and have commanded me to cut it . . ."[4] He was "thus *disturb'd,*" as he later sums it up, with "silly ridiculous Fancies, and Thousands of unreasonable and nonsensical Delusions."[5]

It was "put in her mind"; it was "hinted"; Trosse was "disturbed." Phenomenologically, we usually feel ourselves to direct our thoughts and receive our perceptual experience. Yet the language in each of these accounts indicates thought processes in the receipt of which their subjects are as passive as in their receipt of perceptual experiences.

Experiences of unbidden thoughts and alien commands are typical of psychosis, now as much as then. Phenomenologically, psychiatric symptoms often involve ruptures and divisions within consciousness, and inner voices, thoughts, and feelings are not merely framed, but *experienced,* as alien. Caution is required here, then: an epistemic indeterminacy prevents us from unreservedly attributing the depiction of the self/symptoms relation to framing, rather than treating it as a phenomenologically accurate report. This indeterminacy makes for ambiguity and confusion as we try to interpret narratives such as these.

That said, the particular framing in these narratives whereby such thoughts are directed *as if from an unearthly external agency* in a form of possession, a framing common to early modern memoirs, is less frequently found in memoirs nearer to our own time. By the modern era different conceptual possibilities suggest themselves, and other ideas and assumptions—including some sense of the proprietary self as owner of and constituted by the totality of its experiences and corporeal states—seem to have gained salience.

This more recent conception emerges in John Perceval's 1838 memoir, written after a year in a private madhouse that followed upon an episode of severe disturbance. Perceval looks back on earlier states of hallucination and delusion and judges them to have resulted from a "natural but often erroneous . . . confused judgement," a source within himself which is not himself.[6] The mind, Perceval explains, is "a piece of excellent machinery," and "there is a power in man, which independent of his natural thought and will, can form ideas upon his imagination—control his voice—and even wield his limbs." His recovery from this condition comes, as Perceval understands it, when he recognizes he can resist the directives from this unconscious source. "On one occasion . . . I yielded my voice to the power upon me, and forthwith I uttered the most gross and revolting obscenities, by the influence of a similar power." But now, he chose to be silent "rather than obey." Finally, he says, he was cured of the "folly that I was to yield my voice up to the control of any spirit . . . without discrimination, and thus my mind was set at rest in great measure from another delusion; or rather, the superstitious belief that I was blindly to yield myself up to an extraordinary guidance was done away."[7]

Although not attributing them to any agency external to his body, Perceval denies his symptoms are his, and in that sense he "disowns" or "alienates" them. This kind of framing is regularly found in later writing such as the following, reported in the middle of the twentieth century. The author apparently speaks of experiences similar to Kempe's, Trosse's, and Perceval's here, yet reasons not to the presence of an alien agency but to a state of compromised personhood and a sense of objectification: "Things just happen to me now and I have no control over them. I don't seem to have the same say in things any more. At times, *I can't even control what I want to think about.* I am starting to feel pretty numb about everything because I am becoming an object and objects don't have feelings."[8]

From the same era comes Lisa Wiley's *Voices Calling* (1955), in which she describes "darkness . . . closing in" and frames the relation between her self and her symptoms in terms of depletion and deadness: "I could see everything and saw it as it was, but it was all a dead, lifeless mass. I was dead mentally, having no conscience of anything and having no emotion. I could still think and apparently reason but it was all silent thoughts. . . . There was no future and no past. Everything was just an endless black nothingness . . ."[9] The alienation of her mental states here, it seems, renders them unreal or even nonexistent for their subject.

John Custance's long memoir about his manic-depressive condition, *Wisdom, Madness and Folly* (1952), provides a final illustration of a symptom-alienating framing from these mid-twentieth-century memoirs. Speaking of the preceding manic period, he describes experiencing "unearthly joys." But of his depression, he remarks: "A crumpled pillow is quite an ordinary everyday object, is it not? One looks at it and thinks no more about it. So is a washing rag or a towel tumbled on the floor, or the creases on the side of a bed. Yet they can suggest shapes of the utmost horror to the mind obsessed by fear. Gradually my eyes began to distinguish such shapes, until eventually, whichever way I turned, devils [appeared] which seemed infinitely more real than the material objects in which I saw them."[10] Recounting what he experienced, imagined, and saw, Custance employs a more active voice than is found in early modern narratives, and leaves no doubt that his own mind is the source of his hallucinated "devils." Custance positions all his experiences within a psychiatric understanding. This was illness. Though painful, exhilarating, and *seemingly* unearthly, his experiences were merely the symptoms of a disordered brain.

These ways of representing symptoms as alienated from the self, sometimes no more, perhaps, than reports of the actual phenomenology of unbidden and alienated states, must also be distinguished from another kind of framing, this one as apparent in premodern as in contemporary memoirs: *reframing*. Most mental illnesses are episodic. Few such memoirs are completed, although they have sometimes been begun, during the severest throes of disorder.[11] (Such episodes might prevent and eclipse the writing, or not last the time it takes.) In reading these works, we must be alert to the inevitable reconfigurations imposed on all self-narratives in their retelling, but very often heightened, here, by efforts to explain or excuse states so extreme, unsought, unwelcome, and stigmatized.

Moralistic and religious reframing typifies early modern memoirs such as Trosse's. A previous self, disordered and sinful, is viewed from the perspective of one morally restored or saved. While not denying the presence of illness, when he looks back on the "Sin and Folly" of his youth ("going from Place to Place . . . prating and drinking"), Trosse sees the presence of disorder as invited, and made possible, by his own iniquities, for all that its seat was a disordered brain. "A crack'd Brain," in his words, was "impos'd upon by a deceitful and lying Devil."[12]

Attitudes in our times are less immediately moralistic, if still stigmatizing. And although a repositioning of self with respect to symptoms can be found in contemporary narratives, that repositioning is construed in a different way. What were seen in the throes of the episode as reasons, and as "my reasons" for "my" conclusion, "my" resolve, or "my" action, are represented—with the shift in standpoint provided by recovery—as more like invasive and alien states bearing no comprehensible connection to the self. My experiences become things that befell me—or things I mistakenly thought were "my" experiences, reasons, and actions.[13] (Thus the assertion: "It was my depression talking, not me.")

Adding to the complexities of interpretation introduced thus far, memoirs from our present era introduce new elements, such as the reductionistic assumptions of modern biological psychiatry where symptoms are dismissed as the meaningless causal products of a disordered brain. These assumptions are almost inescapable given the ubiquity, authority, and influence of medical psychiatry today. Moreover, the medical psychiatric perspective *enforces its own adoption*. Understood as a failure to acknowledge the medical nature of one's condition, "lack of insight" is uniformly treated a sign of illness. Very often it is only by acknowledging that their experiences are medical symptoms of underlying pathology, and thus acceding to the presuppositions of the medical perspective, that patients can demonstrate restored health or evidence of healing.

This influence of the medical model is self-consciously acknowledged in Lauren Slater's *Prozac Diary* (1998). "Having lived with chronic depression," she writes, "a high-pitched panic, and a host of other psychiatric symptoms since my earliest years, I had made for myself an illness identity, a story of the self that had illness as its main motive. I did not sleep well because I was ill. I cut myself because I was ill." "Illness, for me," she says, "had been the explanatory model on which my being was based."[14] Slater looks back here, transformed by Prozac to the unexpected experience of wellness. This description easefully employs the psychiatric language of "chronic depression" and "symptoms," and nods toward the explanatory power and reductionistic tone of psychiatric framing. Yet— as is true of many such sophisticated, contemporary memoirs—there is a tone of irony, and we sense the author's reservations over this limiting identity she had woven for herself.

The reductionistic aspect of a medical framing and the coercive way it is imposed are often more openly challenged by today's memoirists. Writing of his breakdown, Peter Campbell charges the medical psychiatric system with disempowering patients and thwarting their capabilities:

> By approaching my situation in terms of illness, the system has consistently underestimated my capacity to change and has ignored the potential it may contain to assist that change. My desire to win my own control of the breakdown process and thereby to gain independence and integrity has not only been ignored—it has been thwarted. The major impression I have received is that I am a victim of something nasty, not quite understandable, that will never really go away and which should not be talked about too openly in the company of strangers.[15]

And of her experiences with a diagnosis of schizophrenia, Patricia Deegan observes: "*My identity had been reduced to an illness* in the eyes of those who worked with me. . . . [T]reating people as if they were illnesses is dehumanizing. Everyone loses when this happens. . . . People learn to say what professionals say; 'I am a schizophrenic, a bi-polar, a borderline, etc.' . . . [M]ost professionals applaud these rote utterances as 'insight.' . . . [T]he great danger of reducing a person to an illness is that there is no one left to do the work of recovery."[16]

Campbell's and Deegan's narratives exemplify a growing, new emphasis. In the era of identity politics, group identification and self-identity have come to receive unparalleled attention; the question "Who am I?" is inescapable. Similarly inescapable, as we saw earlier, is the influence of medical framing, bringing an increased interest in the disease status of mental disorder and hence in "symptoms" in the medical sense. Today, the relation between self and symptoms is frequently addressed in memoirs such as these with explicit and sustained attention.[17]

Contemporary Models

One or the other of two apparently incompatible frameworks or "models" representing the relationship between self or identity and symptoms is to be found in many of today's first-person descriptions.[18]

On a "symptom-alienating" model, we find distancing and controlling metaphors. The person describes living and strives to live "outside," rather than being pulled "inside," the illness; the illness and its symptoms are at most a peripheral aspect of the whole person. Essential to recovery is hope, and the hope of everyone with mental illness is the absence ("remission") of all symptoms. Thus symptoms are alienable from, rather than integral to, the self. Through an active process of "recovering" or taking back an identity hitherto reduced to these symptoms, the symptoms are controlled ("managed"), their effects and importance minimized and diminished. Often, showing the influence of medical psychiatry, symptoms appear as the meaningless by-products of inherent biological disorder with no intrinsic interest or relevance to the person from whose dysfunctional brain they emanate.

Rhetoric from the "recovery" movement echoes, likely grows out of, but also nourishes this set of assumptions in first-person narratives. And these ideas also underlie new definitions of "recovery": defining a self apart from the symptoms of disorder is said to constitute part of, and has been established to foster, healing.[19] In prescriptions for getting "outside" mental illness, emphasis is placed on resuming "control" and "responsibility" by "managing" symptoms.

In contrast to the symptom-alienating model, some narratives reveal "symptom-integrating" assumptions, a picture of symptoms as less easily alienated and, in some cases, as central to and constitutive of the identity of the person. Instead of alienated and controlled, symptoms are embraced, even valorized. Rather than inconsequential effects of a diseased brain, they are depicted as meaningful aspects of experience and identity. When they are alienated, the goal of recovery is also sometimes understood to be integrating them into the self. Simon Champ, in "A Most Precious Thread" (1999), illustrates the integrative aspect of this kind of narrative, describing how he has come to think about his symptoms. He speaks of a "communication with himself" that allows him to overcome the initial sense of disintegration accompanying the onset of his symptoms. This communication, Champ discloses, "has given me the most precious thread, a thread that has linked my evolving sense of self, a thread of self-reclamation, a thread of movement toward a whole and integrated sense of self, away from the early fragmentation and confusion."[20]

Symptoms are not only integrated and valued but valorized in Simon Morris's narrative "Heaven Is a Mad Place on Earth" (2000), in which he employs the metaphor of deep sea fishing to capture the extreme states wrought by his disorder. "All who have experienced 'deep sea fishing,'" he writes, "will know the sensation of heightened awareness, of consciousness enhanced far better than LSD could ever do it, of feelings of wonder and terror that can't be verbalized . . . and then have these visions which effortlessly outstrip the alienation of daily life dismissed as 'delusion' by some fucking shrink. . . . I was always mad— I hope I always will be. My crazy life is wonderful. The 'sane' really don't know what they're missing."[21]

Although it is found in narratives describing other disorders as well, this symptom-integrating framing is particularly apparent in narratives about depressive states (and in such writing it long predates the current consumer movements). Memoirs such as Kay Jamison's *An Unquiet Mind*, William Styron's *Darkness Visible*, and Meri Nana-Ama Danquah's *Willow Weep for Me* emphasize the depth of appreciation and feeling that come with depression, not only accepting that these moods are integral to who they are, but insisting that there is a value in them. Acknowledging that she is identified with and at least in part constituted by her depression, Danquah writes, "For most of my life I have nurtured a consistent, low-grade melancholy; I have been addicted to despair." Honoring her mood states, she comments, "Depression offers layers, textures, noises. At times depression is as flimsy as a feather. . . . Other times it . . . present[s] new signals and symptoms until finally I am drowning in it. Most times, in its most superficial and seductive sense, it is rich and enticing. A field of velvet waiting to embrace me. It is loud and dizzying, inviting the tenors and screeching sopranos of thought, unrelenting sadness, and the sense of impending doom."[22]

Why should depression, particularly, lend itself to the "integrative" conception of self and symptoms? Speculation here takes at least three distinct directions. First, affective states appear to be more integral to self-identity than cognitive ones: our emotions and moods are not easily separated from our core selves. Mood states, such as depression, are pervasive and unbounded in their psychological effects. In this they differ from beliefs. We may distance ourselves from any given belief in several ways—by doubting or disbelieving rather than embracing it, for example. But no comparable separation allows us to distinguish our moods from ourselves. Moods by their nature color and frame all experience. In this respect, at least while they last, they are inescapably part of us. (Consistent with this, of course, is a subsequent reframing that effects that distance, although arguably such reframing still takes the form of "That person was not me" rather than "That mood was not mine." In contrast, reframing a state when a now-relinquished delusional belief was entertained simply involves saying, as Trosse does in the passage quoted earlier, "Thus was I disturb'd with . . . unreasonable and nonsensical delusions"—not "That person was not me.")

Second, the effect of depression on reasoning and on perceptual, cognitive, and communicative capabilities is often less disabling than is the effect of other severe conditions: moods of despair and sadness may be easier to integrate than the jarring and disruptive intrusion of symptoms such as inner voices. Severe, psychotic depression can occur, and the subtler effects of depressive moods on judgment are not inconsiderable. Nonetheless, reasoning, judgment, and interpersonal communication are not as immediately compromised by most depressive moods as by the delusions and hallucinations associated with other severe disorders such as schizophrenia.

And last, glamorous associations still cling to the notion of melancholia and even extend to today's depression. In the afterglow of the long tradition in which melancholy bespeaks brilliance, creativity, and inspiration, the drawback of depressive moods is not unalloyed. In Styron's memoir, for instance, although emphasizing the excruciating and terrifying aspects of his depression, Dante's *Inferno* is used as a frame and the great depression sufferers of the past are listed, as if to remind the reader of the ennobling value of such suffering.

Some Theoretical Implications

Some additional theoretical implications appear to attach to the models outlined here and may in turn account for their adoption in some cases. For example, theories of self-identity and agency vary. Some analyses portray the "author" of the self-narrative as actively engaged in selecting the experiences that comport with a story she constructs, rather than as passively receiving whatever life experiences she is dealt. On this analysis, arguably, a person's psychiatric symptoms may not even enter her story. The narrative of self-analysis is widely adopted today and seems to play an important part in much of the rhetoric and prescriptions associated with the recovery movements. Other theories of self-identity deriving from Kantian traditions, in which the self is the recipient and proprietor of the

totality of its life experiences, will perhaps better accommodate a symptom-integrating approach, such as in Champ's memoir, than a symptom-
alienating one.

A second theoretical implication of these contrasting models concerns the analogy between psychiatric and other kinds of symptoms.
Much symptom-alienating recovery movement rhetoric is styled on that
of the broader disabilities movement, wherein differences between the
symptoms of bodily and psychiatric disorders are diminished and de-
emphasized. Such a perspective denies psychiatric disorders exceptional
status. Symptom-integrating assumptions, in contrast, seem more hospitable to such exceptionalism. The extent and persuasiveness of the
analogy between ordinary, bodily symptoms and psychiatric symptoms,
then, is at the center of this contrast between symptom-alienating and
symptom-integrating framings of the self/symptom relationship.

Holistic thinking concerned to avoid unacceptable forms of dual-
ism would insist on the strong analogy between all symptoms, whether
they resulted from bodily or psychological dysfunction or disorder. On a
strict, medical understanding, symptoms, in contrast to signs, are by definition psychological and subjective; they are the patient's "complaint" or
avowal—communicative acts. (Signs are observable aspects of the situation, not requiring cooperation or even consciousness from the patient.)
Arguably, then, the statements "I cannot walk on my leg" and "My
thought processes are being interrupted by distracting inner voices"
belong to the same ontological order of things.

Even limiting our focus to symptoms strictly so called, however, the
deficits and problems included among psychiatric symptoms come in
many forms less hospitable to the analogy with the complaint "I cannot
walk on my leg." The silence of catatonia; incomprehensible "word sal-
ads"; neologisms; apparently self-contradictory claims ("I am dead,"
"Someone has stolen my thoughts"); words addressed to unseen or un-
heard others—these bear little resemblance to what we mean when we
think of ordinary, bodily symptoms.

Space does not permit a thorough discussion of these issues. But
at least two seeming differences between psychiatric and nonpsychiatric
symptoms compel our attention. First, the attitudes and expectations
customarily accompanying more ordinary bodily symptoms are not as re-
liably present with psychiatric symptoms.[23] These include the presump-
tion that those experiencing them will (at least in the face of medical
knowledge) accept the disorder status of their symptoms, want to be rid
of them, and want to cooperate in their removal.

Second, psychiatric symptoms regularly compromise the capabilities
required for the expression of any symptoms, so understood: speech and
the shared, intersubjective responses that allow words to convey meanings

successfully, actions to make apparent sense, and understanding and communication to take place. While mental disorder may not often be so devastating in its effects as the aforementioned examples portray, and the statement "My thought processes are being interrupted by distracting inner voices" may be more common than "I am dead" or "Someone has stolen my thoughts," nonetheless, these examples of fundamental dysfunction in the means of expressing and communicating symptoms seem to raise a challenge for the general analogy between the symptoms of psychiatric and bodily disorders.

Conclusion

Some of the factors influencing how illness narratives portray the relation between self and symptoms have been introduced here. Most generally, rather than being mere phenomenological reports, individual narratives reflect the "framing" ideas and explanations accepted and imagined at their given time and place in history. But several further features of these narratives have been shown to complicate our efforts to identify these framings. Because the relation between self and symptoms may itself become disordered as the result of mental illness, any separation between accurate report and cultural framing is problematic and leaves epistemic indeterminacy at the heart of our interpretive efforts. Further interpretive complexity comes from the element of "reframing": these narratives will likely reflect the temporal standpoint from which they were written rather than the framing within which the symptoms were first experienced. These each intersect with the last factor that was our particular focus: the assumptions, ideas, and explanations—including the theory of self and the perceived analogies with bodily symptoms—guiding how the self is seen in relation to its psychological symptoms.

Variation among these narratives vis-à-vis depictions of the self/symptom relation is most obviously attributable to variation in the kind of symptoms experienced, it was pointed out at the outset of this discussion. And here too, we have discovered patterns of interaction with the ideas about the relation between self and symptoms discussed here. The distinctive nature and cultural place of mood states likely explain why memoirs of depression more often adopt symptom-integrating assumptions.

Notes

1. I use the word "symptoms" here for simplicity, and because that will be the main focus of my discussion. In some narratives, the relationship between self and the broader "disorder," "disease," or "illness" also appears, but these terms introduce additional considerations and will not receive systematic analysis here.

2. Symptoms include behavioral dispositions as well as psychological states, but this discussion is limited to examples of the latter.

3. Kempe, *The Book of Margery Kempe*, 183–84 (emphases added).

4. Trosse, *Life of the Reverend Mr. George Trosse*, 30 (emphasis added).

5. Ibid., 32 (emphasis added).

6. Interestingly, although Freud's work on the unconscious was still half a century away, this account seems to anticipate the belief in unconscious mental states framing some twentieth-century narratives.

7. Perceval, *A Narrative of the Treatment Experienced by a Gentleman*, 253.

8. Quoted in McGhie and Chapman, "Disorders of Attention and Perception in Early Schizophrenia," 109 (emphasis added).

9. Wiley, *Voices Calling*, 280–81.

10. Custance, *Wisdom, Madness and Folly*, 58–59.

11. Nijinsky's *Diaries* constitute one valuable exception to this generalization. See *The Diaries of Vaslav Nijinsky*, translated by Kyril FitzLyon, edited by Joan Acocella (New York: Farrar, Straus and Giroux, 1999).

12. Trosse, 30.

13. This raises some epistemic puzzles: particularly when it involves a recurring disorder, such as depression or manic depression, we must ask why the perspective of the later "recovered" author of the illness narrative, which alienates the self from its symptoms, should be privileged over the account of the earlier, ill subject, which did not. (See Radden, *Divided Minds and Successive Selves*, 170–71.)

14. Slater, *Prozac Diary*, 50.

15. Campbell, 56–57.

16. Deegan, "Recovery as a Self-Directed Process of Healing and Transformation," 5–6 (emphasis added). Deegan's discussion illustrates Hilde Lindemann Nelson's work, in *Damaged Identities: Narrative Repair*, on the healing achieved through replacing others' subordinating "master narratives" (You are a schizophrenic) with one's own "counter stories" (I have schizophrenia).

17. See, for example, Read and Reynolds, *Speaking Our Minds*; Barker et al., *From the Ashes of Experience*; and Davidson, *Living Outside Mental Illness*.

18. In using the term "model" here, I mean to suggest a cluster of ideas that are very often found together and that appear to form a harmonious set although they are not joined by entailment.

19. See, for example, Jacobson and Greenley, "What Is Recovery?"; Barham and Hayward, *From the Mental Patient to the Person*, *Relocating Madness* and "In Sickness and in Health"; Corrigan and Penn, "Disease and Discrimination"; and Davidson, *Living Outside Mental Illness*.

20. Champ, "A Most Precious Thread," 120.

21. Morris, "Heaven Is a Mad Place on Earth," 207–08. Some of the political rationale for the "mad pride" model is clarified in the following passage from the UK Mad Pride website: "The word 'mad' is basically a term of abuse. Remember so once was the word 'black.' But people reclaimed the word and used it as a proud badge to be worn along the long march to freedom. There was Black Power. There is Mad Pride."

22. Danquah, 151–54.

23. Some psychiatric symptoms are of course bodily sensations, such as pain and discomfort in the head. So we can at best speak of typical psychological or psychiatric symptoms in these ways.

Bibliography

Barham, Peter, and Robert Hayward. *From the Mental Patient to the Person.* London and New York: Routledge, 1991.

———. *Relocating Madness.* London: Free Association Books, 1995.

———. "In Sickness and in Health: Dilemmas of the Person with Severe Mental Illness." *Psychiatry* 61, no. 2 (1998): 163–70.

Barker, Phil, Peter Campbell, and Ben Davidson, eds. *From the Ashes of Experience: Reflections on Madness, Survival and Growth.* London: Whurr Publishers, 1999.

Campbell, Peter. In Read and Reynolds, eds., *Speaking Our Minds,* 56–62.

Champ, Simon. "A Most Precious Thread." In Barker, Campbell, and Davidson, eds., *From the Ashes of Experience,* 113–26.

Corrigan, P., and D. Penn. "Disease and Discrimination: Two Paradigms That Describe Severe Mental Illness." *Journal of Mental Health* 6, no. 4 (1997): 355–66.

Custance, John. *Wisdom, Madness and Folly: The Philosophy of a Lunatic.* New York: Farrar, Straus and Cudahy, 1952.

Danquah, Meri Nana-Ama. In Rebecca Shannonhouse, ed., *Out of Her Mind,* 151–55. New York: Modern Library, 2003.

Davidson, Larry. *Living Outside Mental Illness: Qualitative Studies of Recovery in Schizophrenia.* New York: New York University Press, 2003.

Deegan, Patricia E. "Recovery as a Self-Directed Process of Healing and Transformation," 2001. http://intentionalcare.org/articles/articles_trans.pdf (accessed August 7, 2005).

Jacobson, Nora, and Dianne Greenley. "What Is Recovery? A Conceptual Model and Explication." *Psychiatric Services* 52, no. 4 (2001): 482–85.

Jamison, Kay Redfield. *An Unquiet Mind: A Memoir of Moods and Madness.* New York: Knopf, 1995.

Kempe, Margery. *The Book of Margery Kempe.* Translated by B. A. Windeatt. 1985. London and New York: Penguin Books, 2000.

"Mad Pride." www.madpride.org.uk/about.htm (accessed June 2004).

McGhie, Andrew, and James Chapman. "Disorders of Attention and Perception in Early Schizophrenia." *British Journal of Medical Psychology* 34 (1961): 103–16.

Morris, Simon. "Heaven Is a Mad Place on Earth." In *Mad Pride: A Celebration of Mad Culture,* edited by T. Curtis et al., 207–08. London: Spare Change Books, 2000.

Nelson, Hilde Lindemann. *Damaged Identities, Narrative Repair.* Ithaca: Cornell University Press, 2001.

Perceval, John. *A Narrative of the Treatment Experienced by a Gentleman, During a State of Mental Derangement.* Volumes I and II. 1838 and 1840. In *The Inner World of Mental Illness,* edited by Bert Kaplan, 235–53. New York: Harper and Row, 1964.

Peterson, Dale, ed. *A Mad People's History of Madness.* Pittsburgh, PA: Pittsburgh University Press, 1982.

Radden, Jennifer. *Divided Minds and Successive Selves: Ethical Issues in Disorders of Identity and Personality.* Cambridge, MA: MIT Press, 1996.

Read, Jim, and Jill Reynolds, eds. *Speaking Our Minds: An Anthology.* London: Palgrave Macmillan, 1996.

Ridgeway, P. "Re-Storying Psychiatric Disability: Learning from First-Person Narrative Accounts of Recovery." *Psychiatric Rehabilitation Journal* 24, no. 4 (2001): 335–43.

Slater, Lauren. *Prozac Diary.* New York: Penguin Books, 1998.

Styron, William. *Darkness Visible: A Memoir of Madness.* New York: Random House, 1990.

Trosse, George. *Life of the Reverend Mr. George Trosse: Written by Himself, and Published Posthumously According to His Order in 1714.* In Peterson, ed., *A Mad People's History of Madness,* 27–38.

Wiley, Lisa. *Voices Calling.* In Peterson, ed., *A Mad People's History of Madness,* 271–83.

Chapter 2

The Language of Madness

Representing Bipolar Disorder in Kay Redfield Jamison's An Unquiet Mind and Kate Millett's The Loony-Bin Trip

Debra Beilke

Which of my feelings are real? Which of the me's is me? The wild, impulsive, chaotic, energetic, and crazy one? Or the shy, withdrawn, desperate, suicidal, doomed, and tired one?

—Kay Redfield Jamison, *An Unquiet Mind*

Writing an autobiography involves "agonizing questions of identity, self-definition, self-existence, or self-deception," as Sidonie Smith has observed.[1] How does an author construct a coherent narrative self out of the messy ebb and flow of existence? Which memories should one ignore and which should one stress? What about important information one does not even remember? How much knowledge does one really have of oneself, after all? Is "authenticity" even possible when constructing an "I" who is both subject and object of the same sentences? While questions such as these—and many others—are inherent to all autobiographical acts, having a mood disorder magnifies the "agonizing questions" of self-representation to an extreme degree. If one is deeply depressed, is this mood an expression of the "true" self or is the self distorted beyond recognition? Does the manic mood, which frequently results in brilliant insights, reveal an aspect of the authentic self that might otherwise remain muted? Or does it alter the "real me" beyond recognition?

The purpose of this essay is to address such questions by analyzing the interconnections between self, language, and mental illness as represented in Kate Millett's and Kay Redfield Jamison's autobiographies. Kate Millett, a feminist writer, activist, and scholar, is probably most famous for her book *Sexual Politics* (1970), a widely influential critique of patriarchy in Western culture. Kay Redfield Jamison, a professor of psychiatry at Johns Hopkins University, is well known as one of the world's foremost authorities on mood disorders. What these two women share, in addition to being extremely successful and influential in their fields, is a psychiatric diagnosis of bipolar disorder.[2] However, the two women relate to this illness—more specifically, to the idea of this illness—very differently. In Jamison's *An Unquiet Mind: A Memoir of Moods and Madness* (1995) and Millett's *The Loony-Bin Trip* (1990), the language of madness strongly shapes these authors' dramatically different representations of what is ostensibly the same disorder. I borrow the term "language of madness" from Jamison's discussion of the power of words in shaping our understanding of mental illness.[3] Jamison uses the term "madness" deliberately, as a way to emphasize the intensity of the experience of mental illness as well as to emphasize the power that language has on our perceptions of illness. While Millett more often uses "crazy" than "mad," I believe she, too, uses these terms deliberately to emphasize their potency.

Because Jamison's and Millett's texts contribute to a long tradition of women's autobiography, it is helpful to read them in the context of recent autobiographical theory. As mentioned earlier, narratively constructing a coherent autobiographical self is a slippery undertaking that requires investing past events with meaning they may not have had when originally experienced. As Anne Hunsaker Hawkins notes, "The assertion that there is a significant difference between the original 'real' experience and the retrospective autobiographical narrative is now a commonplace among critics and theorists of autobiography. Most critics see this difference as caused by the author's creative imposition of order, pattern, and meaning on what is remembered of one's life."[4] Not surprisingly, this imposition of "order, pattern, and meaning" on the flux of experience is colored by the historical and cultural context in which the woman is writing. As Smith points out, the "I" of women's autobiographies "reveals the way the autobiographer situates herself and her story in relation to cultural ideologies and figures of selfhood."[5] While all autobiographers must wrestle with competing forces of signification to construct the narrative "I," people afflicted with mood disorders must confront an additional set of challenges. If, as Estelle Jelinek argues, women's autobiographies have historically been marked by a "multi-dimensional, fragmented self-image colored by a sense of inadequacy and alienation,"[6] a mood disorder makes the sense of fragmented, multiple, defective selfhood all the more dramatic.

How, then, do autobiographical accounts of mood disorders contribute to prevailing theories on the postmodern, unstable, liminal self? Hawkins asks a related question in her study of pathographies: how does serious (physical) illness affect the autobiographical act? Hawkins argues that "neither the self as fiction nor the self as ineffable mystery are adequate formulations for the self encountered in pathographical narrative. . . . Pathography challenges the skepticism of critics and theorists about the self, making that skepticism seem artificial, mandarin, and contrived."[7] Hawkins makes a compelling argument in her book. However, she does not address the issue of mood disorders, which I believe complicates the issue of the self in an interesting way. The ever-changing flux of moods, perceptions, and energies of bipolar illness seems to me to reinforce, even magnify, postmodern formulations of the unstable self.

What is often missing in poststructuralist discussions of the unstable self, however, is an interrogation of the biological components of selfhood. More specifically, while theorists have paid a great deal of attention to the body in terms of race, gender, and sexuality, there has been little discussion of biological components of selfhood such as the biochemical disturbances of mood disorders. Analyzing autobiographical accounts of bipolar disorder can help to rectify this imbalance.

My analysis in this essay is based on certain assumptions. First of all, I accept—at least to a certain extent—the medical model of mood disorders in that I believe there is a biochemical basis to depression and manic depression. However, I also believe that the historical context in which a person lives profoundly colors his or her experience of manic depression. To use an extreme example, if one believes that one is possessed by demons, one will have a very different experience of mania than if one believes one's brain chemistry is out of whack. In emphasizing the importance of a person's perceptions of mental illness, I agree with Dwight Fee, who asserts that depression (and by extension, other mood disorders) is not only a biological and psychological phenomenon, but is also a "*discursive project*," "a reflexive process of self-definition and identity construction . . . an active, interpretive process of culturally informed self-communication."[8] While acknowledging that mood disorders have a material basis, this approach also recognizes that "no matter how it may be disordered, mood must be *interpreted* in order to be experienced."[9]

In their autobiographies, both Millett and Jamison attempt to interpret their experience of bipolar disorder—or, in the case of Millett, the accusation of it. (Millett does not accept her diagnosis of manic depression.) Their constructions of this disorder are multifaceted, but I'd like to focus on the language each writer uses to characterize her struggle with the concept of mental illness. The metaphors Millett and Jamison use not only illuminate their differing conception of mental illness, but also shed light on how they view the source of a person's core identity, or deepest sense of self. In *The Loony-Bin Trip*, Millett lashes out at psychiatry, especially its emphasis on medication and its use of forced hospitalization. However, more interesting to me than her quest to stay out of the "loony-bin" (to use her term) is her quest to avoid the shackles of language: she seems to fear the diagnosis of mental illness—the label, the words—as much as she fears incarceration. I suggest that Millett so deeply fears the diagnosis of mental illness because she conceptualizes her mind and her self as identical. Her mind is her self. Therefore, psychiatric professionals who label her as "sick" are dismissing her core self, her basic identity, as inherently "wrong" or "invalid," and are thus not to be taken seriously.

However, Jamison more easily accepts the diagnosis of manic depression, although she too struggles against lithium because with it she loses her productive hypomanic states and because it causes unpleasant side effects, such as severe nausea and vomiting. This acceptance stems, at least in part, from her academic background in biology and her professional affiliation as a psychologist, and colors her discursive project. Whereas Millett conflates the mind and the self, Jamison distinguishes between them. In constructing her narrative "I," Jamison emphasizes a core identity, a self that exists apart from her mind and apart from her bipolar disorder. Because she is able to separate self from mind and mind from illness, manic depression for her is a disease that, while it causes extraordinary suffering, does not obliterate her core identity.

Kate Millett's *The Loony-Bin Trip* recounts her two experiences of involuntary commitment to mental institutions—one in California in 1973 and one in 1980 while traveling in Ireland. Initially pleading "guilty" to the "charge" of mental illness, Millett did take lithium for several years after the first institutionalization. However, one summer she decided to discontinue taking the drug and told her partner that she was doing so. Most of the book focuses on this summer after stopping the lithium treatment and the harrowing events of the year or so afterward—including her involuntary confinement in an Irish asylum. According to *The Loony-Bin Trip*, friends and family believed that Millett became manic after stopping her lithium and strongly urged her to go back on it. However, Millett believes that the lithium had no effect on her mental state. Rather, when people who knew of her diagnosis found out she was off lithium, they began treating her differently. This condescension, this unstated accusation, Millett argues, made her irritable, which only fed others' belief that she was manic, which made her even more angry and so forth. The cycle of accusation-defense-accusation escalated until her friends and family believed Millett needed to be committed against her will and tried to trick her into entering the hospital.

Millett's text raises a number of provocative issues. For example, part of her project is to suggest that there is no such thing as mental illness and to make a case against "forced hospitalization, drugging, electroshock, [and] definitions of insanity as a crime to be treated with savage methods."[10] As such, Millett is clearly writing within the tradition of antipsychiatry, like critics such as Thomas Szasz, who argues that "what people now call mental illnesses are for the most part *communications* expressing unacceptable ideas, often framed, moreover, in an unusual idiom."[11] For the purpose of this essay, I will set aside the question of whether or not Millett was accurately diagnosed and whether or not enforced hospitalization and medication should be prohibited. Rather, I will focus on Millett's "discursive project" of mental illness, in which she focuses less on her own mental state than on how others perceive her and label her.

The major strategy used by Millett is to compare mental illness to a crime. Or, more specifically, she believes that mental health professionals, along with the general public, treat mental illness as a crime. For instance, she claims that she can "be made to do time at any moment" if she is found "guilty" of being bipolar. It is "[n]ot an 'illness' but a crime; for in fact that's how it's seen. Lithium maintenance is only a suspended sentence. What if I were innocent altogether?"[12] She further suggests that mental illness is treated like a crime in which the individual is guilty until proven innocent: "Of course, madness is worse than a crime; crimes merit trials, counsel, stated sentences if convicted. If acquitted of crime, one is free to go. [With a diagnosis] you will never get acquitted and, as a matter of fact, you are not nearly as innocent as you claim."[13] In fact, one of the reasons Millett decided to stop taking lithium was not only to eliminate the drug's side effects but also to prove herself "innocent" of the "crime" of manic depression. If she were off lithium for a few months without "freaking out" she might be "absolved of the ever-present and proven charge of insanity."[14] Partly because of her construction of mental illness as a crime, Millett's autobiography has the narrative tension of a good crime thriller: she is constantly on the verge of being "busted" and vows that she "will not be cornered again."[15]

Millett's enemy in this crime thriller is not a disease or an aspect of herself against which she struggles. Rather, the enemy is institutionalized psychiatry and the people who buy into its belief system. Echoing Michel Foucault, Millett suggests that "mental illness" is a social construct, an ideology designed to control and punish social dissidents: "How like vengeance it all is, how like all terrible ideologies."[16] Mental institutions and many treatments are means of punishment and control rather than of healing. Lithium is "a form of social control, don't you see, because this psychiatrist thing is in itself a form of social control and very much directed by institutions. Not just schools and companies and hospitals but ultimately the state."[17] Again, Millett's analysis recalls that of Thomas Szasz, who argues that the "psychiatric idiom is actually only a dialect of the common language of oppressors."[18]

For Szasz and Millett, psychiatric labels have no benefit; they serve only to oppress, even dehumanize. Mental illness in general (and bipolar disorder in particular) is, for Millett, merely an accusation made against people based on fear. Furthermore, once the diagnosis is made, it is hard to disprove: "I become not what I am but what I am said to be, as the self flails on, skewered by a pushpin, squirming for credibility even in its own eyes by the end."[19] This statement emphasizes the enormous power psychiatric language has for Millett. Clearly, she does not view manic depression as a disease or even as a disturbance of part of the brain; it is, rather, a deep flaw in the self. Or to be more precise, she believes that outsiders view "mental illness" as a deep flaw in the self. Furthermore, that self seems to be radically unstable and vulnerable, since it is inflated or deflated by the language used to describe it. Millett highlights the power of language to construct reality when she writes, "If only no one had told them I was mad. Then I wouldn't be. They wouldn't imagine it and act accordingly, nor I take exception to their manner, alienating them further. Nor would I have been so vexed and irritated that I probably was crazed."[20]

It must be noted that not everybody views psychiatric labels as destructive or degrading. In his book *The Noonday Demon*, for example, Andrew Solomon discusses a depressed person he interviewed who found the label "depression" empowering:

> The labeling of her complaint was an essential step toward her recovery from it. What can be named and described can be contained: the word *depression* separated Lolly's illness from her personality. If all the things she disliked in herself could be grouped together as aspects of a disease, that left her good qualities as the "real" Lolly, and it was much easier for her to like this real Lolly, and to turn this real Lolly against the problems that afflicted her. To be given the idea of depression is to master a socially powerful linguistic tool that segregates and empowers the better self to which suffering people aspire.[21]

Solomon's argument that psychiatric idiom can be empowering is completely absent from Millett's narrative. So is the notion that people can conceivably benefit from therapy and medication or that some people might *welcome* medical treatment for mental illness.

Rather, her autobiography is suffused with fear—the fear of utter annihilation that awaits the psychiatric patient. I suggest that Millett's relentless fear stems not only from the constant threat of incarceration but also from her belief that mental illness is, if not a crime, then at least an unbearable threat to one's core identity. On the surface, Millett would claim that she is only pointing out how *others* see mental illness. But in so doing, she ignores viewpoints that differ from her own—beliefs of both professionals and other patients who see bipolar disorder not as the sign of a flawed self but as an illness that can be treated. While Millett rightly observes that people are frightened of the idea of madness, it seems to me that she is more frightened of it than the people she criticizes—so scared that she denies its very existence.

Millett projects her own views of mental illness onto her lover when she says: "I am in [Sophie's] view no longer valid. Invalid. Incompetent. Canceled by what I have become to her, a crazy."[22] This language suggests that if she were to acknowledge her mind to be ill, her self or core identity would be "canceled" and "invalid." Later statements reiterate this point. She remarks, for example, that "to lift the judgment against me would be to have my selfhood again, absolved of the ever-present and proven charge of insanity."[23] If she *did* have bipolar illness, this sentence suggests, it would mean her selfhood was obliterated. Obviously this is a deeply threatening thought. When explaining her rationale for writing *The Loony-Bin Trip*, she states that it is "[b]ecause the telling functions for me as a kind of exorcism, a retrieval and vindication of the self—the mind—through reliving what occurred."[24] Her syntax "the self—the mind" suggests that for her, the mind is synonymous, or nearly so, with the self. Later, her syntax again suggests a similar logic: "I turned frantically to what seemed my only other option to save my life, my body anyway, and surrendered *my mind, the spirit, the self.* I sought 'help,' became a lithium patient and lived thereafter a careful existence."[25] Notice she does not say "my mind, my spirit, my self" as in a series, but "my mind, *the* spirit, *the* self," implying these are synonyms for the same thing. If this is true, then of course a diagnosis of mental illness would be a deeply threatening accusation, an invalidation of her identity and one that must be resisted at all costs.

Kay Redfield Jamison's discursive project of manic depression takes a different form than Millett's. *An Unquiet Mind* recounts Jamison's harrowing experiences of recurrent cycles of mania and depression. First diagnosed as manic depressive in her late twenties, Jamison, like Millett, also initially rebelled against her diagnosis and the prescribed use of lithium. Eventually, however, Jamison came to terms with her "madness" (her term) and the need for lithium and has been able to lead a professionally successful and relatively stable life. I suggest that one reason Jamison navigates the stormy seas of her mood disorder relatively well is that she distinguishes between her self—her core identity—and her moods. For her, the core self—whatever that is, wherever it is located—is something separate from her mind. Therefore, if her mind becomes ill, it does not mean that she is fundamentally broken or invalid, as Millett seems to suggest in her own case. Of course, her training as a scientist contributes to this discursive project; she consistently and insistently refers to manic depression as an illness of biological origin: "I believe, without doubt, that manic-depressive illness is a medical illness; I also believe that, with rare exception, it is malpractice to treat it without medication."[26]

When she was first confronted with severe mood swings, however, Jamison was more resistant to the idea that she had a mental illness and more uncertain about how such an illness would alter her core identity. At first, she denied "that what I had was a real disease. . . . Moods are such an essential part of the substance of life, of one's notion of oneself, that even psychotic extremes in mood and behavior somehow can be seen as temporary, even understandable, reactions to what life has dealt. In my case, I had a horrible sense of loss for who I had been and where I had been."[27] In this early stage of her struggle with the illness, Jamison shares with Millett a resistance to separating one's "self" from one's moods, as being labeled bipolar can be a devastating affront to one's identity. Understandably, one sometimes reacts to such a threat by denying that one has an illness and rejecting medication, as both Millett and Jamison did at one point. Jamison observes that "[b]ecause my illness seemed at first simply to be an extension of myself—that is to say, of my ordinarily changeable moods, energies, and enthusiasms—I perhaps gave it at times too much quarter."[28]

Eventually, however, Jamison separates her "real self"—or at least her idea of her real self—from the extremes in moods and behavior she experiences cyclically. Statements such as "I finally was feeling myself again";[29] "England . . . gave me back myself again";[30] and "Each day I awoke deeply tired, a feeling as foreign to my *natural self* as being bored or indifferent to life"[31]—all imply that mood extremes are not an expression of the real self, but of something else. Jamison also suggests that many of her actions during extreme highs and lows (including a suicide attempt) were not the actions of her true self: "These discrepancies between what one is, what one is brought up to believe is the right way of behaving toward others, and what actually happens during these awful black manias, or mixed states, are absolute and disturbing beyond description . . ."[32]

So while Millett makes no distinction between one's "true self" and one's manic or depressed self (all are valid expressions of one's mind, one's self), Jamison's language clearly suggests such a division. She writes, for example, that "I was used to my mind being my best friend. . . . Now, all of a sudden, my mind had turned on me: it mocked me for my vapid enthusiasms; it laughed at all of my foolish plans; it no longer found anything interesting or enjoyable or worthwhile."[33] This phrasing separates the mind, "it," from herself, "me." How, then, to explain the feelings and actions that occur during manias and depressions?

Jamison explains them through the metaphor of bipolar disorder as an outside force, "a fascinating, albeit deadly, enemy and companion."[34] Unlike her sister, who is also troubled by a mood disorder, Jamison does not consider her mood swings to be a reflection of her core identity. Whereas her sister "saw the darkness as being within and part of herself, the family, and the world," Jamison saw the darkness "as a *stranger*; however lodged within my mind and soul the darkness became, it almost always seemed an *outside force* that was at war with my natural self."[35] She continues with this metaphor throughout her memoir. For example, she writes, "I was a senior in high school when I had my first *attack* of manic-depressive illness; once the *siege* began, I lost my mind rather rapidly,"[36] suggesting that she was invaded, as in a war. Later, she notes that "[e]ventually, the depression went away of its own accord, but only long enough for it to regroup and mobilize for the next attack."[37] These military metaphors, I believe, are strategic on Jamison's part; they provide a way for her to conceptualize her problems in a way that does not destroy her identity. While it is certainly horrible to be attacked and invaded by an outside force, it is even worse to believe that one's own core is inherently flawed, that one's self is inferior, wrong, rotten, "criminal," or worthless—common self-perceptions among the depressed.

In conclusion, both of these books raise intriguing questions about the nature of the self in relationship to mood disorders. Not surprisingly, perhaps, they provide no conclusive answers to these questions. Jamison's discursive project of manic depression as an outside force is, at least for her, an empowering construct that allows her to manage successfully her mood disorder and lead a productive life. However, Kate Millett might find Kay Jamison's psychiatric approach problematic.[38] Instead of demonizing the extreme mood swings, Millett might suggest, why not accept them as one more facet of a complex personality? One might also ask of Jamison: if the extreme moods are not an expression of the self, at what point does the real self end and the distortions caused by moods begin? Furthermore, is it ethically possible for me to decide which parts of myself are "real" and which parts are not? Might not this kind of thinking potentially lead to a disavowal of responsibility for my actions?

On the other hand, Millett's discursive project raises questions as well. While Millett's goal is to free the "mentally ill" from the shackles of psychiatric imprisonment, I believe her project can be counterproductive to someone struggling with a serious mental illness. Is the only way to deal with a mood disorder to deny it exists? Is not this a dangerous strategy for people undergoing severe suffering—people who may commit suicide because of their disorder? While there are no easy answers to these questions, one thing seems clear from the study of these pathographies: the way people think, write, and talk about their experiences of mental illness matters a great deal; it profoundly colors how they experience their emotional turbulence.

Notes

1. Smith, *A Poetics of Women's Autobiography*, 5.
2. I am using the terms "bipolar disorder" and "manic depression" as synonyms in this essay. "Bipolar disorder" is the official *DSM-IV* classification; however, Jamison prefers the older term "manic depression."
3. Jamison, *An Unquiet Mind*, 179–84.
4. Hawkins, *Reconstructing Illness*, 15.
5. Smith, 47.
6. Jelinek, *The Tradition of Women's Autobiography*, xiii.
7. Hawkins, 17.
8. Fee, "The Project of Pathology," 75 (italics in the original).
9. Hewitt et al., "Is It Me or Is It Prozac?" 173 (italics in the original).
10. Millett, *The Loony-Bin Trip*, 314.
11. Szasz, "The Myth of Mental Illness," 8.
12. Millett, 32.
13. Ibid., 232.
14. Ibid., 31.
15. Ibid., 29.
16. Ibid., 72. For example, see Foucault, *Madness and Civilization*.
17. Millett, 55.
18. Szasz, "Should Psychiatric Patients Ever Be Hospitalized Involuntarily?" 479.
19. Millett, 71.
20. Ibid., 143.
21. Solomon, *The Noonday Demon*, 343.
22. Millett, 64.
23. Ibid., 31.
24. Ibid., 11.
25. Ibid., 12 (emphasis added).
26. Jamison, 102.
27. Ibid., 91.
28. Ibid., 5.
29. Ibid., 147.
30. Ibid., 158.
31. Ibid., 38 (emphasis added).
32. Ibid., 121.
33. Ibid., 37–38.
34. Ibid., 5.

35. Ibid., 15 (emphasis added).

36. Ibid., 36 (emphasis added).

37. Ibid., 45.

38. In her preface to the reissued *The Loony-Bin Trip* (2000), Millett expresses gratitude for Jamison's *An Unquiet Mind*, but adds the caveat, "though [*An Unquiet Mind*] derives from a conventional psychiatric point of view" (9).

Bibliography

Fee, Dwight, ed. *Pathology and the Postmodern: Mental Illness as Discourse and Experience*. London: Sage, 2000.

———. "The Project of Pathology: Reflexivity and Depression in Elizabeth Wurtzel's *Prozac Nation*." In Fee, ed., *Pathology and the Postmodern*, 74–99.

Foucault, Michel. *Madness and Civilization*. 1965. Translated by Richard Howard. New York: Vintage, 1973.

Hawkins, Anne Hunsaker. *Reconstructing Illness: Studies in Pathography*. West Lafayette, IN: Purdue University Press, 1993.

Hewitt, John P., Michael R. Fraser, and LeslieBeth Berger. "Is It Me or Is It Prozac? Antidepressants and the Construction of Self." In Fee, ed., *Pathology and the Postmodern*, 163–85.

Jamison, Kay Redfield. *An Unquiet Mind: A Memoir of Moods and Madness*. New York: Vintage, 1995.

Jelinek, Estelle. *The Tradition of Women's Autobiography from Antiquity to the Present*. Boston: Twayne, 1986.

Lilienfeld, Scott O., ed. *Seeing Both Sides: Classic Controversies in Abnormal Psychology*. Pacific Grove, CA: Brooks/Cole, 1995.

Millett, Kate. *The Loony-Bin Trip*. 1990. Reissued with a new preface by the author. Urbana: University of Illinois Press, 2000.

———. *Sexual Politics*. Garden City, NY: Doubleday, 1970.

Smith, Sidonie. *A Poetics of Women's Autobiography: Marginality and the Fictions of Self-Representation*. Bloomington: Indiana University Press, 1987.

Solomon, Andrew. *The Noonday Demon: An Atlas of Depression*. New York: Scribner, 2001.

Szasz, Thomas. "The Myth of Mental Illness." In Lilienfeld, ed., *Seeing Both Sides*, 5–10.

———. "Should Psychiatric Patients Ever Be Hospitalized Involuntarily? Under Any Circumstances—No." In Lilienfeld, ed., *Seeing Both Sides*, 475–82.

Chapter 3

Winter Tales

Comedy and Romance Story-Types in Narratives of Depression

Brenda Dyer

In "The Story of 'I': Illness and Narrative Identity," Shlomith Rimmon-Kenan says, "[W]e lead our lives as stories, and our identity is constructed both by stories we tell ourselves and others about ourselves and by the master narratives that consciously or unconsciously serve as models for ours."[1] One can hear the echoes of these master narratives—Tragedy, Comedy, Romance, Restitution, Chaos, Quest, Confession, Regeneration—in almost every account of personal experience with illness, whether published by professional writers or recounted orally to social science researchers in interviews. Ilka Kangas notes that in her interviews with sufferers of depression, the interviewees not only have an individual understanding of their condition but also use shared cultural conceptions of the illness.[2] An aspect of this shared knowledge is the narrative types by which we explain, understand, and indeed experience depression. This chapter looks at these types in the depression memoirs of William Styron and Martha Manning (*Darkness Visible* and *Undercurrents*) and in oral depression narratives from sociological and psychological studies.[3] All of these depression narratives move in and out of several cultural master narratives, but particularly draw on comedy and romance, both the tragicomic romance of Shakespeare's last plays and the medieval quest romance.

Some Narrative Typologies

Northrop Frye's typology of literature is informed by Aristotle's original categories.[4] In his *Anatomy of Criticism,* Frye proposes four categories of

41

literature—comedy, tragedy, romance, and irony/satire—which are "permanent forms embodied in the human imagination."[5] These archetypal categories he sees as broader than literary genres such as drama, poetry, and fiction; he refers to them as "*mythoi* or generic plots."[6] According to Frye, comedy involves overcoming a challenge in order to achieve social harmony, while tragedy ends with the downfall of the hero. The romance protagonist embarks on a dangerous journey in which he or she overcomes several obstacles and, through his or her sufferings, becomes wiser. In the *mythos* of satire/irony, which has a pessimistic tone of chaos and confusion, the "shifting ambiguities and complexities of unidealized existence" cannot be overcome.[7]

In his typology of illness narratives, Arthur Frank does not refer explicitly to Frye, yet his three categories overlap significantly with Frye's. In Frank's restitution narrative, a healthy person becomes sick and then recovers. This might be compared to the comic *mythos* of Frye. In Frank's chaos narrative, however, life never gets better. The protagonist is a victim of bad luck. This narrative lacks the moral coherence of classical tragedy (where the noble hero suffers directly as a result of his fatal flaw) but approximates modern existential tragedy or theater of the absurd. It could also be compared to Frye's *mythos* of irony/satire. Although Frank calls for "honoring the chaos story,"[8] he claims that chaos narratives are incompatible with writing or even telling: "Those who are truly *living* the chaos cannot tell in words. . . . Lived chaos makes reflection, and consequently story-telling, impossible."[9] In Frank's third type, the quest narrative, the illness initiates a spiritual journey, in which the hero "meet[s] suffering head on; [he or she] accept[s] illness and seek[s] to *use* it."[10] This quest/journey motif links Frank's quest narrative with the romance genre of Frye, but Frank does not refer to the dramatic turning point of romance, which is typically a battle against an enemy like a dragon, whether this enemy be real or allegorical.

Another genre that has been identified by genre theorists is tragicomedy, and particularly tragicomic romance. Verna Foster suggests that tragicomedy's "central inherent requirement" is "to offer a more comprehensive . . . understanding of human experience than either tragedy or comedy."[11] In Renaissance tragicomedy, Foster contends, the "individual's self-worth and the meaningfulness of his suffering are ultimately affirmed."[12] In her view, Renaissance tragicomedies are forms of comedy since they "generally work themselves through to some kind of 'happy ending,'" yet evoke tragic and comic responses in the audience, for example, a "painful awareness of the ironic discrepancy between what is and what might have been."[13] Foster categorizes the late plays of Shakespeare as romantic tragicomedies, which incorporate romance materials and "[work] towards . . . comic romantic endings" but have endings in which the happiness "is muted by memories of loss."[14] Another feature of this story-type is that typical "tragicomic inevitability"[15] is complicated by a sense of wonder at miraculous resurrections or reversals. While Frye does not use this term "tragicomedy," his description of Shakespeare's last plays is very similar to Foster's. He distinguishes between six "phases" of comedy; the fifth-phase comedies, which he says we find in Shakespeare's late plays, "do not avoid tragedies but contain them."[16] In this category, there is not a simple cyclical movement from sadness to happiness, but a "bodily metamorphosis and a transformation from one kind of life to another."[17]

The Depression Narrative

Dominant medical/psychiatric discourse poses depression as an illness with a cure through medication, and outcome-based quantitative research does show that medication and psychotherapy significantly help in the treatment of depression.[18] However, this comic structure of "problem—intervention—happy ending" frames only a minority of depression narratives. The particular nature of depression as a commonly episodic, recurrent illness strains the assumptions and parameters of the comic story line. Underlying the comic depression narrative are not only the interests of psychiatry and the pharmaceutical industry but also modern North American ideals of optimism and individual heroism.

While some accounts of depression frame recovery in comic terms—medication, ECT, psychotherapy, and/or God aiding the stricken heroes to rise successfully above their despair and recover definitively from it—many other accounts reflect a tale more akin to romance, in which the protagonist cycles through several obstacles/depressions. Looking at a medical graph showing the "remission, recovery, relapse, and recurrence" typical of unipolar major depressive disorder,[19] one may be reminded of Frye's description of "naïve" romance, "an endless form in which a central character who never develops or ages goes through one adventure after another."[20] Of course, the protagonist of the narrative of chronic or recurrent depression does age over time, but there is no final upward plot trajectory toward a happier ending. Indeed, the inability to manage or make sense of a never-ending and cruel depression may be better storied in what Frank calls the "chaos" genre, which he says is rarely published, possibly because it is not in accord with the North American values aforementioned.[21]

Frye also describes a more sophisticated three-stage quest romance in which there is the "perilous journey and the preliminary minor adventures; the crucial struggle, usually some kind of battle . . . ; and the exaltation of the hero."[22] This quest romance story is manipulated in an interesting way in depression narratives: the narrators often construct as a turning point an intensely internal moment in which the depression, previously seen as an external enemy, is accepted and incorporated into the protagonist's life narrative. In these narratives, "recovery" is incomplete and bears the stamp of past and future suffering. The joy of feeling better is fragile, complicated by the realization that the hero will, in fact, never be better—or as Nancy Mairs puts it, in reference to her own experience of depression: "No hope of a cure, ever, for being me."[23] This lack of closure indicates a degree of irony in the otherwise epiphanic setting of romance.

Depression Narratives as Comedy or Tragicomedy

The two examples of comic or tragicomic depression narratives I shall touch on come from qualitative feminist sociological research. Ingela Skarsater frames her interviews from a comic perspective. Each of the thirteen Swedish women she interviewed had a history of major depression and at least one hospitalization. Although Skarsater uses a disease-and-recovery model, she locates the women's recovery not in medication or therapy per se, but in "tak[ing] charge of their own recovery process."[24] She uses words like "empowerment," "succeed," "change," "choice," "control," and "decision," and writes: "Recovering from depression is a question of making changes in one's life and in oneself as a person . . . tak[ing] risks in trying new activities."[25] There is not a sense here of a circuitous individual journey, struggle, or quest, but rather of "taking charge" and reforming what has gone awry in the social (patriarchal) fabric, with a comic conclusion of renewed membership in the community of women.

Melva Steen's less optimistic account in her depression study is more tragicomic in tone. She interviewed twenty-two women who had been clinically depressed and were in the recovery stage. Most described impoverished childhoods, emotional or physical neglect, and abuse. Adulthood held difficult, abusive relationships and situations. The first turning point in these women's recovery from depression was a life or interpersonal crisis in which the women realized they needed help. This help came in the form of therapy and/or medication. The second turning point occurred when "they stopped trusting the experts . . . and started acting as their own agents."[26] "Setting boundaries, learning to say no and asking for what they needed to get well" completed the recovery process.[27] The upward plot trajectory of both Skarsater's and Steen's interpretations of the narratives is typically comic (or in the case of Steen's downward and upward trajectory, tragicomic), with a happy ending of restored agency in a community. The characters are almost stereotyped stock characters in a feminist fable, their depression construed as arising from an imbalance of personal and social power, and their recovery achieved when this imbalance is rectified through increased personal agency.

Depression Narratives as Tragicomic Romance

While tragedy emphasizes the inevitable or fated triumph of evil and human flaws, and comedy overcomes evil's power, romance acknowledges the reality of human suffering and the necessity of trials and tribulations in the development of moral experience. Thus, while tragedy involves irreversible situations and comedy focuses on alternatives to or reversals of bad situations, romance renders choices as lessons on how to use free will: characters benefit from second chances and fresh starts. In romance, an event with tragic potential leads not to a tragic fall but to a providential experience. For instance, Shakespeare wrote his late plays *Cymbeline, Pericles, The Tempest,* and *The Winter's Tale* in the mode of the tragicomic romance, involving a reversal of fortune for the protagonists, who start well, then seem headed for a tragic catastrophe, and finally celebrate a comic ending.

Foster argues that *The Winter's Tale* demonstrates the tragicomic structure particularly well: there are three acts of tragedy, followed by two acts of reconciliation and comedy. Foster speaks of "tragicomedy's characteristic double vision,"[28] referring to *The Winter's Tale*: here, the apparent death of a major character (Hermione) is not irreversible, but also the happiness of the final reunions is stained by memories of irrevocable loss (for example, in the death of Mamillius). Nature's inevitable cycle is the frame for the play—"things dying" give way to "things new born" (3.3.114)—and tragedy shifts to comedy in ways that emphasize the natural cycles of suffering and liberation. The joy of tragicomic romance is particularly mixed with sadness and a lingering anxiety about the future, a sense that summer declines to autumn and winter again and a sense that experiential lessons learned do, to some extent, compromise the innocence that led to suffering in the first place. As Foster says, the audience remembers "the characters' past suffering and the terrible price that has been paid for sin and error."[29] This is a "universe that allows second chances, even though nothing is ever quite as the characters would like it to be."[30] Foster presents this as a fallen Christian world of redemption rather than one of Edenic bliss.

While William Styron's depression memoir, *Darkness Visible,* contains elements of classical tragedy and comedy, I would argue that it is ultimately a tragicomic romance. That Styron is tempted by the tragic plot for the crafting of his life story is evident from the foreboding first lines: in Paris, 1985, he "[becomes] fully aware that the struggle with the disorder in [his] mind . . . might have a fatal outcome."[31] Upon his glimpse of Hôtel Washington, which he visited thirty-five years before, he feels he has "come fatally full circle."[32] When he puts his journals into the garbage bin in preparing for a suicide attempt, he knows "[he has] made an irreversible decision" and that death is "as inescapable as nightfall."[33] The dramatic turning point comes when, knowing he "could not possibly get [himself] through the following day," he listens to Brahms and realizes "[a]ll this . . . was more than [he] could ever abandon."[34] He uses literary terminology to describe the turning point of his tale, the "near-violent denouement"[35] of near-suicide when he is finally hospitalized. Thus the plot, driving down toward tragedy, turns abruptly and takes an upward direction, as Styron eventually "emerge[s] into light."[36] The turning is away from death and toward life.

The structure of Styron's narrative, then, is not unlike that of *The Winter's Tale* with its tragic first three acts, the hiatus of sixteen years, and the final comic restoration of life that would be meaningless if Leontes did not recognize the significance for himself of the intervening years of repentance. Leontes spends the sixteen years in grieving and remorse: "[T]ears . . . / Shall be my recreation" (3.2.237–38). The seven-week period Styron spends in the hospital parallels this hiatus of time: "For me the real healers were seclusion and time."[37] Styron's recovery seems based on both the healing powers of time and his individual regaining of a will to live. He says, "I knew I had emerged into light. I felt myself no longer a husk but a body with some of the body's sweet juices stirring again."[38] In the dénouement, Styron reframes the "near fatal" disease of depression in tragicomic plot terms, as containing both tragic potentiality and a providentially happy ending: "[D]epression's only grudging favor . . . [is] the eventual passing of the storm . . . its fury almost always fades and then disappears."[39] Further, he identifies his episode of depression as a romance when he adds: "[T]he affliction runs its course, and one finds peace."[40] Styron's allusion to Dante in the last few pages marks his vision as essentially that of tragicomic romance: "For those who have dwelt in depression's dark wood, . . . their return from the abyss is not unlike the ascent of the poet, trudging upward and upward out of hell's black depths and at last emerging into what he saw as 'the shining world'."[41] We see a full revolution from good to bad to qualified good, the movement of tragicomic romance down to hell and then out again into a redeemed world, the happiness of which is qualified by the unforgettable experience of hell.

Styron constructs his experience within medical discourse on depression, in terms of cause and cure, with medication and hospitalization as turning points in the story. He experiences depression as "mysterious," "coming and going" with no reason. He also uses the word "victim" repeatedly, in order to identify how the disease as antagonist affected him, the protagonist. Although the tale is framed as a tragicomic structure, with a happy ending, there is a sense of a powerless protagonist riding the waves of fate rather than a hero learning or being transformed by his suffering. Yet there is an intriguing mixture of agency and surrender at the dramatic turning point. While his recovery seems predicated on bowing to the illness, surrendering himself to it in the hospital, and trusting that it will "run its course,"[42] Styron first makes an existential choice to live, which then prompts the crucial and life-saving decision to check himself into the hospital. This paradoxical merging of heroic, decisive control and resigned surrender marks the turning point of the depression narrative as romance.

Depression Narratives as Quest Romance

The paradoxical sense of resigned agency, or decisive surrender, is beautifully enacted in Martha Manning's memoir *Undercurrents*, in her use of the dragon and battle motif. In her memoir, Manning starts out with a comic restitution structure. As a depressed psychologist, she begins with faith in therapy and medication and does indeed recover from her first episode: "I considered myself 'cured.'"[44] However, as the depression recurs and the medications fail, she enters a potentially tragic plot, in which she is suicidal: "All escapes are illusory. . . . I want to die."[45] She longs for the comic structure, "the smooth ascending slope," but eventually understands that the romance pattern of recovery from depression has "a 'saw-toothed' profile, with numerous peaks and valleys."[46] She uses the quest romance metaphor of the journey in her description of recovery as "a long lonely journey, in all its circuitousness."[47]

What makes Manning's story distinctive is her use of the archetypal figure of the dragon as an externalized doom. Frye speaks of the "central form of quest-romance" as the dragon-killing theme, and mentions that in the book of Job, the sea monster (Leviathan) is closely associated with the "blasted world of struggle and poverty and disease into which Job is hurled by Satan."[48] According to Frye, in some stories the hero kills the dragon in a decisive triumph over death. In other stories, "the dying-god myths," the hero dies fighting the dragon and the final stage involves his cyclical rebirth/resurrection.[49] Manning dips into this romance archetype when she makes reference to the Christian myth of St. Martha and the Dragon. In one version of the medieval French legend, St. Martha sprinkles holy water on the tail of the fire-breathing dragon, Tarasque of the River Rhône, to make it docile, and then leads it back into town with her silken belt. Manning, whose first name is Martha, compares herself to St. Martha and marvels that the saint "all[ied] herself with the thing that she most feared. She gave the object of her fear something that it needed and wanted."[50] That is, in order to appease the dragon, St. Martha befriended it. Manning admits she is full of terror of depression returning in the future: "I hate that dragon. It is my enemy." Yet the legend "moves [her] deeply" and "illuminates an entirely different way of thinking about [depression]."[51]

In fact, in the conclusion of the memoir, it appears that Manning does bow to the dragon. She finally recognizes the "limits of [her] effort and will," that "[t]o know the force of the avalanche and [her] powerlessness over it is to feel [herself] in brand-new territory."[52] When she declares, "There is no getting away from a wave that's got your name on it. . . . The tide will come and go," we have the profound view, typical of romance, of the cyclical and impermanent nature of existence itself.[53] She also realizes that she will never return to the Edenic innocence of her life before depression:

> For so long now I have waited to get back to baseline and return to exactly the same point from which I originally set out on these travels. My criterion for healing has been to be able to pick up right where I left off, like midpage in a novel. . . . [But] I'm never going to get back to that page. . . . I'm in an entirely new book now, most of it unwritten.[54]

Thus the romance plot, whose goal is to take a hero/ine through a series of learning experiences, results here in Manning's increased acceptance of depression as a travel companion in a new landscape, a larger narrative that includes both descent and ascent.

For Manning, this stage of "recovery" from depression includes a spiritual transformation that brings her into a gratitude for the present moment: "The ability to breathe and to be is such a tremendous gift that anything lacking in our lives is cheap in comparison."[55] For the first time in her life she understands her alcoholic sister's recovery as a "surviving minute by minute."[56] She is even able to see the gifts of her depression, as she describes the epiphany of realizing that "one of the great dividends of darkness is an increased sensitivity to the light."[57] Her epiphany, like Styron's, recognizes the paradox of surrendering agency in order to take control of a life.

The concept of surrendering as a pivotal part of depression recovery is richly developed in sociologist David Karp's *Speaking of Sadness*, a phenomenological study of depression based on his personal experience and his interviews with fifty people who had received a physician's diagnosis of depression. His description of the illness "careers" of chronically depressed people recalls Frye's definition of "naïve romance" as an endless sequence of adventures: "Chronically depressed people are constantly in the throes of an illness that is tragically familiar, but always new . . . a nearly continuous process of construction, destruction, and reconstruction of identities."[58] However, while Frye's naïve romance hero never develops, for Karp the heroes of depression careers do undergo a transformation;

although the *plot* does not unfold in an upward comic movement to full recovery, there is a sense of progress in *character* through these episodes of identity reconstruction. Karp argues that once people learn to live with the depression, they "often respond to pain in a more spiritual fashion, trying to find ways, if not to embrace it, at least to incorporate depressive illness into their lives. Thus, the process of adaptation moves full circle. It starts with diversion and ends with incorporation."[59] Through the repeated experience of suffering, people move from "the medical language of cure and toward the spiritual language of transformation."[60] What Karp refers to as "epiphanies," transcendent vertical moments, punctuate the forward movement of a horizontal plot. Aristotle in his *Poetics* describes the ideal tragic plot as one in which the moment of reversal (the turning point) coincides with the moment of recognition or insight (the epiphany). In Karp's narratives, there appears to be no plot reversal: not much changes except the sufferer's response to his suffering. Epiphany rather than reversal marks the encounter with the dragon of depression; the beast is befriended rather than slain. As Karp puts it, "[F]or me depression is akin to being tied to a chair with restraints on my wrists. . . . [I]t took me a long time to see that I only magnified my torment by jerking at the restraints."[61] In the world of romance, where time is cyclical rather than linear, these out-of-time epiphanies are possible.

Echoing Karp's description of the "depression career" as involving "assessing self, redefining self, reinterpreting past selves, and attempting to construct a future self,"[62] Rita Schreiber describes the process of depression recovery for twenty-one women as involving six stages of "redefining self." Before the women sink into depression, they experience being "clued out." The first turning point in the road to recovery is "seeing the abyss," which is recognizing that something is wrong and taking action to get help. The second turning point is "clueing in," "when the woman's consciousness about her self and her world change[s], often quite suddenly." In the final stage, the woman "see[s] herself as a whole person . . . [S]he has a history that enriches who she is, and a part of that history is her experience with depression."[63] These turning points seem to resemble the epiphanies of the spiritual journey or quest romance, a narrative depicted by the researcher visually as a jigsaw puzzle, rather than as a story line or graph.[64]

Conclusions

Frank characterizes as restitution narratives those illness narratives with a comic story line: "Yesterday I was healthy, today I'm sick, but tomorrow I'll be healthy again." He finds this "culturally preferred narrative" in television commercials, sociological studies, and medicine, but critiques its hegemony: "Medicine's hope of restitution crowds out any other stories."[65] In a similar critique of the modern monomyth of depression recovery, Jeffery Smith states, "[N]ot everyone was listening to Prozac; or perhaps it simply wasn't speaking to thousands who wanted to hear from it. This underscores what is perhaps the most noxious effect of biological psychiatry: it has reduced the ancient melancholic narrative to one story. . . . But we need more stories than just this one."[66] Most of the depression stories discussed in this chapter draw on not the comic narrative but rather the tragicomic romance or quest romance.

Frye describes romance as involving two worlds: an "idyllic world" of happiness and a "night world" involving separation, loneliness, and pain.[67] The conclusion is not a return to idyllic happiness but rather an incorporation of the lessons of the night: "The . . . world of romance reminds us that we are not awake when we have abolished the dream world: we are awake only when we have absorbed it again."[68] This integrating principle in romance is expressed in depression narratives as a merging of personal agency with existential surrender. Karp says that when he stops struggling against his chains, he finds relief. One has the image of the heroic traveler struggling along the up-and-down circular plot trajectory of the quest romance, meeting the dragon of depression yet again, and simply dropping out of the plot for a while to sit with the enemy. Frank calls this movement a "shift from the hero as Hercules to the hero as Bodhisattva, from the hero of force to the hero of perseverance through suffering."[69] As Smith says about his own recovery from depression, "I had conquered nothing, mastered nothing, transcended nothing. I had simply settled into something that had been waiting for me—who knows how long?—and made the descent it seemed to require."[70] This resigned descent seems a necessary preliminary to any significant ascent into wisdom, as the dialectical struggle between comedy and tragedy inspires the synthesis of romance.

In the rhetoric of depression recovery narratives, there seems to be a conception of the self as capable of self-learning and repositioning, but not of "authoring" one's life. As Paul Ricoeur states, while "we learn to become the *narrator of our own story* [we do so] without completely becoming the author of our life."[71] Andrew Solomon describes his depression experience as bringing about greater self-knowing rather than victory over the illness: "It was . . . in depression that I learned my own acreage, the full extent of my soul."[72] In romance narratives of depression, the protagonists are forced to give up their roles as autonomous heroes who can conquer the obstacles of depression. Instead, they must reposition themselves in the context of a tragicomic universe, one in which they incorporate depression into their lives and welcome spring while it lasts, knowing that winter will come again.

Notes

1. Rimmon-Kenan, "Story of 'I,'" 11.
2. Kangas, "Making Sense of Depression," 86.
3. These studies can be found in Karp, *Speaking of Sadness*; Schreiber, "(Re)defining My Self"; Skarsater et al., "Women's Conceptions of Coping"; and Steen, "Essential Structure and Meaning."
4. In the fourth century BC, Aristotle identified "Epic Poetry and Tragedy, Comedy also and Dithyrambic poetry" as fundamental "modes of imitation." *Poetics*, 7.
5. M. H. Abrams's phrase in *A Glossary of Literary Terms*, 109.
6. Frye, *Anatomy of Criticism*, 162.
7. Ibid., 223.
8. Arthur Frank, *The Wounded Storyteller*, 109.
9. Ibid., 98 (italics in the original).
10. Ibid., 115 (italics in the original).
11. Foster, *The Name and Nature of Tragicomedy*, 1.
12. Ibid., 13.
13. Ibid., 13–14.
14. Ibid., 53.
15. Ibid., 65.
16. Frye, *Anatomy of Criticism*, 184.
17. Ibid.
18. See Lam and Kennedy, "Evidence-Based Strategies."
19. An up-and-down movement is shown on the medical graph in E. Frank et al., "Conceptualization and Rationale," 853. The graph represents the typical "remission, recovery, relapse, and recurrence" of major depressive disorder.
20. Frye, *Anatomy*, 186.
21. Rimmon-Kenan develops an interesting explanation for the paucity of chaos illness narratives (23), mainly hypothesizing that would-be narrators of these narratives are silenced by social expectations to "get well," and may "conceal disruption under a semblance of continuity and/or victory" (14). She critiques Arthur Frank's assertion that chaos and narrative are incompatible, and wants to "make room for illness narratives without epiphanies and for writing that does not overcome chaos" (24).
22. Frye, *Anatomy*, 187.
23. Mairs, "On Living Behind Bars," 212.
24. Skarsater et al., 433.
25. Ibid.
26. Steen, 84.
27. Ibid., 85.
28. Foster, 67.
29. Ibid., 78.
30. Ibid., 127.
31. Styron, *Darkness Visible*, 3.
32. Ibid., 4.
33. Ibid., 64–65.

34. Ibid., 66–67.
35. Ibid., 8.
36. Ibid., 75.
37. Ibid., 69.
38. Ibid., 75.
39. Ibid., 73.
40. Ibid.
41. Ibid., 84.
42. Ibid., 73.
43. Foster, 65.
44. Manning, *Undercurrents*, 59.
45. Ibid., 99.
46. Ibid., 145.
47. Ibid., 151.
48. Frye, *Anatomy*, 189.
49. Ibid., 192.
50. Manning, 195–96.
51. Ibid., 195–96.
52. Ibid., 186.
53. Ibid., 194.
54. Ibid., 186.
55. Ibid., 167.
56. Ibid., 178.
57. Ibid., 161.
58. Karp, *Speaking of Sadness*, 75.
59. Ibid., 108.
60. Ibid., 127.
61. Ibid., 124.
62. Ibid, 56.
63. Schreiber, "(Re)defining My Self," 484, 486–87.
64. Ibid., 473, figure 1.
65. Frank, *The Wounded Storyteller*, 83.
66. Smith, *Where the Roots Reach for Water*, 113–14.
67. Frye, *Secular Scripture*, 53, 55.
68. Ibid., 61.
69. Frank, 134.
70. Smith, 272.
71. Ricoeur, "Life: A Story," 437 (italics in original text).
72. Solomon, *The Noonday Demon*, 24.

Bibliography

Abrams, M. H., ed. *A Glossary of Literary Terms.* 7th ed. Forth Worth, TX: Harcourt Brace College Publishers, 1999.

Aristotle. *Poetics.* In *Aristotle's Theory of Poetry and Fine Art,* translated and edited by S. H. Butcher. 4th ed. New York: Dover, 1951.

Foster, Verna. *The Name and Nature of Tragicomedy.* Aldershot, UK: Ashgate, 2004.

Frank, Arthur. *The Wounded Storyteller: Body, Illness, and Ethics.* Chicago, IL: University of Chicago Press, 1995.

Frank, E., R. Prien, and R. Jarrett. "Conceptualization and Rationale for Consensus Definitions of Terms in Major Depressive Disorder: Remission, Recovery, Relapse, and Recurrence." *Archives of General Psychiatry* 48 (1991): 851–55.

Frye, Northrop. *Anatomy of Criticism: Four Essays.* Princeton, NJ: Princeton University Press, 1957.

———. *The Secular Scripture: A Study of the Structure of Romance.* Cambridge, MA: Harvard University Press, 1976.

Hawkins, Anne Hunsaker. *Reconstructing Illness.* 2nd ed. West Lafayette, IN: Purdue University Press, 1999.

Kangas, Ilka. "Making Sense of Depression: Perceptions of Melancholia in Lay Narratives." *Health* 5, no. 1 (2001): 76–92.

Karp, David. *Speaking of Sadness: Depression, Disconnection, and the Meanings of Illness.* Oxford: Oxford University Press, 1996.

Lam, Raymond W., and Sidney Kennedy. "Evidence-Based Strategies for Achieving and Sustaining Full Remission in Depression: Focus on Metaanalyses." *Canadian Journal of Psychiatry* 49, no. 3, suppl. 1 (2004): 17S–26S.

Mairs, Nancy. "On Living Behind Bars." In *Unholy Ghost,* edited by Nell Casey, 181–213. New York: HarperCollins, 2002.

Manning, Martha. *Undercurrents: A Life Beneath the Surface.* New York: HarperCollins, 1994.

McAdams, Daniel P. *The Stories We Live By: Personal Myths and the Making of the Self.* New York: William Morrow, 1993.

Ricoeur, Paul. "Life: A Story in Search of a Narrator." In *A Ricoeur Reader: Reflection and Imagination,* edited by Mario J. Valdés, 425–37. Toronto: University of Toronto Press, 1991.

Rimmon-Kenan, Shlomith. "The Story of 'I': Illness and Narrative Identity." *Narrative* 10, no. 1 (2002): 9–27.

Schreiber, Rita. "(Re)defining My Self: Women's Process of Recovery from Depression." *Qualitative Health Research* 6, no. 4 (1996): 469–91.

Skarsater, Ingela, Karina Dencker, Ingegerd Bergbom, et al. "Women's Conceptions of Coping with Major Depression in Daily Life: A Qualitative, Salutogenic Approach." *Issues in Mental Health Nursing* 24 (2003): 419–39.

Smith, Jeffery. *Where the Roots Reach for Water: A Personal & Natural History of Melancholia.* New York: Farrar, Straus and Giroux, 1999.

Solomon, Andrew. *The Noonday Demon: An Atlas of Depression.* New York: Scribner, 2001.

Steen, Melva. "Essential Structure and Meaning of Recovery from Clinical Depression for Middle-Adult Women: A Phenomenological Study." *Issues in Mental Health Nursing* 17 (1996): 73–92.

Styron, William. *Darkness Visible: A Memoir of Madness.* New York: Random House, 1990.

Chapter 4

"Repenting Prodigal"

Confession, Conversion, and Shame in *William Cowper's* Adelphi

Hilary Clark

In the last years of his life, from 1797 to his death in 1800, the poet William Cowper suffered from paranoid delusions, hearing voices and believing that God was preparing terrible punishments for him. The poet's beloved companion of thirty years, Mary Unwin, had died, and he could no longer look back on his life's work with any pleasure. Over the years, by leading a quiet, regulated, rural life with Mrs. Unwin, he had survived repeated episodes of suicidal melancholy; further, writing poetry forced him to "look out into the world that was not part of his circle of damnation."[1] Now despair closed the circle again. Whereas after his first illness he had expected divine punishment for the sin of attempting suicide, now "[h]is 'unforgiveable sin'. . . was his failure to follow God's command to kill himself."[2]

William Cowper is perhaps best known for his last poem, "The Castaway," whose line "We perish'd, each alone" is declaimed by the melancholy Mr. Ramsay in Virginia Woolf's *To the Lighthouse* (1927). Cowper is also known for his memoir of his first madness, written in 1766 or 1767 but not published until after his death.[3] The memoir is a narrative of madness and recovery; it is also a narrative of Christian conversion drawing on the conventions of spiritual autobiography,[4] an account primarily of the author's conversion but ending with his brother John Cowper's conversion on his deathbed. Charles Ryskamp points out that "it had become the custom for one recently converted to write the story of his newly found faith."[5] Yet critics have argued that in Cowper's case these two memoirs—of recovery from madness and conversion from sin—appear to conflict, even as the author attempts to make them one narrative, reconstructing every event in his illness and recovery as being orchestrated by God in order to bring him, "the repenting prodigal," back into the fold.[6] In other words, he presents his recovery as a spiritual one, a return to God's love and health. The conflict between two narratives, I would suggest, is a symptom of unresolved shame and reflects the stigma associated with insanity and suicide in Cowper's time (as now).

The memoir clearly belongs to the confessional genre, its chief precursor being Saint Augustine's *Confessions*, in which the author recounts his early sins and conversion to Christianity. I will address the author's strategies in confessing to stigmatized states, such as paranoid delusions and despair, and to attempts at suicide—an act traditionally seen, from the Christian perspective Cowper adopts, as a terrible sin.[7] That the audience of such a confession would have been disapproving or shaming is suggested by the fact that Cowper did not publish the memoir during his lifetime. Indeed, a scene of (potential) public shaming is central to the story told: the young man fears an impending examination involving "the narrowest scrutiny," in the House of Lords no less, "touching [his] sufficiency" for a Clerkship.[8] The anticipation of public shaming arouses in him such horror that he is driven to attempt suicide to escape the event. I will investigate the strategies the author draws on to avoid the return of shame in confessing—strategies to deflect negative judgment, including his own, "tormented" and "self-accusing"[9] as he was, and present a self not utterly abject but worthy of love and redemption. A "flight from shame,"[10] from humiliation, motivates these confessions. Yet shame is closely related to shamelessness, and both are involved in the act of confession. The "shameless" act of confessing, before a real or imagined audience, to the "shameful" state of madness threatens to undermine Cowper's spiritual autobiography and the comforting moral dichotomies in terms of which the author represents his recovery and conversion.

In the memoir, Cowper first skims over his life from childhood up to the onset of his breakdown of 1763. He describes childhood years of being sent away from his family and "native Place": his mother dying when he was six,[11] he was sent away to school, enduring still-vivid bullying; after two years he was sent from that school to live with the family of an oculist, then after two more, he moved on to Westminster School. When he left Westminster at the age of eighteen, he moved to London to study law—a field for which he was unsuited, as signaled by a year-long "dejection of spirits": "Day and night I was upon the rack, lying down in horrors and rising in despair."[12] Recovering, he lived the life of a young gentleman in London until the need to make a living became pressing. Nominated by a friend for the Clerkship of the Journals at the House of Lords, he was told to expect an intimidating examination in the House in order to demonstrate his fitness for the position. He was filled with anxiety: "They whose spirits are formed like mine, to whom a public exhibition of themselves on any occasion is mortal poison, may have some idea of the horror of my situation; others can have none."[13] As the examination loomed, he was once again "a soul upon the rack," facing public scrutiny and "rejection for insufficiency,"[14] exposure to the world as a shameful impostor.

He looked to madness as his only way out, much as a child hopes for illness to avoid a test or a bully at school: "My chief fear was that my senses would not fail me in time enough to excuse my appearance in the House, which was the only purpose I wanted [madness] to answer."[15] However, madness did not oblige him right away, so he turned to suicide, undertaking a series of failed attempts by laudanum, by knife, and by hanging. With the last attempt, which almost killed him, he achieved his purpose: he was relieved of the Clerkship and hence the feared examination. Nonetheless, he now became truly delusional, fearing God's punishment for the sin of attempting suicide: "[T]hat distemper of mind which I had before so ardently wished for actually seized me."[16] Terror of God's punishment and despair of attaining salvation were to mark his suicidal depressions for the remainder of his life. Although during his stay at Dr. Nathaniel Cotton's hospital he did recover, and upon his conversion to the Gospel "the cloud of horror" passed away, he never escaped the cloud entirely: "Oh that this ardour of my first love had continued! But I have known many a lifeless and unhallowed hour since—long intervals of darkness interrupted by short returns of joy, and peace in believing."[17] When Cowper wrote these words he had more than thirty years yet to live, years that were marked by recurring and worsening attacks of melancholy and a dogged conviction of being abandoned by God.

In the eighteenth century, madness had well-established cultural meanings. For those writing about madness, a "well-developed . . . rhetoric" and familiar set of stereotypes came into play.[18] Satires drew on the commonplace of the close relationship between madness and sanity in order to skewer extravagant attitudes and excess in society.[19] There was also the traditional connection between madness, genius, and insight; however, real insanity was stigmatized, and the insane were figures both to mock and to fear. Bedlam represented "one meaningful boundary" between sanity and insanity;[20] it had become a spectacle or theater of madness, visitors flocking there to view the inmates and, in doing so, confirm their own sanity. Those, like Cowper, writing from the perspective of recovery—a return to sanity, "cooler judgment," and "perfect health"[21]—confronted the difficulty of conveying their earlier suffering without drawing on humiliating stereotypes of mad people. How does Cowper confess to derangement—fascinating on stage and in literature but shameful in reality, exposing the sufferer to ridicule and imprisonment in an asylum, to be "treated" there with abuse and grotesque "cures"? As well, in Cowper's case, there is the problem (and irony) of being "cured" by conversion to the Evangelical faith—at a time when "enthusiasts were increasingly denounced by their enemies as mad," their "inner light" suspect in the light of reason.[22]

Autobiographies of mental illness have at all times drawn on certain strategies of shame management, that is, defensive rhetorical strategies whereby the writer can confess to returning from a stigmatized experience defined as sanity's shadow "other," a suffering that nonsufferers are often quick to deny or to judge. A "language of negotiation" is used in maintaining the self's integrity "in the face of invasion" by an imagined shaming audience,[23] this rhetoric varying, of course, depending on historical and cultural context. However, every story of recovery draws on the myth of rebirth and involves a process of "autobiographical reconstruction," which interprets "a chaotic, absurd, or violent past as a meaningful, indeed necessary, prelude to the structured, purposeful, and comparatively serene present."[24] As Cowper puts it: "[B]lessed be the God of my Salvation for every sigh I drew, for every tear I shed, since thus it pleased Him to judge me here that I might not be judged hereafter."[25] While depression narratives in the late twentieth and early twenty-first centuries may draw on the authority of psychiatry to define and justify depression as a treatable mental illness, eighteenth-century (and earlier) narratives had an equally powerful explanatory framework within which to present the experience of madness: the Christian context of "temptation, transgression, and salvation" conveyed in the genre of spiritual autobiography, a context in which suffering could be made meaningful.[26]

The spiritual autobiographer presents himself as "as an actor in God's drama, playing a part that retrospectively makes perfect sense,"[27] that of the sinner led back into the fold, whose every suffering turns out to have been preordained. As Cowper puts it, "God ordered everything for me like an indulgent father."[28] Such a "highly conventionalized" framework, Spacks suggests, "may embody efforts to control the possibly dangerous forces of fantasy"[29]—those forces of aggression, desire, and delusion that threaten to lure us away from God. Cowper as spiritual autobiographer encloses his memoir, including his account of childhood, firmly within this Christian framework and speculates on God's intentions throughout, interpreting each event retrospectively as a sign of these larger designs.

The very first sentence of the memoir is an observation that throughout the author's life, up until his thirty-second year and the onset of his troubles, he had no "serious impressions of the religious kind," nor "bethought [himself] of the things of [his] salvation."[30] He acknowledges exceptions to this conclusion—times when "the seeds of religion" he picked up might have sprouted—but on the whole presents the heart of the young Cowper as lacking in contrition, having "become proof against the ordinary methods which a gracious God employs for our chastisement."[31] Heightening the young Cowper's ignorance and sinfulness, the author emphasizes his inability to pray or appreciate the benefits of prayer when these appeared: for instance, the author interprets as God's work the lifting of a depression upon a change of scene, and he ascribes the young Cowper's ingratitude to Satan's influence: "I think I remember somewhat of a glow of gratitude to the Father of Mercies for this unexpected blessing. . . . But Satan and my own wicked heart quickly persuaded me that I was indebted for my deliverance to nothing but a change of season and the amusing varieties of this place."[32] Along with this inability to pray, Cowper is careful to emphasize his schoolboy expertise in "the infernal art of lying," exhibiting "a total depravity of principle" under the influence of "the father of lies."[33]

The more benighted the sinner, of course, the more glorious the redemption. Despite all the young man's sins, God did not abandon him. Drawing on the conventions of spiritual autobiography, Cowper presents himself as passively taken up in God's design for his redemption, which included chastisement—in the form of madness—along the way. According to the author, one way God communicated this design was through omens, signs, and dreams. For instance, the young Cowper was warned away from his "inveterate habit of rebelling against God" by "an emblematical representation of [his] great danger," a striking vision of a sheepdog forcing a sheep to the edge of a cliff, "from whence if he had fallen, he must have been dashed to pieces."[34] The author presents himself as bound by conscience to confess these visions that "cannot . . . be accounted for otherwise than by supposing a supernatural agency"—bound by conscience to tell the truth, even if these "facts . . . may expose me to the suspicion of enthusiasm."[35] Later, he interprets a dream he had at the height of his suffering as a message of damnation: a dream of being excluded from prayers in Westminster Abbey, an "iron gate . . . flung in [his] face with a jar that made the Abbey ring."[36] Satan heightened these sufferings worthy of Job, "pl[ying him] close with horrible visions and more horrible voices."[37]

Cowper's interpretation of his madness as a stage in God's benevolent design—a design at work since his childhood—can be read as a strategy for deflecting shame and defending his integrity of self, particularly against those delusions that threatened the sufferer's sense of identity by dividing him in two and pitting one side of him (suicidal) against the other (self-conserving). He presents himself as not invaded by irrational forces but carried along in a larger and infinitely wise design working for his salvation. This interpretation is particularly important, and noticeable as a strategy, when he writes about his suicide attempts. Planning one's own death is a process of self-abjection so beyond the pale of the usual interests and desires of the self that, for the author it seems, its memory brings extreme anxiety—provoking defenses such as the elaborate religious interpretation that he undertakes.

On the one hand, this rationalization has the despair, suicide attempts, and anguish afterward as being God's design, His punishment for his failure to repent. On the other hand, it has the *failure* of the suicide attempts as being a sign of God's design, His providence and mercy. Indeed, the author presents God as actively intervening and foiling each attempt, to the point where—even at the point of taking his own life— the desperate man notices that something is up. For instance, we read of his attempt to drink off a phial of laudanum:

> But God had otherwise ordained. A conflict that shook me to pieces almost suddenly took place. . . .Twenty times I had the phial at my mouth and as often received an irresistible check, and even at the time it seemed to me that an invisible hand swayed the bottle downwards as often as I set it against my lips. I well remember that I took notice of this circumstance with some surprise, though it affected no change in my purpose.[38]

The author "well remembers"—that is, retrospectively interprets—his suicidal self as being powerless before God's will that he be held back from the brink, in order to see the light in due time. Satan made him do it and God saved him from doing it: this narrative of passivity and rescue allows the author to avoid the shame of confessing to what were clearly active attempts at self-murder. Going to the apothecary's shop, for instance, and putting on a "cheerful and unconstrained" mask, he "managed [his] voice and countenance so as to deceive" the man and obtain the laudanum.[39] He actively sought opportunities to execute his suicidal purpose. After the failed laudanum attempt, he hid a knife in his bed and was astonished when his attempts to stab himself failed; then he attempted to hang himself but failed when his garter (used as a noose) broke. These failures the author attributes to Providence, just as the attempts themselves he attributes to a "Satan . . . impatient of delay";[40] in sum, he had little to do with the whole process. To the post-Freudian reader, it is clear that he was extremely conflicted in attempting suicide, both actively planning his death and just as actively thwarting these plans. Indeed, A. Alvarez has described this sequence of suicide attempts as "a horrifying holding operation" seeking "more to forestall death than to bring it about"; Cowper "attempted suicide in order not to die but to drive himself mad"[41]—and hence avoid the feared scene of humiliation at the Bar of the House of Lords. Ironically, he was successful on both counts—freeing himself, but only into greater bondage.

Rather like this conflict in his motives for suicide, a struggle having uncanny results (the poisoning hand stayed, the knife and the noose/garter broken), there is in the memoir as a whole a conflict between the spiritual autobiographer—Cowper as the piously passive yet controlling interpreter of his own life—and the remembered sufferer, a character tormented with delusions and messy, ambivalent desires. This is a conflict between the author and his former mad self, a self he realizes is still all too close. Ironically, the author's attempted flight from shame—a defensive drive to interpret his suffering and thereby put it at a distance—is undercut by a shameless desire to tell, to expose all, to spin the story out and seduce the reader, even at the risk of incurring that reader's negative judgment.

Einat Avrahami has described the literary confession as "an ambivalent rhetorical mode" in which the penitent author "tempt[s] . . . readers with the allure of power that comes with the authority to judge the confession."[42] One reason Cowper's narrative still fascinates today, I think, is that it seduces us in this manner: we judge not only the conflicted confession itself but also the actions of the desperate young man—fearing (or, exasperated, hoping) each suicide attempt will be the last, while knowing, of course, that the author lived to tell all. Cowper the author has Cowper the character fail repeatedly to recognize God's signs, thus extending the narrative and building up suspense. Although the author identifies God's hand in the "failures"—the autobiographer "[s]electing, repressing, interpreting his experience"[43]—this salvage work doesn't stop poor William from blundering shamelessly on. A conflict is evident, then, between the telling of events and the interpretation that accompanies it, that anxiously adopts the convert's new perspective. Here interpretation functions as correction, in both linguistic and penal senses: in the religious tradition, the practice of confession offers "absolution for faults and omissions while simultaneously policing the contents of consciousness."[44] On a personal level, interpretation fashions an acceptable reading of events that would otherwise hold a meaning too dreadful to contemplate: the sufferer's humiliating failure—he could not kill himself, even after three tries—and utter "unlovability."[45]

Besides the interpretive and justifying purpose of the spiritual autobiography, another purpose of such narrative is to testify to readers of God's power and mercy in transforming a life, so that they, too, might repent and be saved. As Spacks puts it, the narrator "dedicates his imagination to the effort of leading man to God by demonstrating how he, the hero of his narrative, has been led."[46] A testimonial purpose is extremely common in illness narratives from Cowper's time up until the present. As Cowper was passive before God in his illness, he will now actively testify, tell his story, in order to show others the ways of God. If *this* sinner can be saved, then so can anyone. This more "public" or other-oriented role of the spiritual autobiography is evident in the narrator's concluding address to the reader: "If the Lord gives me life, I shall not in this place make an end of my testimony to His goodness; at some future time I shall resume the story. . . . Peace be with thee, reader, through faith in the Lord Jesus Christ. Amen."[47] Motivating this public testimonial is not only a concern for the souls of others but also a flight from personal shame: as testimony, the memoir transforms the abjection recounted, the remembered anxiety, confusion, terror. Such testimony functions as a defense against abjection, performing a "heroic transcendence of shame"—in Léon Wurmser's view, the motive of creativity in general.[48]

That a number of critics have seen a conflict, in Cowper's confession, between what it purposes to do and what it actually does—between its religious-testimonial aim and its recording of stigmatized experience—is an indication not of aesthetic failure, as Barrett Mandel concludes,[49] but of the complexity of the illness experience itself, which can never be entirely resolved in narrative. Horrifying, seductive, frustrating, and sometimes even funny,[50] Cowper's memoir enacts in its contradictions the conflicted experience of shame itself—so central to the experience of illness, particularly mental illness—in which the impulse to hide from scrutiny defends against not only the negative judgment of others but also the perverse, "shameless" impulse to expose oneself to such contempt.[51] "Telling all," like any penitent to his confessor, the author exposes his most abject experiences of derangement, yet he does so in a carefully plotted manner—one calculated to seduce the reader into reading on, "exploit[ing] the highly charged contents of his confession as a means of undermining his audience's resistance" to reading about such experiences.[52] At the same time, just as the penitent slips into a confessional, the author retreats in shame behind a religious interpretation of events and the conventions of the spiritual autobiography.

In its contradictions, then, Cowper's memoir both reveals and conceals the truth about his illness. In doing so, it is not a failed enterprise. As long as stigma attaches to mental illness, any memoir by a sufferer will be a document of shame—enacting shame, defending against it, but most importantly, as narrative art, striving to transcend it.

Notes

1. Ingram, *The Madhouse of Language*, 158.
2. King, *William Cowper*, 267.
3. King and Ryskamp, in *The Letters and Prose Writings of William Cowper*, xxiii–xxvi, outline the rather convoluted textual history of *Adelphi*. In his lifetime, Cowper let those closest to him read his memoir in manuscript: these included Mary Unwin, John Newton (his spiritual mentor), Lady Hesketh (his cousin), Martin Madan (his cousin), and Judith Madan (his aunt), whose daughter Maria Cowper copied it into her mother's Common Place Book. After the poet's death in 1800, the account of his brother John Cowper's deathbed conversion was published

first, as it was not controversial. It seems Newton made excisions in the earlier part of the memoir at some point, decorum dictating some "significant cuts": "The more ghastly aspects of Cowper's attempts at suicide and his behavior while in a suicidal frame of mind" were deleted, in order to make the memoir "more readily sympathetic to some of its first readers, and less objectionable to his family" (xxv). Two rival editions of Cowper's memoir appeared in 1816, both derived from the expurgated version. The unexpurgated manuscript in Mrs. Madan's Common Place Book was presented to the Bodleian Library in 1967 (King, "Cowper's *Adelphi* Restored," 293). The King and Ryskamp edition is based on this "restored" version.

4. On the characteristics of the spiritual autobiography, see Spacks, "The Soul's Imaginings," 424–46. Two earlier narratives in this tradition, by George Trosse and Hannah Allen, can be found in Ingram, *Patterns of Madness*, 11–17 and 29–35.

5. Ryskamp, *William Cowper*, 174.

6. *Adelphi*, 44. He also sees himself as Lazarus returned from the dead (38).

7. In *The City of God*, St. Augustine had harsh words on suicide: in his view it is "a detestable crime and a damnable sin" (quoted in Colt, *The Enigma of Suicide*, 158). His arguments shaped the Christian view of suicide for centuries. However, views on suicide were beginning to change in Cowper's time; his contemporary David Hume briskly dismantled Christian arguments against suicide in his essay "On Suicide"—not published, however, until after Hume's death, and "promptly suppressed" (Colt, 174).

8. *Adelphi*, 15.

9. King and Ryskamp, xxiii.

10. Adamson and Clark, *Scenes of Shame*, 10. Confession is also linked to guilt, of course, and critics have addressed this issue: for example, see Brooks, *Troubling Confessions*, and (on Cowper in particular) Morris, "The Uses of Madness." On the close relationship between, but not identity of, shame and guilt, see Adamson and Clark, 23–27.

11. Ann Cowper died in 1737, at the age of thirty-four, after giving birth to Cowper's younger brother John. King, *William Cowper*, chapter 1.

12. *Adelphi*, 8.

13. Ibid., 15.

14. Ibid., 16–17.

15. Ibid., 18.

16. Ibid., 32.

17. Ibid., 40.

18. Ingram and Faubert, *Cultural Constructions of Madness*, 4.

19. Ibid., 2.

20. Ibid., 7.

21. Recalling delusions he had "while in a state of insanity," Cowper emphasizes that he is "recollecting them now and weighing them in my cooler judgment, which I thank God was never more its own master" (35). In a letter to Joseph Hill, his friend and benefactor, written in June 1765 after his release from Dr. Cotton's asylum, Cowper claims "that by the Mercy of God I am restored to perfect Health both of Mind and Body." King and Ryskamp, 94–95.

22. DePorte, *Nightmares and Hobbyhorses*, 34.

23. Ingram, *The Madhouse of Language*, 106.
24. On the myth of rebirth in spiritual autobiography and in pathography, see Hawkins, *Reconstructing Illness*, chapter 2. The quotation is from E. B. O'Reilly, *Sobering Tales: Narratives of Alcoholism and Recovery* (Amherst: University of Massachusetts Press, 1997) in Maruna and Ramsden, "Living to Tell the Tale," 129–30.
25. *Adelphi*, 34.
26. Ingram, *The Madhouse of Language*, 120.
27. Spacks, "The Soul's Imaginings," 425.
28. *Adelphi*, 42.
29. Spacks, 425, 427.
30. *Adelphi*, 5.
31. Ibid., 6–7.
32. Ibid., 9–10.
33. Ibid., 7–8.
34. Ibid., 11–12.
35. Ibid., 13, 12.
36. Ibid., 28.
37. Ibid., 31.
38. Ibid., 21.
39. Ibid., 19.
40. Ibid.
41. *The Savage God*, 157.
42. Avrahami, "Impacts of Truth(s)," 168.
43. Spacks, 425.
44. Brooks, *Troubling Confessions*, 111.
45. Wurmser, *The Mask of Shame*, 292: "Unlovability has been seen as the core of shame, the basic flaw."
46. Spacks, 425.
47. *Adelphi*, 46.
48. Wurmser, chapter 14, 291–307.
49. Mandel, "Artistry and Psychology in William Cowper's *Memoir*," 442.
50. Spacks admits that a summary of the character's failing attempts at suicide might have a "Marx Brothers flavor," but she insists that in Cowper's telling the story "contains no comic elements" (430). I am not sure I agree.
51. Felicity A. Nussbaum sees the contradictions in Cowper's memoir as being more cultural in nature. See "Private Subjects in William Cowper's 'Memoir.'"
52. Avrahami, 167. Avrahami is writing about Harold Brodkey's illness autobiography, *This Wild Darkness: The Story of My Death* (New York: Metropolitan Books, 1996), but her comments are applicable to the rhetoric of illness autobiographies generally.

Bibliography

Adamson, Joseph, and Hilary Clark, eds. *Scenes of Shame: Psychoanalysis, Shame, and Writing.* New York: State University of New York Press, 1999.
Alvarez, A. *The Savage God: A Study of Suicide.* London: Weidenfeld and Nicolson, 1971.

Augustine, Saint. *Confessions*. Commentary by James J. O'Donnell. Oxford: Clarendon Press, 1992.

Avrahami, Einat. "Impacts of Truth(s): The Confessional Mode in Harold Brodkey's Illness Autobiography." *Literature and Medicine* 22, no. 2 (Fall 2003): 164–87.

Brooks, Peter. *Troubling Confessions: Speaking Guilt in Law and Literature*. Chicago: University of Chicago Press, 2000.

Colt, George Howe. *The Enigma of Suicide*. New York: Summit Books, 1991.

Cowper, William. *Adelphi*. In King and Ryskamp, *The Letters and Prose Writings of William Cowper*, Volume 1, 3–61.

DePorte, Michael V. *Nightmares and Hobbyhorses: Swift, Sterne, and Augustan Ideas of Madness*. San Marino, CA: Huntington Library, 1974.

Hawkins, Anne Hunsaker. *Reconstructing Illness: Studies in Pathography*. 2nd ed. West Lafayette, IN: Purdue University Press, 1999.

Ingram, Allan. *The Madhouse of Language: Writing and Reading Madness in the Eighteenth Century*. London: Routledge, 1992.

———, ed. *Patterns of Madness in the Eighteenth Century: A Reader*. Liverpool: Liverpool University Press, 1998.

Ingram, Allan, and Michelle Faubert. *Cultural Constructions of Madness in Eighteenth-Century Writing: Representing the Insane*. London: Palgrave, 2005.

King, James. "Cowper's *Adelphi* Restored: The Excisions to Cowper's Narrative." *The Review of English Studies* 30, no. 119 (1979): 291–305.

———. *William Cowper: A Biography*. Durham, NC: Duke University Press, 1986.

King, James, and Charles Ryskamp, eds. *The Letters and Prose Writings of William Cowper*. Volume 1. Oxford: Clarendon Press, 1979.

Mandel, Barrett John. "Artistry and Psychology in William Cowper's *Memoir*." *Texas Studies in Literature and Language* 12 (1970): 431–42.

Maruna, Shadd, and Derek Ramsden. "Living to Tell the Tale: Redemption Narratives, Shame Management, and Offender Rehabilitation." In *Healing Plots: The Narrative Basis of Psychotherapy*, edited by Amia Lieblich, Dan P. McAdams, and Ruthellen Josselson, 129–49. Washington, DC: APA, 2004.

Morris, John N. "The Uses of Madness: William Cowper's Memoir." *American Scholar* 34 (1965): 112–26.

Nussbaum, Felicity A. "Private Subjects in William Cowper's 'Memoir.'" In *The Age of Johnson*, edited by Paul Kushin, 307–26. New York: AMS Press, 1987.

Ryskamp, Charles. *William Cowper of the Inner Temple: A Study of his Life and Works to the Year 1768*. Cambridge: Cambridge University Press, 1959.

Spacks, Patricia Meyer. "The Soul's Imaginings: Daniel Defoe, William Cowper." *PMLA* 91, no. 3 (1976): 420–35.

Wurmser, Léon. *The Mask of Shame*. 1981. Northvale, NJ: Jason Aronson, 1994.

Chapter 5

Leonid Andreev's *Construction of Melancholy*

Frederick H. White

Leonid Nikolaevich Andreev (1871–1919) was one of the most successful Russian writers of the period 1902–1914. This success was measurable in both financial reward and popular acclaim. His short stories, plays, and novel were eagerly read by the public, and lively debates about these works, which often focused on contemporary issues, appeared in the pages of newspapers and journals. Russia's political and social climate was very volatile at the turn of the century, and Andreev seemed to capture the raw emotions of this period. In many ways, Andreev was a celebrity with all the obtrusive media coverage that we associate with that status. This intense scrutiny was made all the more difficult due to Andreev's occasional episodes of mental illness. During his lifetime, he was diagnosed and treated as an acute neurasthenic, a condition that today would be associated with depression, fatigue, and/or anxiety.[1]

This essay will explore, within the critical framework of illness narrative theory, how as a young man Andreev described his illness experience in his diaries.[2] In the early years, prior to his first hospitalization in 1901, Andreev was still searching for answers and did not have a clinical vocabulary for his condition. He often associated his depression with personal problems, but did have an intuition that his prolonged episodes of melancholy could be of a more severe nature.

The tendency of scholars examining these formative years prior to literary success is to connect Andreev's pessimistic outlook to an early interest in the philosophy of Arthur Schopenhauer and Eduard von Hartmann; to suggest that his chronic drinking was a reaction to his poverty and failed romances; and to understand his attempts at suicide as a culmination of all these—philosophical Pessimism, poverty, excessive drinking, and romantic failures.[3] Little has been made of his bouts of depression as the possible source of most of these problems. This essay offers the alternative possibility that Andreev's reading of Schopenhauer, his drinking, and his desperate desire to find love were *in reaction to* his mental illness, not the cause of it as is often argued.

This distinction is important for understanding how Andreev interpreted and gave meaning to his own life because, in turn, his constructs influenced the depiction of madness in many of his literary works.[4] Andreev's narratives (both in his diaries and literary works) offer further insight into how illness informed his perception and depiction of reality. This essay concentrates on only the first stage of this development—prior to literary success and before Andreev gained a clinical vocabulary for his condition—in order to understand his initial construction and narrativization of illness.

"Disease" is the clinical term for a medical condition; for example, cancer is a disease. "Illness," however, is the experience of being sick—the lived experience of certain ailments.[5] It is in view of this distinction that we can talk about illness narrative as the explication of how it feels to be ill—what one experiences physically, emotionally, and psychologically when one suffers from a disease such as cancer or, as in this instance, from depression. Illness narrative makes public a private experience, competes for an individual voice against the powerful voices of medicine, and balances the illness experience against the life as a larger whole.[6]

It is within this critical framework that Andreev's early diaries can be read, in order to investigate how he perceived his episodes of depression. His first recorded illness experience was on March 16, 1890, when he wrote of "fits" that lasted for about a week or two. He described how he would walk around like a madman, not able to think, speak, experience joy or happiness, as if a gloomy color covered everything.[7] He thought about suicide, but could not bring himself to act upon this idea. Andreev wrote that these fits came in the form of strong emotions and influenced all of his words and actions. What bothered him was the seeming meaninglessness of life, and he was left feeling as though he had a double.[8] In an attempt to reconcile these fits, Andreev turned to the philosophy of Pessimism, identifying his double as a pessimist and thoughts of suicide as pessimistic.

One element of an illness narrative such as Andreev's diary must be its contextualization.[9] Narratives are understood to be constructions, performances, enactments, plots and counterplots, which emphasize action, motive, event, and process within a social context.[10] Hayden White argues that although events are value neutral, when we organize them into a coherent structure to make a story, we assign value and meaning to them.[11] In examining Andreev's diaries, one must be aware of the ways in which he creates meaning, perceives cause and effect, and attempts to plot his episodes of depression within the context of his life.

Philosophical Pessimism offered Andreev a way to rationalize his depressive episodes. Schopenhauer in *The World as Will and Representation* suggests that we are not in control of our individual lives. We are all driven by the Will—the force of both the inorganic and organic worlds. According to Schopenhauer, our wants are without satiation: thus suffering, frustration, and a sense of deficiency are always present. Desire, passion, hate, hunger, sleepiness are only manifestations of the Will. Life, therefore, is tragic, full of misery and pain. Hartmann in *The Philosophy of the Unconscious* locates the Will in suffering and the Idea in order and consciousness. Over time, Idea prevails over Will, but paradoxically intellectual development increases our capacity for pain. Hence, ultimate happiness is not attainable and we will eventually shed this illusion and commit collective suicide. For both philosophers, the underlying nature of the world is the Will feeding and preying upon itself; the world is filled with more pain than pleasure. In these philosophies, the individual has little if any hope to escape this misery—suicide and self-overcoming being the only options.

In the philosophies of Schopenhauer and Hartmann, Andreev found an explanation for his depressive episodes, when life seemed meaningless and full of pain. Andreev's own illness experience seemed to support the philosophical ideas of Pessimism; therefore, he conceptualized his illness within this philosophical framework, often contemplating suicide as his only option.

On March 21, 1890, Andreev wrote that he was experiencing a quickly changing mood of the soul, feeling more despondency than joy. There did not seem to be any reason for these feelings, so Andreev suggested that possibly they were caused by a "stimulus" from his internal world. He believed that life's pointlessness was at the heart of all of his problems, and he looked to the pessimistic philosophy of Hartmann for answers. Once he began to feel better, he wrote: "All of this time there has been a void in my head, an inability to think about anything serious."[12]

In May 1890, Andreev experienced an episode of depression with thoughts of suicide. He believed that a bicycle was the only thing that would free him from this mental lethargy: "Terribly vile:—boring; it would be better if there was some kind of misfortune, rather than this foul mood. There seems to be only one escape—this is a bike."[13] Andreev's feelings of depression were combined with his feelings of love for Zinaida Nikolaevna Sibileva and his anxiety about school examinations; nonetheless, he realized that his depression sprang from within.

For the month of June 1890, Andreev's emotional energy was spent on Zinaida Nikolaevna. His high and low moods were perceived as a reflection of the ever-changing state of their relationship. On June 6, however, Andreev felt that his life was quickly leading toward suicide. Although he had just passed exams, was on vacation, and planning to buy a bike, he was experiencing boredom and sorrow. Instead of thinking about the positive things in his life, Andreev could only think about shooting himself in the head: "If this current mood were to continue only a week without relief, I would start drinking and would kill myself,—but no, a new day will dawn, not quite as difficult, and the thought of suicide will recede, but then when this sorrow begins again—I am forced to start all over again and little by little I become conscious of the necessity of suicide." This cycle of depression made him feel "like a squirrel on a wheel."[14]

A week later, Andreev felt poorly while returning by train from Smolensk. He noted that with physical pain there are ways to express what one feels, but there are few expressions for mental pain; saying that one is "bored" is not enough: "I am not even bored . . . I am sickened; everyone and everything has become hateful; before me I see nothing that is positive."[15] The next day Andreev wrote that he doubted that he could be cured of his condition as others are cured of diseases. In this entry, Andreev struggles with how to perceive and express his episodes of depression. Concepts associated with physical ailments were not applicable to what he was experiencing.

In October 1890, after a seemingly final break with Zinaida Niko-laevna, Andreev sank into an especially severe period of depression.[16] For most of the month, he self-medicated with alcohol. On October 22 he was drunk and wrote that he felt foul: "Oh God, how painful; I would like to cry but there are no tears and something oppresses and stands on top of [me]."[17] However, Andreev soon found love with Liubov' Niko-laevna Tukhina, and this brought him out of his despair. In November, looking back on his behavior of October, Andreev blamed it on his poverty.[18] However, on February 18, 1891, he concluded several self-reflective entries with a discussion of his psychological condition, stating that his gloomy mood was organic in nature and not connected to the conditions of his life. Andreev claimed that he grew melancholy both when circumstances went his way and when they went against his wishes. These melancholic moods were even worse when they appeared at his moments of success. Suicide seemed the only escape from this cycle of melancholy and boredom, but he lacked the will to carry it out.

The death of Andreev's father in 1889 and the ensuing financial difficulties caused Andreev to remain in Orel while his friends went to university in Moscow and St. Petersburg. He became the sole bread-winner for his family, and it was due to these financial responsibilities, so he claimed, that he did not kill himself. In 1891, Andreev went to St. Petersburg, where Zinaida Nikolaevna was studying, and entered the Law Faculty. Although reunited with friends, he was still impoverished and very much in love, and his periods of depression were often worsened by these two sources of tension.

In a diary entry of September 24, 1891, Andreev wrote that his psychological condition was constantly changing and he was afraid it would eventually lead him to the madhouse. Feeling that he had reached a critical stage, Andreev noted: "[S]ymptoms of genuine neurasthenia are appearing in me."[19] Almost a week later, Andreev wrote that there was something broken in his core, that again he was experiencing melancholy for no apparent reason. It was not a severe form of melancholy, just a dull internal pain, which had the potential to become very sharp and tortuous. He thought again about suicide, but felt that he could not leave his mother. The next day he wrote that he felt physically and mentally ill, but he did not know why; however, he was beginning to perceive his depression as an internal defect and less as a philosophical state of being.

On November 29, 1891, he wrote: "I feel very bad. So bad, that I do not even know of what this badness consists."[20] Shortly after this, Andreev returned home to Orel, where he began drinking heavily and talking of Pessimism and days without happiness. On December 20 he wrote that his life would end in one of three ways: madness, suicide, or complete moral decline. His boredom and melancholy were alleviated only by vodka.

In February 1892, Andreev returned to St. Petersburg where his depression was fueled by his feelings for Zinaida Nikolaevna and his loneliness. Drunk for several days, Andreev wrote that there was something odd in his head, some kind of strange feeling that had made him feel as if he were sitting and looking at himself—his double.[21] During this period of depression, Andreev attempted suicide and spent several days in the hospital. Once he was released, his problems with Zinaida Nikolaevna and examinations continued to influence his "abominable life."[22] Even with these external factors, Andreev associated his problems with a feeling of emptiness: "It is not people who are guilty that I am alone, it is I, my emptiness and insipidness."[23]

More and more, Andreev expressed the idea that he had some kind of internal defect.[24] He still held to philosophical Pessimism as the context for his illness experience, but Andreev was now looking for a cure for this perceived flaw. Suicide was one possibility, but finding a sympathetic companion who could cure him of his problems seemed to emerge as a more desirable option. In an entry of August 24, 1893, Andreev wrote that he felt like an acrobat on a high wire. On one side was suicide and on the other was madness. He suggested that his latest love, Evgeniia Nikolaevna Khludeneva,[25] was his balance: "Where goes the balance, there I go—but drop it and kaput? . . . Kaput means the end."[26]

In many earlier entries, Andreev wrote that his romantic successes and failures were the cause of his high or low moods; however, he was finally sensing that his mental health was the underpinning and that his relationships only exacerbated his condition. This might seem a minor distinction, but the illness experiences had remained consistent—boredom, loneliness, and thoughts of suicide—and only the "balances" (that is, his romantic interests) had changed. We should not discount Andreev's feelings for various women, especially Zinaida Nikolaevna, but realizing that these women were chosen to stabilize his mental condition changes the way in which we must understand his notions of love and relationships. For Andreev, love was often impulsive and resulted in great emotional demands placed on the woman. Just as quickly as he fell in love, he could become completely dispassionate, depending on his changing mood.

Andreev's belief that love could cure his condition probably stems from his relationship with his mother, Anastasiia Nikolaevna. Their relationship was extremely close, and it provided Andreev with comfort during his periods of depression. The importance of Anastasiia Nikolaevna's role in Andreev's life is evident in the fact that she lived with her son almost his entire life.[27] In a pathography of 1927, Dr. Ivan Galant noted Anastasiia Nikolaevna's "exclusive love for her oldest son Leonid" (although she had five other children) and suggested that this exceptional relationship caused Andreev's obsessive love for his first wife.[28]

Throughout his life, Andreev depended on his mother and two wives as emotional stabilizers. They helped to even out his psychological condition, but did not cure or eliminate his periods of depression. Maxim Gorky, a friend and fellow author, wrote after Andreev's death about their turbulent relationship and how he could not offer Andreev the emotional support he demanded. However, Gorky noted that Andreev's first wife did act as his friend's balance:

> She understood perfectly the need for a maternal, supportive attitude toward Andreev; she immediately and profoundly felt the significance of his talent and the agonizing fluctuations of his moods. She was one of those rare women who, at the same time as being a passionate mistress, does not lose the ability to love with a mother's love. This double love armed her with a subtle instinct, so that she was well able to distinguish between the genuine complaints of his soul and the clanging words of capricious passing moods.[29]

Boris Zaitsev, another friend and fellow writer, made a similar observation: "Th[e] influence [of his first wife] calmed his stormy, passionate, and sometimes not too stable nature."[30] While Pessimism may have been the way in which Andreev rationalized his bouts of depression, vodka was his medicine and, he hoped, love would provide the cure.

In the fall of 1893, Andreev left St. Petersburg and enrolled at the university in Moscow in the Law Faculty. Andreev's move was partly motivated by financial need. In Moscow, he was given some financial aid, but this did not alleviate his periods of melancholy. In January 1894, Andreev again tried to commit suicide. His friends blamed it on a failed romance and his drunkenness, constant themes in Andreev's struggle with depression.[31] For two years, Andreev lived alone in Moscow, a difficult time dominated by his poverty and pathological drunkenness. During this period there was at least one more attempted suicide, caused, so his friends thought, by his love for Nadezhda Aleksandrovna Antonova.[32] In 1895, the arrival of Andreev's mother in Moscow drastically improved his situation, providing a calming effect.

This same year, Andreev published a story entitled "He, She and Vodka." In this story, the character He hates himself and turns to drink as an alternative to suicide. He thinks that his ideal She will "save" him from his despair. Each time he meets a woman, He stops drinking. When he realizes that this woman cannot save him, He returns to drink. Finally He finds She, but both are married to other people.[33] This drives him nearly mad. He returns to drink and eventually is beaten to death.[34] The story is naïve but does provide yet another narrative response to Andreev's illness experience. Many of the same themes are found in Andreev's diaries. Loneliness and boredom lead to thoughts of suicide, excessive drinking, and the idea that somehow the ideal woman will alleviate despair.

In March 1896, Andreev finished his coursework, but asked that he might delay taking his exams. That summer, he rented a country house and began studying. He also met Aleksandra Mikhailovna Veligorskaia, who would become his wife in 1902. There is a gap of nearly four years in Andreev's diaries, but when his personal narrative resumes on March 27, 1897, he is in final preparation for his exams. In April, Andreev wrote in one entry: "Bouts of momentary fear occur, such that cold sweat appears. But this is not a fear of my exams, failure—all of that is nonsense, but a fear of what is going on in my head."[35] He eventually passed all of his exams, but could not enjoy this because his nerves were shattered.[36] One of the reasons for Andreev's lack of joy was that he was again searching for a new balance, falling in love, which was always an emotionally taxing process for him.

In July, Andreev complained of heart palpitations and the feeling that he had gone insane.[37] In August, he returned to the idea of a double and he claimed that love might be able to unite this division.[38] He believed that the ideal woman would heal him of his condition. However, far from providing Andreev with peace, romantic adventures agitated him further. At one point, he had three different women within his sights: Zinaida Ivanovna,[39] Nadezhda Aleksandrovna Antonova, and Aleksandra Mikhailovna Veligorskaia.[40] Ever searching for the balance that would allow him to walk the tightrope above his depression, Andreev placed his faith in romantic relationships. Love and illness were conflated yet again, and Andreev was quite often broken-hearted. The illness experience in most cases remained the same; the external contexts for the depression might have varied, but the actual experience did not. Clearly, I am suggesting that Andreev's low moods were greatly influenced by biochemical factors, more than by romantic failures.

Even as he began to experience literary success and his relationship with Aleksandra Mikhailovna matured, Andreev continued to experience bouts of depression.[41] From January 25 to March 22, 1901, Andreev was hospitalized under the care of Professor Mikhail Cherinov.[42] Friends had to convince him to check into the university clinic, where he was diagnosed as suffering from acute neurasthenia.[43] One friend writes of this experience: "He left the clinic renewed and energetic, got himself a bike, and started to exercise. But only a month later the same Andreev was facing me, with the inextinguishable flicker of despair and doubt in his beautiful eyes, with a grimly set mouth."[44]

Andreev's struggle with depression continued for the rest of his life, although the issue was complicated by his growing literary success and personal celebrity. Unlike the Decadents who wished to play the role of the mad genius, Andreev did not want to be stigmatized as insane or sick. He wanted his struggle with mental illness to remain private. Therefore, the diary played an important role for Andreev in exploring his illness experience and in conceptualizing his periods of depression. In these entries he transformed events into stories, providing cause-and-effect explanations, in order to make sense of his real world. However, this narrative was only a first draft of the life story that would be presented later in final draft form for friends, lovers, relatives, and so on, and ultimately would find its way into his literary works. Andreev wrote in one entry: "It's as if the very nature of the diary is contrary to the introduction of any kind of later amendment, but, in reading it several months later, I am so outraged by the role I play in this diary, that I absolutely cannot remain silent."[45] The process of revising and editing his first draft diary entries occurred rather quickly. Therefore, the immediacy of these entries, especially in the context of illness narrative, provide a unique look at the process by which Andreev confronted and dealt with his depression and also (re)fashioned himself for his various audiences.

The diaries offer personalized interpretations, which are important for gaining perspective on Andreev. His relationship with depression following literary success seems to have been mediated for a particular audience, making it difficult at times to get a clear understanding of his actual condition. When it came to his reading public, Andreev denied his condition and defended his sanity. Andreev was not insane and therefore took offense to reports that he had gone mad. To family and friends, he often complained of various illnesses (heart problems, toothaches, fatigue) but rarely within the context of mental illness. In his literary works, madness and abnormal behavior are prevalent themes, but Andreev rebuffed critics' autobiographical interpretations. Only in his diaries do we find a personal narrative, relatively unmediated, about his relationship with depression.

Reading Andreev's early diaries within the critical framework of illness narrative theory allows one to suggest that melancholic episodes were the impetus for much of his behavior. From the diaries, one can argue that Andreev's readings of Schopenhauer and Hartmann were a way to rationalize his own feelings of futility and boredom brought on by depression. Pessimism gave meaning to Andreev's illness experience. As well, Andreev's excessive drinking was often caused by depressive episodes. Self-medication is a common response when treatment is lacking; alcohol and drugs are often abused specifically to counteract the symptoms of mental illness.[46] Finally, Andreev himself said that he looked to various women to save him from himself. As in his story, the women in Andreev's life were numerous, and in each one he hoped to find the ideal. Poverty clearly was a factor that exacerbated Andreev's situation; however, one can argue that it was not the cause of his depression, as his episodes of melancholy continued well after he had achieved great wealth and material comfort.

One might look at these conclusions and still wonder whether philosophical Pessimism caused depression or depression caused an interest in Schopenhauer. However, as scholars explore the effects of illness on the individual, there is a greater understanding that experience is mediated through various narratives (social, cultural, philosophical), contextualizing that experience and thereby giving meaning to the larger life. Therefore, it is important to understand Andreev's attempt to bring coherence to his illness experience, both for the scholar working on Andreev's life and literary works, and for those interested in how mental illness was negotiated before psychiatry and psychoanalysis were widely available options. In the absence of modern medications, treatments, and therapies, Andreev gave meaning to his depression with philosophical Pessimism, self-medicated with vodka, and looked to love for a cure. I am making this distinction because I believe that recognizing the strong impact that bouts of melancholy had on Andreev's personal life and literary output opens up the nuanced moments of embedded autobiography in his texts, which served him as a type of creative therapy and allow us to contextualize the theme of madness in Andreev's literary works.

Notes

1. For Andreev's medical history, see Frederick White, "«Tainaia zhizn'» Leonida Andreeva: Istoriia bolezni." The awareness and understanding of mental illness in Russia at the turn of the century was very limited. Mental disorders were only vaguely understood, and conditions such as depression were considered to be the result of nervous exhaustion. It was believed that the expenditure of and/or the depletion of bodily energies as a result of excessive living caused emotional problems. This condition of mental deterioration resulting from a depleted nerve force came to be referred to as neurasthenia.

2. Andreev kept a more or less regular diary at two stages in his life: from 1890, when he was in school in Orel, Russia, to 1901, when his first collection of stories was published; and from the outbreak of the First World War to his death in 1919.

3. The idea that Schopenhauer's philosophy influenced Andreev's perspective on life began with Georgii Chulkov and Maxim Gorky. Chulkov makes this connection in his literary portrait of Andreev, *Kniga o Leonide Andreeve*. Gorky then used a similar explanation in his introduction to the English translation of Andreev's novel *Sashka Jigouleff*. The sociological approach, which blames Andreev's poverty and failed romances for his depressive moods, is used by most Soviet scholars; for example, see Iezuitova's introduction to "Pis'ma k neveste," 180.

4. Andreev wrote several works that are unambiguously about mental illness: "Phantoms" ("Prizraki," 1904) describes life in a mental asylum; "Red Laugh" ("Krasnyi smekh," 1905) explores the madness of war; "The Thought" ("Mysl'": story 1902, play 1914) examines the distinctions between sanity and insanity against the background of criminal homicide; "The Life of Vasilii Fiveiskii" ("Zhizn' Vasiliia Fiveiskogo," 1903) suggests that mental illness is a form of divine punishment; "He" ("On," 1913) has a main character who is mentally ill; and *Ekaterina Ivanovna* (1913) probes the boundaries between madness and moral/social decadence.

5. Kleinman, *The Illness Narratives*, 3–6; Frank, *At the Will of the Body*, 13.

6. Frank, "Reclaiming an Orphan Genre," 2.

7. LRA (Leeds Russian Archive), MS. 606\E. 1 *12 March–30 June 1890; 21 September 1898*: March 16, 1890.

8. The issue of the "double" in Andreev's early diaries is a complex one, which cannot be fully addressed in this essay. Briefly, the theme of an internal and external "I" often occurs in the diaries: sometimes Andreev's double taunts him from a distance and sometimes he is inside Andreev's head, banging and scraping. This interpretation may spring from Fedor Dostoevsky's *The Double*, where the character Goliadkin develops a double as part of his mental illness. The double is a symbol of Goliadkin's madness and may have provided Andreev with a way in which to describe his own experience. In 1908, Andreev uses the double in his play *Black Maskers* to represent psychological conflict. This is not to suggest that the double does not have a long literary tradition prior to Dostoevsky or that Andreev is simply mimicking Goliadkin. Instead, I would suggest that in an attempt to provide a narrative for his depression, Andreev may have turned to

a plot structure that he knew in order to bring meaning to his experience. The double seems to be a way in which Andreev can conceptualize the normal external (healthy) and abnormal internal (ill) selves.

9. Fee, "The Broken Dialogue," 3.

10. Garro and Mattingly, "Narrative as Construct and Construction," 17.

11. H. White, "The Historical Text as Literary Artifact" in *Tropics of Discourse*, 81–100; introduction to *Metahistory*, 1–42.

12. MS. 606\E. 1: March 26, 1890.

13. Ibid., May 10, 1890.

14. Ibid., June 6, 1890.

15. Ibid., July 13, 1890.

16. LRA, MS. 606\E. 2 *3 July 1890–18 February 1891*: October 5, 1890.

17. Ibid., October 22, 1890.

18. Ibid., November 13, 1890.

19. Generalova, "Leonid Andreev, Dnevnik 1891–1892," 98.

20. Ibid., 120.

21. Ibid., 132.

22. Generalova, "Dnevnik Leonida Andreeva," 257.

23. Ibid., 267.

24. Ibid., 289; LRA, MS. 606\E. 6 *26 September 1892–4 January 1893*: January 4, 1893; LRA, MS. 606\E. 7 *5 March–9 September 1893*: March 19, 1893.

25. Andreev simply refers to "Evgeniia" in his diary, so it is my assumption that he is referring to E. N. Khludeneva.

26. LRA, MS. 606\E. 7: August 24, 1893.

27. Leonid Andreev died in 1919, and Anastasiia Nikolaevna Andreeva died in 1920.

28. Galant, "Evroendokrinologiia velikikh russkikh pisatelei i poetov. L. N. Andreev," 226 and 228.

29. Gor'kii, *Kniga o Leonide Andreeve*, 53.

30. Zaitsev, *Kniga o Leonide Andreeve*, 129.

31. Fatov, *Molodye gody Leonida Andreeva*, 85.

32. Ibid., 87–89.

33. It is actually not clear if She is married or simply "in love" with another man. Either way, He is driven mad by the thought that She loves another man.

34. Andreev, "On, ona i vodka," 1.

35. LRA, MS. 606\E. 8 *27 March 1897–23 April 1901; 1 January 1903; 9 October 1907*: April 28, 1897.

36. Ibid., May 28, 1897.

37. Ibid., July 12, 1897.

38. Ibid., August 25, 1897.

39. Zinaida Ivanovna's surname is unknown.

40. MS. 606\E. 8: October 15, 1897.

41. Ibid., January 3, 1899; December 25, 1899; April 14, 1900; November 1, 1900.

42. Andreeva, "Trudnye gody," 3.

43. Azov, "Otryvki ob Andreeve," 5.

44. Ibid.
45. LRA, MS. 606\E. 3 *27 February–13 April 1891; 5 October 1891; 26 September 1892*: October 5, 1891.
46. See Khantzian, "The Self-Medication Hypothesis of Addictive Disorders."

Bibliography

Andreev, Leonid. "On, ona i vodka." *Orlovskii vestnik* 240 (September 1895): 1.
———. *Sashka Jigouleff.* Translated by Luba Hicks. Edited and introduced by Maxim Gorky. New York: Robert McBride, 1925.
Andreeva, Rimma. "Trudnye gody." *Orlovskaia pravda* 275 (November 1971): 3.
Azov, V. [V. A. Ashkinazi]. "Otryvki ob Andreeve." *Vestnik literatury* 9 (1920): 5.
Chulkov, Georgii. "Vospominanii." In *Kniga o Leonide Andreeve*, 105–24. Berlin: Z. I. Grzhebin, 1922.
Fatov, N. *Molodye gody Leonida Andreeva.* Moscow: Zemlia i Fabrika, 1924.
Fee, Dwight. "The Broken Dialogue: Mental Illness as Discourse and Experience." In *Pathology and the Postmodern: Mental Illness as Discourse and Experience*, edited by Dwight Fee, 1–17. London: Sage, 2000.
Frank, Arthur W. *At the Will of the Body: Reflections on Illness.* Boston: Houghton Mifflin, 1991.
———. "Reclaiming an Orphan Genre: The First-Person Narrative of Illness." *Literature and Medicine* 13, no. 1 (Spring 1994): 1–21.
Galant, Ivan. "Evroendokrinologiia velikikh russkikh pisatelei i poetov. L. N. Andreev." *Klinicheskii arkhiv genial'nosti i odarennosti* 3, no. 3 (1927): 223–38.
Garro, Linda C., and Cheryl Mattingly. "Narrative as Construct and Construction." In *Narrative and the Cultural Construction of Illness and Healing*, edited by Linda C. Garro and Cheryl Mattingly, 1–49. Berkeley: University of California Press, 2000.
Generalova, N. "Dnevnik Leonida Andreeva." In *Literaturnyi arkhiv: Materialy po istorii russkoi literatury i obshchestvennoi mysli*, edited by K. Grigor'ian, 247–94. St. Petersburg: Nauka, 1994.
———. "Leonid Andreev, Dnevnik 1891–1892." In *Ezhegodnik rukopisnogo otdela Pushkinskogo doma na 1991 god*, edited by T. Tsar'kova, 81–141. St. Petersburg: Akademicheskii proekt, 1994.
Gor'kii, Maksim. "Vospominaniia." *Kniga o Leonide Andreeve*, 5–72. Berlin: Z. I. Grzhebin, 1922.
Hartmann, Eduard von. *The Philosophy of the Unconscious.* 1931. Reprint. Westport, CT: Greenwood Press, 1972.
Iezuitova, L. "Pis'ma k neveste: Iz neizdannoi perepiski Leonida Andreeva." *Zvezda* 1 (1968): 179–207.
Khantzian, E. J. "The Self-Medication Hypothesis of Addictive Disorders: Focus on Heroin and Cocaine Dependence." *American Journal of Psychiatry* 142 (1985): 1259–64.
Kleinman, Arthur. *The Illness Narratives: Suffering, Healing and the Human Condition.* New York: Basic Books, 1988.
Schopenhauer, Arthur. *The World as Will and Representation.* Vols. 1 and 2. Translated by E. F. J. Payne. New York: Dover Publications, 1966.

White, Frederick H. "«Tainaia zhizn'» Leonida Andreeva: Istoriia bolezni." *Voprosy literatury* 1 (2005): 323–39.

White, Hayden. *Metahistory: The Historical Imagination in Nineteenth-Century Europe.* Baltimore: Johns Hopkins University Press, 1973.

————. *Tropics of Discourse: Essays in Cultural Criticism.* Baltimore: Johns Hopkins University Press, 1978.

Zaitsev, Boris. "Vospominaniia." *Kniga o Leonide Andreeve*, 125–46. Berlin: Z. I. Grzhebin, 1922.

Archival Documents

Leeds Russian Archive, MS. 606\E. 1 *12 March–30 June 1890; 21 September 1898.*

LRA, MS. 606\E. 2 *3 July 1890–18 February 1891.*

LRA, MS. 606\E. 3 *27 February–13 April 1891; 5 October 1891; 26 September 1892.*

LRA, MS. 606\E. 4 *15 May–17 August 1891.*

LRA, MS. 606\E. 6 *26 September 1892–4 January 1893.*

LRA, MS. 606\E. 7 *5 March–9 September 1893.*

LRA, MS. 606\E. 8 *27 March 1897–23 April 1901; 1 January 1903; 9 October 1907.*

II

Gender and Depression

Chapter 6

Storying Sadness

Representations of Depression in the Writings of Sylvia Plath, Louise Glück, and Tracy Thompson

Suzanne England, Carol Ganzer, and Carol Tosone

In autobiographical narratives of depression it is not uncommon for authors to refer to their suffering as "unspeakable." This sense of incommunicability—that others cannot understand what one is experiencing—fosters feelings of profound isolation and compounds the suffering. In attempting to explain to herself the causes of the suffering and to find relief, the woman with serious depression grasps desperately for some way to think coherently about the experience—to make sense of it all in order to plan an escape from the pain. Especially poignant is the fact that the sufferer, who feels disconnected from her thoughts, is trying to *think* her way out of the dilemma. Once the depressed woman realizes or is informed that she has a diagnosis of depression, however, the complex and unique experience and the internal dialogues are subordinated to the discourses of the *DSM*, therapeutic practices, and the larger culture. These discourses serve to foreground an internalized identity as a depressed self, and one's life narrative is reframed by a schema dominated by symptoms, treatments, medications, and therapies. All disturbances of emotion, cognition, relationships, and roles are attributed to the depression, and the meaning of small daily events and the flux of everyday life is drawn from one grand interpretive frame—depression.

Autobiographical accounts of depression plus clinical experience suggest that the figurative language—the images and metaphors used by the sufferer to describe depression—may be an attempt to resist the grand medical-psychiatric narrative and its attendant theories and practices, and to reclaim the individuality and richness of the experience of suffering. These accounts also suggest that the most profound existential questions that a woman in the throes of serious depression asks herself emerge in the context of the small prosaic activities and artifacts of daily life. This intersection of the poetic and the prosaic in writings about personal experiences with depression provides an alternative frame for interpretation of these writings, one that has implications for opening new space in theory and therapeutic practice.

Drawing upon postmodern thinking on narratives and pathologies of the self, we continue in this chapter an ongoing inquiry focused on narratives of depression; our aim is to illuminate aspects of depression and recovery that are often hidden from view and not taken into account by current theories and practices. Our purpose is not to generalize or impose some overarching explanatory system on these stories but to be attentive to the expressions of subjectivity and meaning-making in the context of powerful cultural archetypes and meta-narratives, and to create an ear for the voice of the "other." We create that listening space by focusing on figurative language and the details of everyday life. Our methods are interpretive, drawing from literary, psychoanalytic, and feminist traditions of inquiry. Within the general frame of interest described here, each of us has chosen an author and has developed her reflections independently. Carol Tosone, a social work educator, has chosen Sylvia Plath, whose work she draws upon in her teaching. Carol Ganzer, an educator and social worker in independent practice as well as a published poet, has chosen the poet Louise Glück. Suzanne England, a social work educator, whose interest is in autobiographical accounts, has chosen a memoir by the journalist Tracy Thompson. We have focused on women authors for several reasons, the foremost being that we feel close to "our" authors—their narratives and poems resonate with our own experiences as women. Secondly, we have chosen women because of our ongoing interest in expressions of the prosaic and "ordinary" in narratives of illness and disability—aspects that in the lives of women are often played out in intimate domestic spaces. And we are curious about how, or whether, these authors connect the "feminine dilemmas" of their lives with their depression.

Transcendence through Tragedy: Sylvia Plath and the Perfection of Selfhood

On the wintry London dawn of February 11, 1963, Sylvia Plath placed cups of milk beside her sleeping toddler daughter and infant son, sealed their bedroom with tape and towels, then turning on the gas, placed her head inside the oven.[1]

There are few more poignant scenes from literary life where symbolic enactment mingles prosaic domestic details with disturbing, incongruent imagery. The beckoning, womblike oven serves as metaphor for the domesticity that both suffocated and liberated Plath. Paradoxically, her most commanding and highly acclaimed work, *Ariel* (1966), was created within the precincts of her domestic experience. As a poet, however, Plath felt ill equipped to deal with mundane, everyday life and flirted for many years with the allure of nonexistence.

During her brief thirty years of life, Plath wrote for the survival of her sanity, corresponding with family and friends, making regular journal entries, and writing a semi-autobiographical novel, *The Bell Jar* (1966). She is best known for her riveting and haunting poetry, particularly in her collection *Ariel*.[2] During her lifetime, however, Plath's work met with uneven reviews. She surrendered to the promise of peace provided by the oven gas, never knowing that *The Collected Poems of Sylvia Plath* (1981) would receive the Pulitzer Prize for Poetry, a distinction rarely awarded posthumously.

Plath's body of work has been categorized as confessional in genre, an approach whereby the author commits herself to the "concept of salvation through agonized purgation of a naked ego." She wrote her first poem following the untimely death of her father when she was eight years old. Although her idealization of and mourning for her absent father provided the impetus for much of Plath's writing, her earlier works focused on adherence to form and structure and lacked the true affective resonance of childhood. Through her exposure to Robert Lowell's writing class in 1958, where she befriended fellow poets George Starbuck and Anne Sexton, Plath "plunged into the cauldron of childhood."[3]

Here she encounters the father as Colossus; she utilizes the metaphor of a gigantic, decaying statue situated on an isolated island, inhabited only by the daughter and her reparative yet ambivalent memories of her father. Rosenblatt observes that while early on the father is idealized and mourned, in her later poems metaphors such as "vampire," "jailor," and "Nazi torturer" represent the father-husband. Germanic cruelty and blackness succeed early idealistic imagery of the father as tragic casualty. Whereas the early father is depicted as an "innocent victim of deathly external forces," corresponding to her father's actual death due to complications of diabetes, the father archetype of the later poetry "has been transformed into an agent of death."[4]

In "Daddy," Plath's mourning and melancholy yield to metaphorical rage and revenge, precipitated by her husband's infidelity and their subsequent estrangement. A vampire father-husband-bastard meets a fitting fate:

If I've killed one man, I've killed two—
The vampire who said he was you

And drank my blood for a year,
Seven years, if you want to know.
Daddy you can lie back now.

There's a stake in your fat black heart . . .[5]

In "The Jailor," marriage is equated with imprisonment, and Plath implies
that all humankind is victimized by a harsh and capricious universe:

Indeterminate criminal,
I die with variety—
Hung, starved, burned, hooked.

I imagine him
Impotent as distant thunder,
In whose shadow I have eaten my ghost ration.[6]

Plath's Nazi metaphors and related imagery of imprisonment and exe-
cution suggest a universal and unchanging patriarchal domination mirrored in the domicile.

In large measure Plath's collected writings suggest a rebuff of domesticity as culturally defined and enforced. Especially in the composition
of *Ariel*, when poems were written at the rate of several each day, she boldly
and defiantly freed herself of the shackles of domesticity, unleashing a lifetime of pent rage. And Plath offers rich metaphors and prosaic details to
portray her disdain and distrust of the married state. In "The Couriers," for
example, "[t]he snail on a leaf stands for the sluggish and dull domestic
life; the sealed tin of vinegar symbolizes the enclosure and 'sourness' of
marriage; and the gold ring represents the wedding ring with its lying
promise of bliss."[7] Weddings and funerals are interchangeable; in *The Bell
Jar*, for instance, the protagonist Esther Greenwood is wary of her suitor's
courting rituals, maintaining that his true intentions are "to flatten [her]
out underneath his feet like [his mother's] kitchen mat."[8]

Pregnancy and childbirth are construed as a martyr's acts. Like Esther, Plath feared the loss of creativity and selfhood that would result
from marriage and motherhood. In *Letters Home* (1975), Plath's mother
acknowledges Sylvia's loss of self in the complex, symbiotic nature of
their relationship, noting that her daughter sometimes blended parts of
her (mother's) life with her own. In considering the psychological im-
port of pregnancy on Plath's relationship with her mother, Al Strangeways argues that the pregnant daughter returns to a state of oneness with
the mother, where boundaries are ambiguous.[9]

In contrast to her mother, who sacrificed her life to raise the children following her husband's death, Plath was determined to have it all and refused to choose between career and home life. When Plath's husband left her for another woman, Plath faced the possibility of repeating her mother's fate; this prospect, coupled with the initial American publisher's rejection of *The Bell Jar*, dampened her artistic spirit. Unable to bear these outcomes, Plath turned to suicide as the only viable option.[10]

In the poem "Ariel," Plath chooses for herself the image of "God's lioness" with attendant liberating powers:

And I
Am the arrow,

The dew that flies
Suicidal, at one with the drive
Into the red

Eye, the cauldron of morning.[11]

Her suicide was a merciless act of self-destruction carried out in order to attain perfection, tranquility, and freedom from intrapsychic and interpersonal persecution. Sadly and ironically, Sylvia Plath's symbolic transformation and transcendence, initiated in her poetry, required her own death.

A fig tree, the core metaphor in *The Bell Jar*, represents the dilemma of a bright, marriageable young woman in the 1950s, who must choose only one of a myriad of desirable options. Esther laments, "From the tip of every branch, like a fat purple fig, a wonderful future beckoned and winked. . . . a husband and a happy home and children . . . a famous poet . . . a brilliant professor . . . [an] amazing editor . . . Europe and Africa and South America . . . an Olympic lady crew champion . . . I saw myself sitting in the crotch of this fig tree, starving to death, just because I couldn't make up my mind which of the figs I would choose."[12] Given the opportunities, today, for women to inhabit both domestic and professional worlds, Plath's critics, readers, and fans are left with the question of whether she would have made the choice of death today.

Louise Glück:
Survival and Transcendence

The narrative constructed by the poet Louise Glück in her poems gives voice to felt experience, yet it does so in an oblique way. The poems do not so much tell a story directly as suggest a state of foreboding, an intensity of feeling about human experience. Her poetry has been characterized as bearing "witness to intimate occasions—subtle, psychological moments captured by the austerity of her diction."[13] Her poems are spare and minimal; their cryptic and laconic voice, threaded through imagery, leaves imprints and clues for the reader to follow. She acknowledges that she is "attracted to ellipsis, to the unsaid, to suggestion, to eloquent, deliberate silence. The unsaid . . . is analogous to the unseen. . . . Such works inevitably allude to larger contexts; they haunt because they are not whole, though wholeness is implied."[14] Glück's poetry is haunted by sadness and loss, conveyed through imagery, metaphor, and associations. For Glück, "poems are autobiography, but divested of the trappings of chronology and comment."[15] She often writes about the commonplace, the prosaic: family life, small domestic occurrences. Nature is never far from her thoughts; one collection, *The Wild Iris* (1992), is a meditation on a garden peopled by disembodied voices. Against this backdrop of quotidian experience we trace a narrative thread of sadness, hints of a struggle to survive and transcend.

In her early poem "Dedication to Hunger," Glück references her battle with anorexia, remembering "touching, at fifteen, / the interfering flesh / that I would sacrifice / until the limbs were free."[16] In *Ararat* (1990), alluding to the mountain where Noah's Ark settled after the floodwaters dissipated, Glück writes about her family relationships infused with sorrow and loss—the death of her father and childhood memories of sibling rivalry with her sisters, the dead one she replaced and the living one her mother preferred. In one of the more transparent poems, "Mirror Image," she writes:

> Tonight I saw myself in the dark window as
> the image of my father, whose life
> was spent like this,
> thinking of death, to the exclusion
> of other sensual matters,
> so in the end that life
> was easy to give up, since
> it contained nothing.[17]

It is through this gaze into the dark glass that Glück, comparing her own life with her father's emotionally empty life, gives voice to her own struggle with darkness, the "easeful Death."[18]

The theme of loss pervades Glück's books. *Meadowlands* (1996) chronicles the breakup of her second marriage. Here the narrative is more linear, more direct; the familiar monologue of the lyric poet is replaced by a dialogue between quarreling partners. The story is interlaced with imagery from the *The Odyssey*, Penelope waiting for Odysseus to return. In

Glück's narrative, however, the husband continues to wander and the modern couple separates. In *Vita Nova* (1999) the poet heralds spring but "this time / not as a lover but a messenger of death."[19] The poet has moved from rural Vermont to Cambridge, but elements of the past still haunt her. *The Seven Ages* (2001) reprises and recapitulates the themes of the first eight books: "Desire, loneliness, wind in the flowering almond—/ surely these are the great, the inexhaustible subjects."[20]

A more recent work by Glück, *October*, a sequence published first in *The New Yorker* and then as a chapbook in 2004, is a meditation on the theme of endings. Although the speaker identifies herself by the pronouns "I" and "my," we sense neither time nor place, only the season of ending with "the wind's cries, whistling over the bare ground."[21] There is violence, but we never learn the details; they are embedded in the growing silence, sown in the wind: "It does me no good; violence has changed me. / My body has grown cold like the stripped fields." The speaker looks to the earth for hope, but there is no resolution, no redemptive moment in the poet's embrace of nature:

> What others found in art,
> I found in nature. What others found
> in human love, I found in nature.
> Very simple. But there was no voice there.[22]

Once the world gave her pleasure, "Beauty / the healer, the teacher—." But now the poet resigns herself to the barrenness: "Death cannot harm me / more than you have harmed me, / my beloved life."[23] The narrative moves from winter to spring, but the speaker finds "[t]he light has changed; / middle C is tuned darker now. / And the songs of morning sound over-rehearsed."[24] It is not the light of spring that she sees but the twilight of autumn, a growing darkness. In the final poem of the sequence, the speaker compares herself to the earth, which is "bitter; I think / sunlight has failed her." The sun no longer provides "affirmation," and "the brilliance that made all life possible / becomes the cold stars." The poem ends obliquely with the moon rising over the "coldness and barrenness" of the earth.[25] The only beauty or hope that survives does so in the coldness and darkness.

From this brief overview of her work, we can trace Glück's depressive narrative through the natural images that lend visual description to a somber tone delivered at times in the poet's voice, at other times in the disembodied voice of the other. Glück's narrative is one of absence or lack, what is lost. We enter the narrator's interior life; we bear witness to the depression that lies just under the surface, embodied in the bleak images and plangent voice of the poet. Writing about the experience of watching her house burn down in 1980, Glück claims she had been waiting "twenty years . . . to undergo the losses I knew to be inevitable. . . . Actual loss . . . was a release, an abrupt transition from anticipation to expertise. . . . I watched the destruction of all that had been, all that would not be again, and all that remained took on a radiance."[26] It is this radiance that shines through in her poems, no matter how dark they are, and serves as an antidote to the depression. Hope runs like a second, minor narrative thread through her work, a voice often stilled but rising in brief moments, as the disembodied voice of white lily in *The Wild Iris* signals hope: "I live to return: / this one summer we have entered eternity. / I felt your two hands / bury me to release its splendor."[27]

Tracy Thompson:
Fear of Abandonment and Annihilation

In *The Beast: A Journey through Depression,* Tracy Thompson writes of being a survivor of depression: "Inside, I am a battlefield—Waterloo after Napoleon, Vicksburg after the siege."[28] Describing her years of suffering from depression, Thompson interweaves the story of her desperate struggle to understand and overcome this "psychic freight train of roaring despair"[29] with reflections on her life and work as a writer, and on her emerging consciousness about the sources and meaning of her deep need to be "normal"—to feel safe, secure, and loved.

When she was fourteen, Thompson began writing a private journal; in the journal, the teenage girl writes that she aims "'to put down the cause of my depressions and to see if I can help myself that way. . . . It sounds horrible, and it is, but a couple of times I have thought how nice it would be to kill myself!!!'"[30] In her teens, Thompson self-medicated her insomnia by taking a combination of codeine-based cough medicine and Valium. Soon she was taking fistfuls of Sominex each night. Later, involved in a mutually destructive relationship with a man she calls Thomas, she put together a plan to kill herself: "[M]y preparations were like strapping on a parachute in an airplane that was about to crash; the whole time I was preparing to hurl myself out the door, I clung to the hope that something would happen at the last minute to forestall that terrible necessity." Postponing suicide that night, she went to work the next day and typed a note to herself: "'Right now I am thinking I want to die.'"[31] When she realized what she had written, she called Thomas and agreed to be hospitalized.

Thompson's lifeline is her writing—she writes her way through the depression and, in spite of its debilitating symptoms, is able to build and maintain a successful career as a journalist. In her narrative, the prosaic is not expressed in a domestic context; indeed, we get very little sense of her as someone who shops, cooks, exercises, or cares for a pet. However, she writes in satisfying detail about her work life—the writing projects, office politics, and her relations with other journalists.

Growing up in the 1960s in a Southern fundamentalist family, Thompson's earliest recollections "are like sunlight through a tree, dappled with dread."[32] Both of her parents had suffered, when young, the loss of their own parents from death or abandonment; although they showed it in quite different ways, they were likely depressed themselves. Thompson's sense of dread and impending doom as a child was not surprising, given the histories and personalities of her parents.

Thompson adored her father, a successful, jovial man with whom she would joke and wisecrack, much to their mutual delight, but he frightened her with his bursts of rage and dark fury over some inconsequential thing, "a lawn mower that wouldn't start, the mayonnaise jar left open on the kitchen counter. . . . In him I sensed a deep, unfathomable anger—perhaps because, even then, I sensed that I had it too."[33] Thompson's father had grown up in a family of "death and abandonment."[34] When he was a small child, his mother "went to bed and stayed there for a decade," and in doing so "simply gave up on life."[35] Piecing together the family story, Thompson discovers that before her father was born there was a sister, who died at age three after toppling a pot of boiling water from the stove. Shortly afterward Thompson's grandfather abandoned the family and now, having no one to care for him, her father was sent to live with an aunt.

Thompson's mother lost both her parents when she was quite young, and endured years of poverty and abuse. Thompson says her mother "loved her Savior with the fervor of an abandoned child," yet trusted no one and lived in anxious anticipation of apocalypse. On a family trip, her mother refused to describe one of her terrible nightmares except to say that Thompson and her sister were in it, and that "'[t]he sun was blood-red, like it was the end of the world.'" Thompson believed the dream to be an omen of the Second Coming, and was convinced she would be "left behind." A fearful and anxious child, Thompson awaited what her fundamentalist church termed the Rapture with "horror and dread"; that she feared the "end time," when the faithful would be taken up to heaven and non-believers left behind, "was proof of [her] difference from others. And different . . . meant defective."[36]

Thompson's fear of annihilation by some irrational evil force and certainty of her defectiveness were nearly confirmed when, barely into her teens, she was hit by a speeding car. Though her injuries were extensive and serious, to her, the worst "was to [her] face: something metal on the car had left a ragged tear of skin that opened just below the hairline above my left eye and exposed the whole left side of my skull, miraculously missing the eye." Three months after nearly being killed, Thompson was "walking without a limp" but had a jagged red scar over a quarter of her face that turned the left corner of her eye "into a distorted squint."[37] She remembers longing to hear her father say she was pretty, but knowing it would never happen, "I didn't even ask. When I came home from the hospital, he had picked me up in his arms and carried me into the house, but I felt no comfort in his touch, only embarrassment. . . . Inside, my rage retreated to a dark corner of my mind."[38]

Thompson is silent on the matter, but one assumes that the visible scar faded in time. However, her fear of not being loved by a man remained a deep psychic scar. Her Southern-bred image of "Woman as Wife" was in some tension with her desire for a career as a writer, but there is never any question that "[m]arriage was the glass slipper, the charm that would break this evil spell" of self-doubt and fear of never being loved.[39] It is her father's adoration that Thompson wants from men, but as she realizes years later, her clinging self-involvement and anger made the love and security she so desperately desired impossible.

Thompson draws on striking metaphors and imagery when describing the depth of her fear and despair, as well as the relief of recovery. As the subtitle of her memoir reveals, she views her life with depression as a "journey through" it and the depression itself as a "Beast" that lies in wait to devour her.[40] Using imagery eerily reminiscent of the "end times," she conveys her suffering with the image of moving through space toward death and annihilation, a powerless "speck in that vastness."[41] After losing three men, including her father, upon whom she "depended . . . for [her] self-worth," Thompson felt "like someone had opened the hatch in [her] spacecraft; outside, the blank universe loomed—cold, airless, and incomprehensible."[42] She also associates depression with dangerous waters. In a dream, she is at the edge of the ocean at night, the only thing visible a boat in the near distance "lit like a festival." She starts out on a small raft for the pleasure boat but is caught up in the current: "The waters were going to suck me down into some huge waterfall that somehow existed below the surface, a silent, downward rush of current."[43] Later, as she begins to recover with the help of Prozac, Thompson first notices a "moment of silence" in her brain; with imagery reversing the descent of her frightening dreams, she writes, "I was a body floating to the surface of the water, and then my face felt the air and I breathed, for the first time in a long time, a long cool draft of oxygen."[44]

Writing Depression

We began this inquiry not to speculate about the intrapsychic lives of the authors or to seek common themes, but to surface and highlight the authors' use of metaphor, imagery, and the homely details of everyday life in conveying their experience. Their creative use of language gives a sense of intimacy that engenders empathy, and the prosaic elements elicit a woman-to-woman familiarity and connection. What we found to be significant for treatment and recovery is that these writers give voice to their depression. It is in speaking the "unspeakable suffering" of depression that one begins to recompose the narrative, to trace the threads of the story from the past to the present and to find a way to make new sense out of old material. The imagery and details of everyday life provide the space for reflection and transcendence. Depression is only one piece of each writer's experience. Paying attention to prosaic quotidian moments allows her to contextualize the depressive feelings within a frame of life that is moving and changing rather than fixed and static.

The complexities of our responses to these writings are too great to cover here, but what is evident is the overarching theme of the transcendence of suffering through writing. Thompson begins writing a journal at fourteen, not only to try to understand her depression but also to prepare for a writer's vocation. Later she is rescued from suicide by seeing her own words on a computer screen. Glück's poetry of searching for hope and healing in nature, and finding only loss and barrenness, transcends the fear of death itself and allows the reader in turn to confront and transcend, in beauty, the silence and emptiness of depression. Plath, too, created a legacy of writing that has transcended her suffering and her brief life. Through their writings these women speak possibility into our lives and give us hope in the liberating and transcending power of our own words.

Notes

1. Wagner-Martin, *Sylvia Plath*, 243.
2. Her other collections of poems include *The Colossus and Other Poems* (1962), *Crossing the Water* (1971), and *Winter Trees* (1971).
3. Butscher, *Sylvia Plath*, 17.
4. Rosenblatt, *Sylvia Plath*, 111–12.
5. Plath, *Collected Poems*, 224.
6. Ibid., 227.
7. Rosenblatt, 109.
8. *The Bell Jar*, 89.
9. Strangeways, *Sylvia Plath*, 145.
10. Wagner-Martin, 233.
11. *Collected Poems*, 239–40.
12. *The Bell Jar*, 80.
13. Diehl, *On Louise Glück*, 1.
14. Glück, *Proofs & Theories*, 73.
15. Ibid., 92.

16. *Descending Figure*, 32.
17. *Ararat*, 63.
18. John Keats, "Ode to a Nightingale," line 52.
19. *Vita Nova*, 2.
20. *The Seven Ages*, 67.
21. *October*, 8.
22. Ibid., 10–11.
23. Ibid., 12.
24. Ibid., 13.
25. Ibid., 17–18.
26. *Proofs & Theories*, 106.
27. *The Wild Iris*, 63.
28. Thompson, *The Beast*, 46.
29. Ibid., 4.
30. Ibid., 5.
31. Ibid., 145–46.
32. Ibid., 18.
33. Ibid., 28.
34. Ibid., 23.
35. Ibid., 22.
36. Ibid., 19–20 (all quotations in this paragraph).
37. Ibid., 30.
38. Ibid., 32–33.
39. Ibid., 44–45.
40. Ibid., 4.
41. Ibid., 41.
42. Ibid., 72.
43. Ibid., 41.
44. Ibid., 249.

Bibliography

Butscher, Edward, ed. *Sylvia Plath: The Woman and the Work.* New York: Dodd, Mead, 1977.

Diehl, Joanne Feit, ed. *On Louise Glück: Change What You See.* Ann Arbor: University of Michigan Press, 2005.

Glück, Louise. *Ararat.* New York: Ecco Press, 1990.

———. *Descending Figure.* New York: Ecco Press, 1980.

———. *Meadowlands.* Hopewell, NJ: Ecco Press, 1996.

———. *October.* Louisville, KY: Sarabande Books, 2004.

———. *Proofs & Theories: Essays on Poetry.* Hopewell, NJ: Ecco Press, 1994.

———. *The Seven Ages.* New York: Ecco Press, 2001.

———. *Vita Nova.* Hopewell, NJ: Ecco Press, 1999.

———. *The Wild Iris.* Hopewell, NJ: Ecco Press, 1992.

Plath, Sylvia. *Ariel.* New York: Harper and Row, 1966.

———. *The Bell Jar.* London: Faber and Faber, 1966.

————. *The Collected Poems of Sylvia Plath.* Edited by Ted Hughes. New York: Harper and Row, 1981.

————. *The Colossus and Other Poems.* New York: Knopf, 1962.

————. *Crossing the Water.* London: Faber and Faber, 1971.

————. *The Journals of Sylvia Plath.* Edited by Ted Hughes and Frances McCullough. New York: Dial Press, 1982.

————. *Letters Home: Correspondence, 1950–1963.* Edited by Aurelia Schober Plath. New York: Harper and Row, 1975.

————. *Winter Trees.* New York: Harper and Row, 1972.

Rosenblatt, Jon. *Sylvia Plath: The Poetry of Initiation.* Chapel Hill: University of North Carolina Press, 1979.

Strangeways, Al. *Sylvia Plath: The Shaping of Shadows.* Madison, NJ: Fairleigh Dickinson University Press, 1998.

Thompson, Tracy. *The Beast: A Journey Through Depression.* New York: Penguin, 1996.

Wagner-Martin, Linda. *Sylvia Plath: A Biography.* New York: Simon and Schuster, 1987.

Chapter 7

"Addiction got me what I needed"

Depression and Drug
Addiction in Elizabeth Wurtzel's Memoirs

Joanne Muzak

In her 2002 memoir, *More, Now, Again: A Memoir of Addiction*, Elizabeth Wurtzel professes that she "didn't see addiction coming"—that, despite what she describes as "previous troubles with drug abuse," addiction did not register as a possible outcome of the prescribed Ritalin use that led her to the compulsive use of both licit and illicit stimulants, for which she eventually sought professional medical treatment.[1] On one occasion, however, Wurtzel contemplates the possibility that she unconsciously willed herself into this addiction. She contrasts her heroin use, which she describes as carefully controlled and regulated by the fear of "being a junkie," with her use of Ritalin: "I didn't see the Ritalin creeping up. I thought it was a free ride." She immediately reconsiders this perception of the genesis of her addiction: "Or maybe not. Because addiction got me what I needed."[2]

Then, in one of the book's most intriguing passages, Wurtzel describes how her drug addiction has made manifest the interminable emotional pain that she has always experienced as depression:

> All those years of depression got people to worry about me. But now they're scared. They're really scared. They used to worry that I might get sad enough to kill myself, but no one ever believed I'd really do it, not even me. But now they are scared that I am just going to end up dead. They're afraid that they will find me dead. And they mean it. I see the way they look at me. I see fear.
>
> Finally, people take my sorrow seriously.

> . . . *Drugs put the fear of God into people the way a bad mood,*
> *even one that goes on for a decade, just does not. You can always*
> *wake up feeling better; that's always the hope with a depressive. But*
> *no one around me harbors that hope any longer. They are petrified.*
> *They are disgusted. At long last, my pain is a serious matter.*
> *I've won.*[3]

Wurtzel's insight into the very different perceptions people have of her depression versus her drug addiction keenly illustrates the differences between depression and addiction as cultural constructs. While in mainstream Western culture both are currently referred to as "diseases" or "illnesses"—and while both behaviors or conditions are seen to be "pathological" responses to, or at least reflections of, unbearable psychic pain—drug addiction and depression do not have the same cultural currency as signs, symptoms, or expressions of emotional pain. To Wurtzel's mainly white, upper- and middle-class friends and family, drug addiction—although it induces fear and disgust—is more understandable as a manifestation of emotional pain than depression is. Drug addiction, with its popular connotations of moral degeneration and physical deterioration, speaks more loudly than depression. The visible cues of drug use and addiction, such as track marks and an emaciated body, are easier to interpret as signs of emotional pain than the utter passivity exhibited by the depressive. The corporeality of addiction makes it more tangible, more believable, more "real" than depression. The drug addict, particularly the white, upper-middle-class addict, is afforded the possibility of recovery (and redemption) by the supposedly destigmatizing discourse of Western medicine, which conceptualizes addiction as a treatable disease. However, the depressive, especially the depressed woman, occupies a more ambiguous position as an in-valid invalid.

This essay examines how the discourses of depression and drug addiction intertwine not only in Wurtzel's account of her drug addiction in *More, Now, Again,* but also in her description of depression in her earlier memoir, *Prozac Nation: Young and Depressed in America* (1994). When I began working on these memoirs, I anticipated that Wurtzel, having published *Prozac Nation* eight years before *More, Now, Again,* would see and articulate a relationship between her drug addiction and her depression in her memoir of addiction. After all, *Prozac Nation* is a thoughtful chronicle of her experiences of depression as a young woman and a complex account of how depression comes to shape her identity. In *More, Now, Again,* however, mainstream concepts and narratives of drug addiction efface any explicit discourse of depression and eventually render depression virtually immaterial to her drug addiction. What makes the negation of depression particularly noteworthy in *More, Now, Again* is the persistence of the discourse of drug addiction through both memoirs. "Recreational" drug use is almost as constant a presence in *Prozac Nation* as depression, and, more significantly, Wurtzel uses drug addiction throughout that book to conceptualize her depression. In both memoirs, drug addiction subsumes depression. What does this unbalanced discursive relationship tell us about the cultural currency of depression relative to that of drug addiction?

Discursive Resemblances between Depression and Drug Addiction

The discourses of depression and drug addiction tend to overlap within expert realms and within personal, experiential narratives.[4] Biomedical conceptions arguably dominate contemporary accounts of both conditions. Neurobiological theories, which explain depression and drug addiction in terms of alterations in the same neurotransmitter systems,[5] have increasingly shaped the popular discourse on these conditions and resonate in autobiographical narratives of depression and drug addiction.

As is evident in mainstream Western culture's labeling of depression and drug addiction as "mental disorders," psychiatry is currently the loudest voice among the many disciplines engaged with these concepts. Its biomedical models also inform the popular discourse on both conditions: depression is understood, in lay terms, as a "chemical imbalance" in the brain, rooted primarily in "abnormally low levels of serotonin";[6] likewise, drug addiction is popularly accepted as a "disease," although, to most, the biomedical basis of the "disease" of addiction is much more ambiguous than the single-cause biochemical explanation of depression.[7] Nonetheless, because of medicine's social authority, the disease model of addiction is widely, and often blindly, accepted.[8] Both the biochemical theory of depression and the disease model of addiction cite neurobiological, physiological, and genetic factors as the basis of these problems.[9] Depressives and addicts are said to "inherit" a "tendency toward abnormal chemical functioning."[10]

Proponents of these theories often declare that depression and addiction "strike . . . indiscriminately at all ages, races, creeds, and classes."[11] According to this rhetoric, the "indiscriminate" nature of these "diseases" reduces the stigma attached to both conditions and thus alleviates the sufferer's debilitating feelings of guilt and shame. It is important to recognize, however, that these "disease" theories more readily accommodate the middle and upper classes. We tend more willingly to apply the disease concept of addiction to white, middle- and upper-class addicts than to addicted Aboriginal prostitutes, for example. Disease models of addiction allow those who already occupy privileged socioeconomic positions to construct a socially acceptable addict identity as a "sick," rather than a weak-willed or inherently bad, person.

While biopsychosocial models appear to offer broader, less reductionist frameworks within which to understand depression and drug addiction, like biomedical models they construct depression and drug addiction as similar conditions.[12] These are upheld as exemplary biopsychosocial problems: "Depressive illness is probably the best example of a psychobiological disorder where nature and nurture interact in its genesis,"[13] and with a multidetermined etiology, "addiction . . . is the quintessential biobehavioral disorder."[14]

A discursive resemblance between the conditions is also noticeable in subjective accounts. Depressives and drug addicts alike represent their respective behaviors as simultaneously illnesses and identities. While such "illnesses" are frequently understood to interfere thoroughly with "the capacity of the self to be itself,"[15] they nonetheless function as a "site of *self-production*, a hermeneutic location . . . [in which] to construct meaning and build personal significance."[16]

Moreover, depressives and drug addicts often describe their experiences in comparable terms, using similar metaphors and narrative trajectories. Metaphors of entrapment, descent, and darkness predominate in accounts of both depression and drug addiction. These metaphors aptly convey the despair, isolation, and helplessness that both depressives and addicts report as their governing affective states. "Imprisoned" in and by their conditions, and overwhelmed by feelings of self-loathing, loneliness, and powerlessness, both depressives and addicts narrate a "downward spiral" into "darkness" until they inevitably "hit rock bottom." "Recovery" begins only once they accept themselves as "sick" and therefore in need of medical intervention. This is, of course, an oversimplification of the varied and complex ways that people narrate their experiences of suffering. Still, the similarities in the subjective discourses of these conditions provide an intriguing counterpoint to the differences in their broader cultural currencies.

That is, despite the resemblance between disciplinary and subjective discursive constructions of depression and drug addiction that I have sketched here, depression and drug addiction have divergent value and utility when they get taken up as constructs by mainstream culture. Wurtzel's memoirs incorporate dominant concepts of depression and drug addiction as "illnesses": she accepts the biochemical conception of depression by the end of *Prozac Nation,* and she embraces the disease model of drug addiction by the end of *More, Now, Again.* But for Wurtzel, and in general, drug addiction registers as the more valid condition and serves as a more potent identity narrative.

PROZAC NATION: Drug Addiction in Depression

Published during the "memoir boom" of the mid-1990s, *Prozac Nation* was met with mixed reviews.[17] Unfavorable reviews focused almost exclusively on Wurtzel herself, rather than addressing the book as an account of a young woman's attempt to understand her depression. Granted, she frequently paints an unflattering self-portrait, which she readily acknowledges. Reviewers who attack Wurtzel personally as "a self-absorbed slacker" represent her accounts of depression as stereotypical feminine ranting and whining.[18] While she effectively communicates "the full gravity of depressive episodes"[19] as well as their consequences, and compellingly examines her family relationships and the cultural and historical issues associated with growing up in the late 1960s and 1970s as major factors underlying her depression, reviewers have more often been concerned with how "(un)likeable" or "relatable" Wurtzel is.[20] Discussions like these threaten to nullify her depression as a material experience. The reviews that trash *Prozac Nation* by attacking Wurtzel personally provide a useful context for my analysis; they illustrate effectively the distrustful and hostile culture that women face when they attempt to relate and examine their experiences of depression.

Wurtzel uses drug addiction as a paradigm for conceptualizing her depression because depression does not signify as much as addiction does as a legitimate problem or expression of emotional pain. She incorporates the discourse of drug addiction into her narrative of depression in an effort to validate her experiences of depression.

"Longing to be a junkie"

Wurtzel writes openly about her illicit drug use, most of which occurs during her freshman year at Harvard and shortly thereafter, during an internship as the arts reporter at the *Dallas Morning News* in the summer of 1987.[21] She characterizes her drug use as "abuse": "I was loading myself with whatever . . . I could find, doing whatever I could to get my head to shut off for awhile. . . . It wasn't just recreational drug use."[22] Wurtzel recognizes her drug use as "self-medication," as a response to her depression, but her friends and family frequently suggest that she has a "drug problem." Their comments provoke her into explanations of her drug use, in which she reasserts depression as her fundamental problem. Despite this insistence, she contemplates drug addiction nostalgically, wishing for a "drug problem" instead of depression.

In a particularly prophetic passage early in *Prozac Nation*, Wurtzel recounts her conception of her depression as an eighth-grader:

I found myself *wishing* for a real ailment, found myself longing to be a junkie or a cokehead or something—something
real. If it were only a matter of keeping me away from my bad
habits, how much easier it all would be. . . .

[I]t seemed to me that if I could get hooked on some drug,
anything was possible. I'd make new friends. I'd have a real
problem. I'd be able to walk into a church basement full of fellow sufferers, and have them all say, Welcome to our night-
mare! We understand![23]

These words resonate with Wurtzel's assertion in *More, Now, Again* that
"addiction got [her] what [she] needed." She draws on cultural constructs of drug addiction as a tangible and distinct condition that signifies as an obviously serious problem, in contrast to her ambiguous and
ubiquitous depression. She imagines that, as an addict, her suffering
would be validated and that she would be offered community.

Wurtzel's perception of the community to which she would belong
as a drug addict is important. Many female addicts express a desire to mit-
igate a crushing sense of non-belonging, to end a horrible loneliness, as a
major motivation for their drug use. The "drug addict" or "junkie" label,
as stigmatizing and derisive as it is, offers a distinct identity and a sense of
community when feelings of loneliness and marginalization are unbearable. Twelve-Step groups, for instance, promise community and a discourse around which to shape an identity.[24] In contrast, social withdrawal
and a sense that the self is deficient or absent characterize depression.[25]

Wurtzel also wishes for addiction in response to her friend David's
suggestion that she "has a drug problem and need[s] professional help."
At the end of a bad psilocybin mushroom trip, she responds to David's
concerns: "What I wouldn't give to have a drug problem. . . . What I
wouldn't give for it to be that simple. If I could check into rehab and
come out the other end okay, I'd be thrilled."[26] Although she oversim-
plifies what it means to resolve a "drug problem," her comments reflect a
common perception of addiction. For those who have health insurance
and/or the money for treatment, a protocol for dealing with addictions
exists. This perception of drug addiction as a remediable medical problem informs Wurtzel's wish for a "drug problem."

Later in the same passage, she describes her depression as a "vise
[that], no matter what, just wouldn't let go."[27] In most popular cultural
narratives of illicit drug addiction, the drug beckons, seduces, and hooks
the user; it just won't let go. She applies this narrative to her depression
in order to convey how debilitating it really is.

In the first half of *Prozac Nation*, then, Wurtzel frequently wishes for
drug addiction to be her primary problem: drawing on the disparate cul-

tural currencies of drug addiction and depression, she conceptualizes her depression as antithetical to drug addiction. Later on in the book, she uses addiction figuratively to liken her thoughts and behaviors as a depressive to those of an addict. By the end of *Prozac Nation*, with clinical overtones, she describes depression as an addiction: "Depression is an addiction the way many substances and most modes of behavior are."[28] In the next section, I focus on how Wurtzel arrives at this conclusion, and what its implications are.

"Depression Junkie"?

The paralysis of her depression does not prevent Wurtzel from being anxious to find a way out of it. Searching her mind for a solution to her pain, she recounts a conversation with her friend Samantha: "If I were an alcoholic," she tells Samantha, "I'd be saying I want a drink, but since I'm me I don't know what it is I want. But I want it right now!"[29] Wurtzel's reference to alcoholism lends a sense of urgency and compulsion to her depression, which at this point appears as a dire and perhaps addictive behavior.

Calling depression an addiction requires an understanding of addiction that is preoccupied neither with illicit drugs nor with the stigma associated with their use. Many cultural critics have noted the expansion of the concept of addiction in the last decades of the twentieth century. As Eve Sedgwick notes, "Not only every form of substance ingestion, but more simply every form of human behavior [has recently been brought] into the orbit of potential addiction attribution. . . . [I]t is now become a commonplace that, precisely, any substance, any behavior, even any affect may be pathologized as addictive."[30] Expanded to include "non-substance-related activities" such as exercise and work, as well as affects such as love and fear, the addiction concept has been imbued with "the capacity to represent a wide of range of psychological phenomena."[31] But what are the consequences of bringing depression under this broad framework of addiction? What happens to the cultural significance of depression when it is framed as addiction?

These questions resonate with Wurtzel's comparison of herself to a recovered alcoholic. She recounts a transformation, around the age of fifteen, in her perception of her depression: it "had already fundamentally changed me. . . . My morose character would not ever go away because depression was everything about me. It colored every aspect of me so thoroughly, and I became resigned to that . . . [and] in a strange way, this resignation allowed me to stabilize."[32] "All this pain" simply became "a fact of [her] life," and Wurtzel appeared to be "a perfectly normal teenage girl."[33] Then, with the hindsight of adulthood, Wurtzel compares herself as a depressed teenager to a "recovered alcoholic who gives up drinking but still longs, daily if not hourly, for just another sip of Glenfiddich or Mogen David or Muscadet; I could be a depressive who wasn't actively depressed, an asymptomatic drone for the cause."[34] The effectiveness of this simile relies on the reader's familiarity with the rhetoric of addiction recovery, which presents the "recovered alcoholic" as always an alcoholic. This notion is a product of Twelve-Step discourse and is a popular tenet of contemporary concepts of addiction. A person can be an "active addict" or a "recovered addict," but even in "recovery" the label indicates that she retains her addict identity; she lives with the notion that addiction always lurks as an opportune virus, awaiting fatal lapses in self-surveillance in order to reassert itself. As Wurtzel suggests, the "recovered alcoholic" is preoccupied by, and must always be on guard against, longings for just a taste of her "drug of choice." Although this comparison leaves the reader wondering for what the "recovered depressive" longs, the implication is that depression is a permanent condition that "defines even asymptomatic intervals," dictates one's identity, and requires constant self-surveillance.[35] As troubling as this depiction is, such discourse of addiction lends legitimacy to depression: aligning the experience of depression with the experiences of a "recovered" alcoholic, "instituting" it, places depression and the depressive within a well-established discourse. At this point, Wurtzel has no discourse outside of addiction that could provide such validation.

Near the end of *Prozac Nation*, Wurtzel's depression is authenticated and sanctioned by two events. First, she receives a formal diagnosis of "atypical depression" and a prescription for Prozac, which makes her feel "much less lonely"; and, second, her mother refers to Wurtzel's depression as "a real problem," which dramatically affects her.[36] Before these events, she "never felt [she] had a right to be depressed."[37] However, shortly after depression becomes a "truth" for her,[38] and just as the Prozac begins to improve her mood and affect, she makes what she describes as a "wimpy attempt" to kill herself in the washroom outside her psychiatrist's office.[39] It is her analysis of this suicide attempt that leads her to conclude that "depression is an addiction."[40]

Wurtzel reasons that the suicide attempt was a last effort to hold on to the depressed person she had been for so many years: "The idea of throwing away my depression, of having to create a whole personality, a whole way of living and being that did not contain misery as its leitmotif, was daunting. . . . How would I ever survive as my normal self? And after all these years, who was that person anyway?"[41] Echoing her psychiatrist, she reflects, "It was so hard for me to formulate a way of being and thinking in which the starting point was not depression. Dr. Sterling agrees that it's hard, because depression is an addiction the way many substances and most modes of behavior are, and like most addictions it is miserable but still hard to break."[42] The all-encompassing character of depression (in conjunction with the authority of her doctor) appears to be the primary basis of her claim that depression is an addiction.

More broadly, however, this moment represents the culmination of Wurtzel's use of the discourse of drug addiction in her narrative of depression. Her earliest references to drug addiction—her nostalgic wish for a drug problem—suggest that drug addiction is more readily perceived as a legitimate illness and manifestation of severe psychic and emotional pain than depression is. Moreover, drug addiction promises community and a legitimate identity whereas depression, as Wurtzel has experienced it up to this point, is a "complete absence."[43] Eventually, however, the differences between drug addiction and depression as cultural constructs are elided as she likens her thoughts and behaviors as a depressive to the urgent and compulsive behavior of the addict, and the all-consuming nature of depression to the supposedly tyrannical and permanent nature of addiction. Conspicuously absent, of course, are the more stigmatizing representations of drug addiction as a voluntary and deliberately "immoral" behavior pursued by inherently "bad," "hedonistic," and otherwise "deviant" and "worthless" individuals; these connotations threaten to stigmatize rather than legitimate depression when it gets subsumed under the discourse of addiction. But in this concluding moment where Wurtzel names depression as an addiction, what is perhaps more disturbing than the possibility of stigma is the ease with which, after over three hundred pages of explication, depression becomes simply another addiction, another "pathology" over which the sufferer has no control except in seeking "proper" medical treatment.

MORE, NOW, AGAIN: "Addiction fulfils that need"

In *More, Now, Again*, Wurtzel rarely refers to her experience of depression. She acknowledges it as one "circumstance" among many that "got [her] started on [her] addiction," but she does not construct a direct, causal relationship between her depression and her drug addiction.[44] Eventually, she understands drug addiction as a distinct and fundamental illness, independent of any source except the compulsive consumption of stimulants and an ambiguous predisposition to such consumption. The only explicit references to depression occur when she attempts to differentiate addiction from depression: "The main difference between depression and addiction, as far as I can tell: depression is full of need and addiction fulfils that need."[45] Recalling Wurtzel's proclamation, "Addiction got me what I needed," I want to conclude with a few remarks about her "need" and how addiction discursively "fulfils that need."

The most telling part of Wurtzel's contemplation of people's discordant perceptions of her depression and her drug addiction is her concluding pronouncement: "At long last, my pain is a serious matter. I've won."[46] This statement suggests not only that drug addiction has cultural currency as an obvious manifestation of emotional and psychic pain, but also that one of Wurtzel's greatest "needs" is to have her pain recognized. She equates her friends' and family's ability to perceive her addiction with a compassionate perception of the pain that underlies it. This (perhaps unstable) equation illustrates the potency of drug addiction over depression as a discursive framework for representing psychic pain. That addiction discursively meets Wurtzel's overwhelming need to have her pain acknowledged points to the absence of a suitable discourse of depression. The discursive resemblances between depression and drug addiction within expert and experiential narratives, as Wurtzel's work demonstrates, do not translate into shared cultural meanings. Drug addiction continues to carry an ominous and legitimate urgency, particularly for the white, middle-class woman who violates normative femininity by being an addict,[47] while the depressed woman, whose apparent passivity *exemplifies* normative femininity, struggles to find a way to tell her story that will validate her experiences and get her what she needs.

Notes

1. Wurtzel, *More, Now, Again*, 153, 25. In Wurtzel's words, Ritalin "was prescribed because I had trouble focusing. . . . Plus, I was tired all the time, my old reliable antidepressants were not working so well, the whole regime needed a boost" (15).

2. Ibid., 153.

3. Ibid., 153–54 (italics in the original text).

4. I do not mean to imply that "expert" accounts are objective.

5. Markou, Kosten, and Koob, "Neurobiological Similarities," 135.

6. Solomon, *The Noonday Demon*, 22.

7. Critics have been debating the scientific legitimacy and the sociopolitical consequences of the disease concept of addiction since its earliest incarnations in the early 1900s. For an insightful discussion of the evolution and the politics of disease models of addiction, see Acker, "Stigma or Legitimation?"

8. Narcotics Anonymous's use of the disease concept exemplifies the uncritical stance of many mainstream advocates of addiction disease models. On their website, NA addresses the question "Is addiction a disease?" with this response: "[W]e treat Addiction [*sic*] as a disease because that makes sense to us and it works. We have no need to press the issue any farther than that."

9. Fee, "The Project of Pathology," 76; Morrison, *White Rabbit*, 184–85.

10. Morrison, 184–85.

11. Styron, *Darkness Visible*, 35.

12. Stoppard, "Why New Perspectives Are Needed," 85.

13. Palazidou, "Depression in Women," 110.
14. Leshner, "Addiction Is a Brain Disease."
15. Cheever, "Prozac Americans," 348.
16. Fee, 85.
17. On the "memoir boom," see Gilmore, "Limit-Cases," 128. Gilmore notes that "memoir in the '90's was dominated by the comparatively young whose private lives were emblematic of unofficial histories . . . [T]he memoir boom's defining subject has been trauma" (128).
18. Schoemer, "To Be Young, Gifted and Blue," 58.
19. Fee, 79.
20. See Perring's and Klinghoffer's reviews of *Prozac Nation*.
21. "Illicit" is not quite accurate. During Wurtzel's freshman year, Ecstasy (MDMA) was still legal, and many of Wurtzel's stories of excessive drug use involve Ecstasy.
22. Wurtzel, *Prozac Nation*, 121.
23. Ibid., 68–70.
24. See Cain, "Personal Stories," and Warhol and Michie, "Twelve-Step Teleology."
25. Later in the same passage, Wurtzel remarks, "Depression was the loneliest fucking thing on earth. There were no halfway houses for depressives, no Depression Anonymous meetings that I knew of" (70). Today, Wurtzel probably would not have too much difficulty locating a group or program for women suffering from depression.
26. Wurtzel, *Prozac Nation*, 177–78.
27. Ibid., 178.
28. Ibid., 329.
29. Ibid., 262.
30. Sedgwick, "Epidemics of the Will," 131–32.
31. Walters and Gilbert, "Defining Addiction," 212.
32. Wurtzel, *Prozac Nation*, 96.
33. Ibid., 96–97.
34. Ibid., 97.
35. Cheever, "Prozac Americans," 349.
36. Wurtzel, *Prozac Nation*, 300, 311.
37. Ibid., 312.
38. Fee, 93.
39. Wurtzel, *Prozac Nation*, 315, 319.
40. Ibid., 329.
41. Ibid., 327.
42. Ibid., 329.
43. Ibid., 22.
44. Wurtzel, *More, Now, Again*, 104.
45. Ibid., 110–11.
46. Ibid., 154.
47. For analyses of the effects of race, class, and gender on the perceptions of addiction, see Campbell, *Using Women*; Humphries, *Crack Mothers*; Kandall, *Substance and Shadow*; and Kohn, *Dope Girls*.

Bibliography

Acker, Caroline J. "Stigma or Legitimation? A Historical Examination of the Social Potentials of Addiction Disease Models." *Journal of Psychoactive Drugs* 25, no. 3 (1993): 193–205.

Cain, Carol. "Personal Stories: Identity Acquisition and Self-Understanding in Alcoholics Anonymous." *Ethos* 19 (1991): 210–46.

Campbell, Nancy. *Using Women: Gender, Drug Policy, and Social Justice.* New York: Routledge, 2000.

Cheever, Abigail. "Prozac Americans: Depression, Identity, and Selfhood." *Twentieth Century Literature* 46, no. 3 (2000): 346–68.

Fee, Dwight. "The Project of Pathology: Reflexivity and Depression in Elizabeth Wurtzel's *Prozac Nation.*" In *Pathology and the Postmodern: Mental Illness as Discourse and Experience*, edited by Dwight Fee, 74–99. London: Sage, 2000.

Gilmore, Leigh. "Limit-Cases: Trauma, Self-Representation, and the Jurisdictions of Identity." *Biography* 24, no. 1 (2001): 128–39.

Humphries, Drew. *Crack Mothers: Pregnancy, Drugs, and the Media.* Columbus: Ohio University Press, 1999.

Kandall, Stephen. *Substance and Shadow: Women and Addiction in the United States.* Cambridge, MA: Harvard University Press, 1999.

Klinghoffer, David. Review of *Prozac Nation*, by Elizabeth Wurtzel. *National Review* 46, no. 21 (1994): 74–77.

Kohn, Marek. *Dope Girls: The Birth of the British Drug Underground.* London: Lawrence & Wishart, 1992.

Leshner, Alan I. "Addiction Is a Brain Disease." *Issues in Science and Technology Online* 17, no. 3 (2001). http://www.nap.edu/issues/17.3/leshner.htm (accessed September 23, 2005).

Markou, Athina, Thomas Kosten, and George Koob. "Neurobiological Similarities in Depression and Drug Dependence: A Self-Medication Hypothesis." *Neuropsychopharmacology* 18, no. 3 (1998): 135–74.

Morrison, Martha. *White Rabbit: A Doctor's Own Story of Addiction, Survival and Recovery.* New York: Berkley Books, 1989.

Narcotics Anonymous World Services. "World Service Board of Trustees Bulletin #17: What Is Addiction?" http://www.na.org/bulletins/bull17-r.htm (accessed September 23, 2005).

Palazidou, Eleni. "Depression in Women." In *Women and Mental Health*, edited by Dora Kohen, 106–32. London: Routledge, 2000.

Perring, Christian. Review of *Prozac Nation*, by Elizabeth Wurtzel. *Mental Help Net*, May 13, 2002. http://mentalhelp.net/poc/view_doc.php?id=1133&type=book&cn=5 (accessed September 23, 2005).

Schoemer, Karen. "To Be Young, Gifted and Blue." Review of *Prozac Nation*, by Elizabeth Wurtzel. *Newsweek* (August 29, 1994): 58.

Sedgwick, Eve Kosofsky. "Epidemics of the Will." In *Tendencies*, 130–42. Durham, NC: Duke University Press, 1993.

Solomon, Andrew. *The Noonday Demon: An Atlas of Depression.* New York: Touchstone, 2002.

Stoppard, Janet M. "Why New Perspectives Are Needed for Understanding Depression in Women." *Canadian Psychology* 40, no. 2 (1999): 79–90.

Styron, William. *Darkness Visible: A Memoir of Madness.* New York: Random House, 1990.

Walters, Glenn, and Alice Gilbert. "Defining Addiction: Contrasting Views of Clients and Experts." *Addiction Research* 8, no. 3 (2000): 211–21.

Warhol, Robyn, and Helena Michie. "Twelve-Step Teleology: Narratives of Recovery/Recovery as Narrative." In *Getting a Life: Everyday Uses of Autobiography,* edited by Sidonie Smith and Julia Watson, 327–50. Minneapolis: University of Minnesota Press, 1996.

Wurtzel, Elizabeth. *Prozac Nation: Young and Depressed in America.* New York: Riverhead Books, 1994.

———. *More, Now, Again: A Memoir of Addiction.* New York: Simon & Schuster, 2002.

Chapter 8

Narrating the Emotional Woman

Uptake and Gender in Discourses on Depression

Kimberly Emmons

This chapter examines the way that cultural commonplaces and metaphors[1]—chief among them that women are the "emotional sex"—are taken up and narrativized in relation to the gendered values of depression. I argue that when speakers take up the cultural commonplace of the excessively emotional woman, they shape narratives of their own identities around and through cultural topoi that originate beyond their immediate speech situations. Such "uptakes"[2] transcend temporal and generic boundaries; indeed, their power lies in their ability to naturalize a set of beliefs or orientations across multiple rhetorical scenes and thus furnish a stock set of roles and scenarios for participating interlocutors, including speakers who appear autonomous agents.[3] For example, far from being direct expressions of individuals' inner experiences, women's narratives about depression—through their uptakes of ideologically loaded topoi—are shaped by the available discourses, and in turn these help construct women's affective lives. In these pages, I will map uptakes of the cultural commonplace of the excessively emotional woman from their presence in government publications into the conversations of two groups of women who narrate their individual and collective understandings of depression as illness in relation to this commonplace.

As others in this volume demonstrate, cultural archetypes and gendered ideologies pervade the discourses surrounding depression. An illness that is accessible primarily through language—through self- and peer-reporting, through diagnostic questions and answers—depression resists quantification and resides somewhere on a continuum that shades from so-called normal sadness and grief into debilitating illness. The legibility of

111

this scale is complicated for women by a commonly held understanding of their predisposition toward excesses of mood. In other words, while depression in men tends to be presented as a stark departure from "normal" feelings or emotions, depression in women is more likely to be understood as an outgrowth of women's complex emotional lives. This discrepancy of interpretation is reflected, I argue, in the particular uptakes of the cultural commonplace of the emotional woman. Here I use *commonplace*, "a common or ordinary topic; a statement generally accepted or taken for granted,"[4] rather than *master narrative* or *archetype* in order to emphasize the daily rituals of talk that rely on unexamined assumptions, and because the term reflects cultural assumptions that only later—through uptake—lend themselves to narrativization.

The commonplace of the emotional woman is available in Western cultures in a variety of genres: from television melodramas to news reporting, from novels to pharmaceutical advertising campaigns. Importantly, this topos encodes a number of understandings and beliefs: that women are ruled by volatile emotions (not only do women feel more emotions, they experience them more forcefully and have less control over them than men do);[5] that such emotions can, and often do, slip across invisible boundaries into illness (hysteria, mania, depression, premenstrual dysphoric disorder); and that these emotions define femininity itself. An unemotional woman might not be vilified or ridiculed but nevertheless will be contained and bracketed off from the definition of woman. The range and forms of emotion available to women are also important for studies of depression: women have permission to be sad, happy, anxious, or even irritable, but full-blown anger and aggression are reserved for men, and pathologized rather than naturalized. Dominant Western discourses of depression draw upon and reinforce common expectations about women's "natural" emotions, but appear to diverge sharply from expectations about men and emotion.[6] So accepted are these gendered assumptions that they pass unrecognized in casual conversation and even in academic investigations and diagnostic sensitivities.[7] My project here is to trace the circulation of these attitudes as they are taken up in texts and talk about depression, and to explore the rhetorical and narrative effects their uptakes precipitate.

Textual Uptakes and the Emotional Regulation of Women

In 2000, the National Institute of Mental Health (NIMH) published the pamphlets *Depression* and *Depression: What Every Woman Should Know.*[8] Although it would be inaccurate to characterize the general pamphlet (*Depression*) as directed primarily at men since it variously targets women, men, adolescents, and the elderly, the second pamphlet suggests that women represent a special case when it comes to depression. Moreover, because the pamphlets are generally comparable—they contain roughly the same number of words, the same major sections, and often-identical paragraphs of explanation—the differences between the two reveal a discursive seam that serves to set women's experiences with depression apart from those of the rest of the population. In fact, as table 8.1 demonstrates, the tone and style of the women's pamphlet is more informal, creating a falsely personal (even condescending in places) relationship with its readers. Certainly, the presence of the women's pamphlet responds to the oft-cited statistic that women are at least twice as likely as men to suffer from and be diagnosed with depression.[9] In doing so, the women's pamphlet is an uptake that (re)circulates the "reality" of women's greater vulnerability and discounts alternative "realities" that describe other populations in relation to depression.[10] The manner in which the women's pamphlet takes up the topic of depression and the commonplace of the excessively emotional woman reflects a strong discursive trend to associate women with depression and consequently to regulate the narratives and experiences of both.

In taking up the cultural commonplace of the emotional woman, *Depression: What Every Woman Should Know* restricts the available narratives that articulate women's experiences and treatment options. In this pamphlet, women's alignment with their emotionality is taken as the starting point for a more complicated understanding of their relationship to depression itself. Because women are emotional by nature—as the commonplace maintains—their slide into depression is harder to recognize: it "seems almost a natural outgrowth of their personalities." This uncertainty in the women's pamphlet, contrasted with the simplicity of recognition in the general pamphlet, calls attention to the ideological force of the commonplace. In the general pamphlet, a failure to "recognize that depression is a *treatable* illness" (emphasis added) is blamed for unnecessary suffering. Patients' failure to act—by seeking treatment—prevents them from returning to a normal, nondepressed state. In contrast, the women's pamphlet characterizes depression *itself* as "often go[ing] unrecognized." Here, the failure is not an ignorance of available treatments but rather an inability to differentiate illness from constitutional emotionality. This discrepancy is characteristic of the rhetorical differences between the two pamphlets: the general pamphlet assumes a clear depressed state or "disorder," while the women's pamphlet represents depression as an unhealthy excess hard to distinguish from normal "ups and downs." These ideological conclusions are reinforced by the syntax of the two pamphlets, for example, in places where each describes what I characterize as an "emotional continuum." The general pamphlet uses four short, declarative sentences in which depression, patients, and symptoms

Table 8.1. Excerpts from NIMH Pamphlets on Depression

	Depression	Depression: What Every Woman Should Know
Introduction	"In any given 1-year period, 9.5 percent of the population, or about 18.8 million American adults, suffer from a depressive illness. The economic cost for this disorder is high, but the cost in human suffering cannot be estimated."	"Life is full of emotional ups and downs. But when the 'down' times are long lasting or interfere with your ability to function, you may be suffering from a common, serious illness—depression."
Recognition	"Unfortunately, many people do not recognize that depression is a treatable illness."	"Yet, because it often goes unrecognized, depression continues to cause unnecessary suffering."
Emotional Continuum	"A depressive disorder is not the same as a passing blue mood. It is not a sign of personal weakness or a condition that can be willed or wished away. People with a depressive illness cannot merely 'pull themselves together' and get better. Without treatment, symptoms can last for weeks, months, or years."	"Up to a point, such feelings [irritability due to stressful life situations, sadness over a 'lost loved one'] are simply a part of human experience. But when these feelings increase in duration and intensity and an individual is unable to function as usual, what seemed a temporary mood may have become a clinical illness."
Dysthymia	"A less severe type of depression . . . involving long-term, chronic symptoms that do not disable, but keep one from functioning well or from feeling good."	"People with dysthymia are frequently lacking in zest and enthusiasm for life, living a joyless and fatigued existence that seems almost a natural outgrowth of their personalities."

serve as grammatical subjects. In the women's pamphlet, however, two longer sentences cast feelings and "a temporary mood" in the subject roles, further displacing both the illness and individual agency for women. The women's pamphlet clearly encourages its audience to seek diagnosis and treatment just as the general pamphlet does, but it also reminds them that their lives are defined by fluctuating emotions that must be closely scrutinized and read for signs of clinical illness, which can seem "simply a part of human experience."

By taking up the commonplace of the emotional woman as "a part of human experience" in a way the pamphlet targeted to the general public does not, the women's pamphlet recirculates and reinforces perceptions about women's constitutive vulnerability to depression. Indeed, the women's pamphlet describes people (oddly enough not using the word "women") with dysthymia, a less severe but chronic form of depression, as "frequently lacking in zest and enthusiasm for life, living a joyless and fatigued existence that seems almost a natural outgrowth of their personalities." Here in the women's pamphlet—and notably not in the general pamphlet where dysthymia is given a more straightforward description including clinical terms like "chronic symptoms"—the disorder is indistinguishable from the individual.[11] Further, the women's pamphlet contains constant reminders of the "natural" highs and lows of women's emotional lives. In the document's first sentence, a woman's life is characterized as "*full* of emotional ups and downs" (emphasis added), and the default expectation is both emotional volatility and affective plenitude; feelings such as sadness at the loss of a loved one or irritability over stressful life events "are simply part of the human experience." Nevertheless, these normal emotional rhythms in women's lives can easily roll into "a serious illness." While the general pamphlet makes a clear distinction between "a passing blue mood" and depression—they are "not the same"—the women's pamphlet conceptualizes depression as just increased "duration and intensity" of such feelings, and invites women to read for the tipping "point" when "normal" emotional fullness becomes a disabling excess.

This need for surveillance, then, is one of the consequences of the emotional-woman commonplace: as volatile emotional beings, women have a constitutive predilection for illness, and even healthy women are subject to this emotional slippage. For if dysthymia and other forms of depression are difficult to recognize—indeed, seem "a natural outgrowth" of a woman's personality—then all of a woman's emotions become suspect, and need to be read and policed closely and remediated aggressively. Something like this suspicion can be read in the recent Celexa advertising slogan, "What's behind that smile?" The print advertisement

shows the head and shoulders of a woman against a blurred floral backdrop. The woman smiles into the camera, and the text asks that we question how she came to be both calm and apparently happy—not the
normal state for a woman—then answers the question by citing the antidepressant. This advertisement, gesturing toward femininity with the floral motif and pastel hues and implying universality by blurring the
background, seems to invite the correlation between pharmaceutical
therapy and emotional equanimity. This woman is smiling because she
has received treatment for depression, which in the words of the advertisement is "more than just feeling sad," but we are encouraged to be sus-
picious of her smile nevertheless, as if happiness and serenity were
unexpected emotional states for a woman.

Beyond fostering intense scrutiny of women's emotional volatility
and plenitude, uptake of the commonplace in the women's pamphlet positions women as patients and victims rather than as agents in their own illness and healing. In the opening of the women's pamphlet, the reader is
warned that when "the 'down' times are long lasting or interfere with your
ability to function, you may be suffering from . . . depression." The pamphlet not only assumes the emotional woman suffers "down times," but
also invites the reader—addressed in the second person—to view herself as
a victim: "*you* may be suffering" (emphasis added). What is more, the
modal *may* contains both possibility and permission: women are rendered
vulnerable to depression and, as a class, authorized to consider themselves
depressed if their emotions exceed the "fullness" and duration they are
being cautioned to expect. At the same time, simply policing one's own
moods is not enough; instead, the pamphlet encourages women to place
themselves under the care of a physician (as implied by the term "clinical
illness" in table 8.1 and made more explicit throughout the pamphlet),
and to abdicate their authority over determining healthy and excessive levels of emotionality. By contrast, the general pamphlet contains two sections on self-help ("How to Help Yourself if You Are Depressed" and "How
Family and Friends Can Help the Depressed Person"), whereas the
women's pamphlet contains only a section entitled "The Path to Healing."
This section's title draws upon the common therapeutic cliché of a journey
toward health, and it replaces the general pamphlet's emphasis on self and
social interventions with the advice for women to seek professional guidance. Indeed, in this section, the woman is called an "informed consumer"
because she "knows her treatment options and discusses concerns with her
provider," not because she has any hope of healing herself. Indeed, this re-
naming of the health professional as a "provider" echoes traditional pater-
nalistic householder roles, further displacing women's agency.

The NIMH women's pamphlet on depression takes up the commonplace of the emotional woman, selecting and recirculating it as an

official discourse that 1) renders women's emotions sites for scrutiny including self-scrutiny and management, since the fine line between emotional fullness and excess of affect also defines the bounds of illness; and 2) invites women to police themselves, but also constructs them as unreliable moderators and interpreters of their own affective lives who thus require professional medical intervention. Keeping in mind this instance of textual uptake of the emotional-woman commonplace in the dominant discourses on depression, I turn now to the conversations of real women to explore the narrative and ideological consequences of women's own uptakes of this commonplace.

Conversational Uptakes and Self-Narration

In a study conducted in Seattle, Washington, in July 2002, I interviewed two groups of women about their experiences with and understandings of depression.[12] The interviews were designed as small, semi-structured group discussions in order to get a sense of how women might be talking with/among their peers about their experiences. I conducted interviews with seven women suffering from mild to moderate symptoms of depression, as measured by the National Institute of Mental Health's CES-D index.[13] The women were students at a large research university— about half undergraduates (four) and the other half graduate students (three). They ranged in ages from about nineteen to thirty-five, and were white (four) and Asian American (three). The women who participated in my study did not know each other before the interviews took place. I digitally recorded and transcribed each ninety-minute interview (transcription conventions appear in the appendix to this chapter). In each of the interviews, I asked open-ended questions ("How do you define depression?"; "Is depression gendered?"; and "What have you heard or read about depression?") in order to elicit general talk about depression.[14]

In the transcripts of both group interviews, the emotional woman commonplace is invoked by individuals and collaboratively reinforced through the discussion. By taking up this commonplace, the participants assume the subjective possibilities implied by it—namely, that women are defined by emotions and live on the uneasy boundary between healthy and ill affective states. Most importantly, the uptake of the emotional-woman commonplace allows it to become part of narrative explanations the women construct about their experiences with depression. In conversation, these women not only take up the idea of the emotional woman, they use it as the basis for apparently authentic, unmediated self-narrations. Uptake in this instance moves the "cultural memory" of the emotional woman to the center of collective and highly personal narratives of depression.

About forty-five minutes into the Group 1 interview, Tiffany responds to my question about whether depression is a gendered phenomenon by introducing examples of men whom she suspects or knows to be depressed, but she concludes her turn with the statement that men are more likely to hide their depression. In an echo of the NIMH pamphlet's attention to the "fullness" of women's emotional lives, all of the participants seem to agree that women are "more sensitive" and more invested in their "rich emotional lives" (figure 8.1). Claire begins to answer my question with the idea that "women are more sensitive," immediately reinforced by Tiffany's latching agreement and further explanation. Paige offers her theory of the importance of "an emotional life" to women, even going so far as to suggest that women and men have difficulty relating to each other because of the differences in their commitment to their emotions.

Claire   You know women are more sensitive too=

Tiff   =yeah that's true women are *definitely* mor- more sensitive

Kim   What do you mean by that?

Tiff   They're more willing to show it I mean they're more willing to like like *feel* the feeling you know what I mean? like? *be:* the feeling ((laugh)) like I don't know that was a really bad description ((laugh))

Paige   ((laugh)) sorry (3.0)

Claire   Well I I think, was only talking about feelings (about gender and) women usually want to talk about it more

Paige   I think women don't, I think men feel things too but (2.0) I think an emotional life is really (.) important for women and most women have really *rich* emotional lives (2.0) but I think that um that's not (.) the case for most men (xx) I think that men's lives are rich in other ways so that sometimes causes a conflict (.) when men and women get together.

Figure 8.1. Women, Group 1 (45:30)

In figure 8.1, the collaborative nature of uptake helps demonstrate the process by which the idea of the emotional woman is naturalized. Gaining support from their peers, the women articulate their understandings in terms dictated by the commonplace itself. As they struggle with the notion of women's greater "sensitivity," they reiterate the gendered ideology inherent in this commonplace. Women are more emotional than men and, in fact, come to be constitutionally identified with their emotions, as in Tiffany's explanation that women are willing to "be: the feeling." And, finally, the women distrust their own emotions, signaled by the nervous laughter following Tiffany's explanation and the numerous pauses and hedges ("I think") in Paige's final turn. In each of these conclusions, the women embody the discursive roles allotted to them by their uptakes and reinforced by documents such as the NIMH pamphlets and the Celexa advertisement.

In the two interviews, statements about women's greater capacities for emotion serve as the basis for self-awareness, as in Tiffany's aforementioned equation, of women with their feelings (figure 8.1). In that Group 1 interview, both Claire and Paige identify themselves as "sad" and "emotional" people. Further, these qualities, though naturalized, are negatively valued, as when Claire describes her depression as a direct result of her tendency to be "over-emotional." This attitude can be read as part of Claire's internalization of the commonplace, particularly when, several minutes later, Paige returns to Claire's statement and asks whether the depression she is feeling colors her self-representation (figure 8.2). Taking up the emotional-woman commonplace proves more than an intertextual reference for these women. Once the topos has been articulated, the women begin to use it heuristically to construct narratives of their own experiences. This, then, is an additional consequence of uptake: not only

---

Paige   Can I ask you a question? (1.0) Like, um sorry um you said earlier that you were that you feel like you're an over emotional person. Do you think that that's your nature or do you think that's (2.0) a st- like a stage that you're in because you feel depressed now or what?

Claire   That's a good question I know I've always been sensitive like I was really sensitive in high school and (1.0) ((sigh)) but when I think about it now that you've asked I think I have been way more emotional this pas:t year or so and maybe that is because I'm (2.0) in a depressed state or something I don't know: cause I wasn't as like crying at little things or being angry at little things or something. I wasn't like that in high school so, I don't know (3.4)

Paige   I wonder about it because I think (1.2) I don't know (.) I don't think I'm like a (1.4) I don't know a: like a moody person but (xxx things) I feel maybe I feel like I cry more than is acceptable ((laughing)) sometimes like um but (1.5) I just was like wondering if it's because I'm (really) depressed and I don't know it or because (1.0) that's just who I am (.)

Figure 8.2. Women, Group 1 (14:35)

are particular kinds of subjectivity suggested and assumed, but certain narrative possibilities are likewise enabled. Crucially, however, this uptake ensures that other narratives are not enabled.

In the excerpt included in figure 8.2, Paige and Claire begin to narrate their self-understandings, adding temporal and causal indices to their descriptions. For Claire, who has "always been sensitive," the conversation with Paige helps her realize that she "has been way more emotional this past year." Placing this information within a time frame additionally helps Claire explore the possible cause of her suffering; she postulates that "maybe that is because I'm in a depressed state or something." Similarly, Paige wonders if she cries "more than is acceptable" because she is "(really) depressed . . . or because . . . that's just who I am." Both women struggle to comprehend their depressive symptoms; both are caught in a narrative explanation of illness shaped by the ideological assumption that women are excessively emotional. Thus the uptake of the commonplace both makes available and restricts the interpretations and self-constructions of these women.

While Paige and Claire are struggling to identify where their emotionality shades into their depressive symptoms, Jennifer, in the Group 2 interview, takes up the emotional commonplace in order to articulate a counter-narrative about depression. Instead of being triggered by her excesses of emotion, Jennifer suggests, her symptoms of depression might have been triggered by the *suppression* of her emotionality. Providing a narrative of loss, Jennifer invokes characteristics of the emotional woman as touchstones in her narrative of the genesis of her current moderate depression. In figure 8.3, the commonplace becomes not the narrative ground from which depression appears to spring, but rather an aspect of personal identity from which the subject has become alienated—and that alienation is both the gist of the narrative and the cause of the illness. Jennifer's narrativization of the emotional woman asserts that she has lost something important to her identity and articulates her desire to return to a more emotional affective state.

In addition to narrating her experience of a loss of "femininity," Jennifer's description points to the self-regulation that all of the women expressed throughout the interviews. While Paige worries about "acceptable" amounts of crying, Jennifer "concoct[s]" her sense of needing to be more rational and less emotional in her self-presentation. Jennifer's word choice fights with her claim to have become more rational, less emotional: the term "concocted" suggests a less-than-systematic process, as do the qualifier "somehow" and the distancing move that places the decision "in [her] brain" rather than in her*self.* Further, Jennifer asserts her desire to get back to "femininity," which she defines in terms of appearance and emotion. These conflicts within Jennifer's narrative demonstrate the limited range

Jenn   You brought up a really good point that I'd forgotten that I
remember, I mean since I've gone back to school and started this
career change and being I mean it's still a very male dominated world
out there. And um, I fe- I somehow in my own brain concocted that I
needed to be more rational, less emotional, um less feminine to be
treated seriously.

Mei   Ohh

Jenn   And, and yeah. And I feel that I've [lost my   ]
                                                                  |
Steph   [(fairness?)]

Jenn   femininity that I am a *woman*.
And, I I think I'm also that's one of my things that I'm striving towards
to to get back. In my twenties, I was always very emotional, um very
feminine and um uh I mean I used to pour on the makeup and y'know
do my hair and everything and do the nails and somewhere that that
just got lo:st. And I don't know how to dress anymore I don't know how
to go shopping ((laughs))

Figure 8.3. Women, Group 2 (60:59)

of options she has in constructing story, yet they also demonstrate her
active use of the available discourses. Thus, women's uptakes of commonplaces like the emotional woman lead to various self-policing maneuvers—
precisely those fostered in the NIMH women's pamphlet. But, these
maneuvers can also be read as the products of active self-fashioning, as Jennifer claims in figure 8.3. In addition, these uptakes offer insight into the
uses individuals make of such discursive topoi. While Jennifer might have
suppressed her emotionality, her uptake in figure 8.3 at least suggests the
possibilities for counter- or at least multiple-narrative formations. While
gendered ideologies are certainly powerful regulatory forces, individuals
not only subject themselves to these forces, they also situate themselves as
agents of them.

My analysis has suggested that what Robyn Fivush and Janine Buckner
call Western culture's "emotion vocabulary"[15]—a vocabulary shaped and reinforced not only by popular recirculations such as movies and television
programming, but also by aggressive pharmaceutical marketing strategies
and even by ostensibly neutral informational genres—necessarily influences women's narratives of their experiences with depression. Discursive
topoi like the emotional woman and the descriptive vocabulary in which

she is most often rendered are regularly taken up in texts and talk about depression. Further, as Anne Freadman argues, uptakes have memories, and these memories follow individual uptakes into new rhetorical situations and into powerful collective and individual narratives. As women seek to narrate their experiences with depression, they also reinscribe commonplaces about gender, emotion, and illness. As agents of this rhetoric—indeed, as narrators of their own affective experiences—women evince real creativity in constructing narratives around the topos of the emotional woman. Yet they nevertheless operate near the discursive limits imposed by this commonplace—offering small revisions and challenges, but unable to tell their stories without it.

APPENDIX: TRANSCRIPTION CONVENTIONS

EXAMPLE	EXPLANATION
Sp 1 I thought you [were saying] Sp 2 [no, I] was talking	Square brackets around speech indicate that the speakers overlapped for the portions bracketed.
Sp 1 she said= Sp 2 =but you didn't say that	Equals signs indicate "latching" where there is no measurable space between speaker's turns.
Sp 1 I *mean* it	Italics indicate some form of emphasis
Sp 1 Yes: I lo:ve chocolate	A colon following a letter indicates an elongation of the sound of that letter.
(.)	A period in parentheses indicates a pause of one-tenth of a second or less.
(0.5)	Numbers in parentheses indicate silences in seconds and tenths of seconds.
((laughing))	Double parentheses indicate transcriber comments or descriptions.
(xxx)	Several "x"s enclosed in parentheses indicate material that is inaudible or otherwise untranscribable.
(happy)	Words in single parentheses indicate transcriber doubt about exactly what was heard.

Notes

1. My focus here is on Western commonplaces. For cross-cultural perspectives on depression, see Kleinman and Good, *Culture and Depression*.

2. "Uptake" describes both the activity of participating in a communicative situation and the artifact that results from that participation; it is a speaker's or writer's decision to respond as well as the content of her or his response. This essay represents an uptake of the editor's call for papers; a reader's choice to adopt or contest some portion of the argument will be another. Yet, uptake is not a simple or unidirectional process. Rather, uptakes work in two temporal directions; in Anne Freadman's words, each discursive intervention "turns back, then turns forward" in order to mark its place within a sequence (see "Uptake," 42). Uptake enables and conditions the work of placing things in sequence—whether temporal, causal, or hermeneutic—and as such it makes discursive topoi like the "emotional woman" available to the narrative activity of individuals and institutions. Uptakes carry with them the power to define narrative situations by enabling affirmations or refutations of the terms of a previous utterance. While speech-act theory describes similar dynamics in the immediacy of the moment of articulation, Freadman's formulation of "uptake" suggests that these dynamics obtain across time and genre as well. Uptakes have "memories—long, ramified, intertextual, and intergeneric memories" (40). The memories transmitted through uptake have the formal power to shape discourse beyond the individual and across time and place. When taken up in talk about depression, the commonplace of the "emotional woman" is coded as a deep-seated, definitional memory—both for individual women's narratives and for collective stories about women's affective realities.

3. As Norman Fairclough notes, the "ideologies embedded in discursive practices are most effective when they become naturalized, and achieve the status of 'common sense'" (see *Discourse and Social Change*, 87).

4. *Oxford English Dictionary*, 2nd ed.

5. See, for example, Fischer, *Gender and Emotion*.

6. For a personal version of this phenomenon, see Real, *I Don't Want to Talk About It*.

7. See Lerman, *Pigeonholing Women's Misery*.

8. In 2002–2003, the National Institute of Mental Health published several additional pamphlets on depression, three specifically targeted at men. In this chapter, I have chosen to compare the two pamphlets published in 2000 because they are the most similar in structure and content, differing primarily in their target audiences. Both pamphlets are still available and unrevised, and neither has a more recent equivalent. While there is not enough space here to explore the additional materials published by NIMH, the information targeted at men reinforces my analysis, suggesting that "men may be more willing to report fatigue, [and] irritability . . . rather than feelings of sadness . . . which are commonly associated with depression in women." In this brief excerpt, feelings are attributed to women, while men report their experiences as symptoms. See NIMH, *Real Men*.

9. See, for example, Nolen-Hoeksema, *Sex Differences in Depression*, 1.

10. In this way, the role of uptake in maintaining cultural commonplaces becomes clear. In order to become (and remain) a commonplace, the discursive object must continue to be taken up in new communicative settings. This circular process implicates all uptake agents (speakers and texts) in the workings of discursive power.

11. It is curious that the women's pamphlet chooses to adopt nongendered terms (for example, "people" and "individuals"). This pattern is striking throughout the pamphlet, which never uses the subject pronoun "she" and uses "her" only twice in twenty-five pages (in both cases "her" is used as a possessive pronoun, referring to "her treatment options" and "her provider"). In the general pamphlet, "she" is used twice, in the phrase "he or she," and "her" occurs six times (three in the phrase "his or her" and three in relation to postpartum depression, which is described in the women's pamphlet as "postpartum mood changes"). These lexical choices place further emphasis on the vocabulary of women's emotions while also distancing women themselves from the text of the pamphlet.

12. This study was approved by the University of Washington Institutional Review Board in May 2002 ("Women, Language, and Depression," Ref. No. 01-1159-C-01).

13. *Center for Epidemiologic Studies Depression Scale* (CES-D). My study was designed to collect language samples from women experiencing what could be termed "sub-clinical" depression: none of the women in my study were under the care of a mental health professional. This population was chosen for their marginal relationship to medicalized discourses on depression but also for their likely participation in more general-interest understandings of depression. The NIMH scale referenced here was used as a benchmark of depressive symptoms. The problematic nature of relying on this diagnostic questionnaire as a genre for selection is the subject of further research and, indeed, formed part of the interview discussion with the participants. They described filling out the survey as both a matter of recognition ("Checking the box was like 'yeah, yeah, I do have this one [symptom]'") and also of realization ("It was kind of a convenient . . . experience. 'Oh, yes, this is what this is . . . this is so validating'"). These comments suggest the power of discursive uptakes in producing narrative explanations and descriptions of experience. As a series of uptakes, the recruiting and selecting of study subjects deserves additional analysis that unfortunately cannot be completed here.

14. This is a limited sample of women's talk about depression and cannot be used to generalize. The subjects are all college or graduate students, a fact that may well influence their language choices. Nevertheless, these interviews provide compelling evidence for how these individuals did take up the commonplace of the emotional woman. The interview methodology was broadly ethnographic, with questions arising from the topics of conversation initiated by the subjects themselves. So, for example, the question of whether depression is a gendered phenomenon was asked only after the women volunteered stories about various men and women that they knew who had experienced symptoms of depression. In this manner, my own influence on the flow and topics of the conversation was minimized.

15. Fivush and Buckner, "Gender, Sadness, and Depression," 223.

Bibliography

Center for Epidemiologic Studies, National Institute of Mental Health. *Center for Epidemiologic Studies Depression Scale* (CES-D). Rockville, MD: NIMH, 1971.

Fairclough, Norman. *Discourse and Social Change.* Cambridge: Polity Press, 1992.

Fischer, Agneta, ed. *Gender and Emotion: Social Psychological Perspectives.* Cambridge: Cambridge University Press, 2000.

Fivush, Robyn, and Janine Buckner. "Gender, Sadness, and Depression: The Development of Emotional Focus through Gendered Discourse." In Fischer, *Gender and Emotion,* 232–53.

Freadman, Anne. "Uptake." In *The Rhetoric and Ideology of Genre: Strategies for Stability and Change,* edited by Richard Coe, Lorelei Lingard, and Tatiana Teslenko, 39–53. Cresskill, NJ: Hampton Press, 2002.

Kleinman, Arthur, and Byron Good, eds. *Culture and Depression: Studies in the Anthropology and Cross-Cultural Psychiatry of Affect and Disorder.* Berkeley: University of California Press, 1985.

Lerman, Hannah. *Pigeonholing Women's Misery: A History and Critical Analysis of the Psychodiagnosis of Women in the Twentieth Century.* New York: Basic Books, 1996.

National Institute of Mental Health (NIMH). *Depression.* Washington, DC: NIMH, 2000. http://www.nimh.nih.gov/publicat/depression.cfm (accessed September 6, 2001).

———. *Depression: What Every Woman Should Know.* Washington, DC: NIMH, 2000. http://www.nimh.nih.gov/publicat/depwomenknows.cfm (accessed September 6, 2001).

———. *Real Men. Real Depression.* 2003. Washington, DC: NIMH, 2003. http://menanddepression.nimh.nih.gov/infopage.asp?id=14 (accessed July 1, 2004).

Nolen-Hoeksema, Susan. *Sex Differences in Depression.* Stanford: Stanford University Press, 1990.

Real, Terrence. *I Don't Want to Talk About It: Overcoming the Secret Legacy of Male Depression.* New York: Simon & Schuster, 1997.

Chapter 9

Fact Sheets as Gendered Narratives of Depression

Linda M. McMullen

Depression has been called the "common cold of psychiatric ills."[1] Although prevalence varies considerably from country to country, depression is one of the most common diagnoses in primary healthcare settings worldwide.[2] In Canada, it is the second most common diagnosis made by office-based physicians,[3] and approximately 4.5 percent of the general Canadian population report having experienced symptoms associated with major depression over a twelve-month period.[4] Although the metaphor of the "common cold" aptly captures the widespread occurrence of depression around the world, it ignores the gendered nature of depression. Studies of general populations, as well as data on users of primary health care, have consistently shown that one and one-half to two times as many women as men report, or receive diagnoses of, depression.[5] In addition to being documented in both community and clinical samples, this difference appears across racial groups[6] and in developing as well as developed nations.[7] The impact of depression is also higher for women, particularly for those between the ages of fifteen to forty-four years. In 2000, one estimate of the burden of depression, based on a combination of the years of life lost due to premature mortality and to disability, placed depression second only to HIV/AIDS in terms of the magnitude of its effect on women in this age group.[8]

Many explanations for this gender difference have been proposed, including biological (primarily genetic or hormonal) influences, personality and cognitive factors such as women's greater need for support and approval from others and their greater tendency to ruminate about problems,[9] and social causes such as interpersonal loss or failure, physical or emotional deprivation, abuse, financial problems or low levels of education.

Typically some combination of biological, psychological, and social variables is implicated, despite long-standing and more recent evidence of the
powerful effects of social determinants in women's depression.[10]

Although the prevalence, impact, and presumed causes of depression for women are well documented and developed, little is known
about how women come to name their distress as depression. Determining that one's suffering can be termed "depression" depends on factors
such as how depression is defined in a particular culture, how diagnoses
are determined, the availability of knowledge about and services for mental health, and the stigma associated with depression. Where resources
permit, people are increasingly using the internet to search for health information, including information on mental health. Data from the
United States indicate that women are more likely than men to access online health information, and that depression is among the most commonly searched health topics.[11]

I have chosen to focus on two "fact sheets" on depression that appear on the website of the Canadian Psychological Association, *Psychology
Works for Depression* (on depression in general) and *Psychology Works for
Postpartum Depression (PPD)*. Both of these fact sheets are intended to supply information on the nature of depression and on the benefits to the
general public of psychological treatments for depression. In light of the
prevalence of depression for women worldwide, I am interested in how
these "official" psychological narratives reference the gendered nature of
depression. To bring this referencing into relief, I compare them to another example of this genre, a fact sheet titled *Women and Mental Health*
that appears on the World Health Organization website.

Online Health Information

The internet has been called "the world's largest medical library."[12] In
addition to thousands of health-related websites, government health
sites, websites of professional health organizations, and personal websites
oriented to health issues, the internet contains millions of citations of
books, journal articles, and personal testimonials. Those who access online health information often report that it affected their own health-
related decisions and behavior as well as those of their family members
and friends. In addition, this information is increasingly being discussed
with healthcare providers. Because of the anonymity of the internet, it is
likely that many people use it as a first step for obtaining information,
particularly in the case of conditions that carry stigma.

Accompanying the significant benefits of electronic access to health
information are problems related to the quantity and quality of this information. The overwhelming amount of material available on almost any
health topic requires that users determine what is relevant and reliable.

Librarians suggest that credible websites are those recommended by healthcare providers, sponsored by official organizations, and displaying clinical evidence. The author should have reputable credentials and be affiliated with a reputable institution; the information should be easy to locate, comprehensive, clear, objective, and situated in the context of disclaimers; and the language should be professional and understandable.[13]

Fact Sheets

Given the limitless nature of cyberspace, it is important that websites (or website information) be tailored to the specific needs of the public, and that users be able to find easily the particular information they are seeking. One means of providing specific information on specific problems is the online fact sheet. Like its print counterpart, the online fact sheet is currently a popular way of presenting expert, state-of-the-art knowledge to a lay audience. In this genre, information is presented in a concise, clear, and to-the-point format, and in language that is highly readable and accessible.[14] In the medical world, fact sheets provide information on the signs and symptoms of, and recommended treatments for, discrete illnesses and medical conditions, and are intended to be read as evidence-based truth as it is currently understood. Under a feature on the website of the Canadian Psychological Association titled *Psychology Works*, members of the Clinical Section of the CPA have prepared a set of fact sheets on over twenty-five common disorders, conditions, or problems currently recognized by clinical psychologists as domains within their professional expertise. Examples include alcoholism, autism, chronic pain, eating disorders, grief, panic disorder, posttraumatic stress disorder (PTSD), relationships, suicide and, as noted previously, depression and postpartum depression. The title page that introduces the *Psychology Works* feature sets the stage for the individual narratives that comprise these fact sheets. By indicating in the opening paragraph that "it is confusing to decide if [one has] a psychological problem" and "to decide what . . . to do about it," this introduction communicates that understanding psychological problems and treating them is the domain of the expert. A subsequent statement that "'Psychology Works' is designed to give you information that you can trust" underscores the message that this feature is intended to provide expert, credible knowledge to the lay person. Reinforcing the substance of the written message is the presence of an explicit acknowledgment that several credentialed persons (designated as Dr.) who are affiliated with reputable organizations (universities, a regional health authority, a health sciences center, committees of the CPA) are responsible for initiating this project. The presence of the logo of the CPA also affirms the legitimacy of the project. With these verbal and visual assurances of credibility, it is reasonable to assume that the summaries comprising the fact sheets are sanctioned by the discipline of psychology—which "works"—and have the status of core or official narratives.

Psychology Works for Depression

For the most part, this fact sheet comprises a single, uncomplicated story line in two parts.[15] It begins with a presentation of what constitutes depression by differentiating clinical depression (or Major Depressive Disorder) from everyday or normal sadness that "almost everyone feels . . . at certain times" and from manic-depression (or Bipolar Disorder). Along with a listing of several symptoms such as "sadness, loss of interest in usual activities, . . . changes in sleep" that, if present for at least a two-week period, are said to confirm the diagnosis of depression, this opening communicates not only that depression needs to be defined, but that it can be defined with a significant degree of precision. The provision of specific figures for the incidence and prevalence of depression for Canadian men (1 percent and 5 percent respectively) and Canadian women (2 percent and 10 percent respectively) following this definition further reinforces that what constitutes depression has achieved a level of consensus among researchers such that enough research has been conducted on the basis of this definition to permit precise estimates. A listing of factors deemed to increase the likelihood that a person will experience depression, for example, "having a parent who has been clinically depressed," "physical illness," "pervasive negative thinking," completes the picture of what depression is. While this final paragraph of the first section of the fact sheet begins with an acknowledgment, "Although **the causes of clinical depression are complex** and vary from individual to individual," the uncertainty in this grammatically subordinated clause is immediately eradicated with the statement that "it is now clear that a variety of factors increase the risk of a person experiencing clinical depression." Again, what is communicated is that through empirical research a considerable amount of evidence and expert knowledge about depression presently exists.

The second section of the fact sheet titled "What Psychological Approaches are Used to Treat Depression?" consists primarily of a selection of approaches to treating depression known as empirically supported treatments, that is, behavior therapy, cognitive therapy, and interpersonal therapy.[16] A brief description of what each therapy involves (for example, "**Cognitive therapy** involves the recognition of negative thinking patterns in depression") and what the anticipated outcomes are (for example, "**Behaviour therapy** helps patients increase pleasant activities") includes a fairly precise indication of success rate, for example, 65 percent in the case of behavior therapy and 67 percent in the case of cognitive therapy. The language is that of instruction and personal change, of correcting old patterns of behavior and thinking, and of teaching new strategies (for example, "**Interpersonal therapy** teaches the individual to become aware of interpersonal patterns, and to improve these through a series of interventions"). The message is clear: these therapies consist of well-defined, individually focused interventions that produce targeted outcomes with empirically demonstrated success rates.

The section on treatment concludes with what can be taken as an obligatory comparison of the effects of psychological treatments with pharmacotherapy ("An important note about psychological treatments for depression is that they are roughly as successful as **pharmacotherapy** for depression"). As with the preceding encapsulations of psychological interventions, this comparison is couched in explicit references to quantitative, empirical data—for example, that "psychological treatments often have significantly lower drop-out rates than pharmacotherapy (approximately 10% in psychological therapies, versus 25–30% in drug therapy)"—or in allusions to such data, for example, that "there is some evidence that cognitive therapy in particular reduces the risk of relapse to those individuals who are treated with drug therapy." This inclusion of references to quantitative evidence warrants the unequivocal declaration that "[p]sychological treatments are effective and safe alternatives to drug therapy for depression." The only slight departure from what is otherwise a smooth narrative on psychological approaches to treatment is that "the evidence is somewhat inconsistent" as to whether combining drug therapies and psychological interventions enhances the success of either treatment alone. A reference to further research on the relative benefits of a combination of drug therapies and psychological treatments being needed orients the reader to potential future developments in the treatment of depression—with the subtext that sorting out when to use various treatments is the type of question that demands attention.

In both content and style, this fact sheet epitomizes the expert narrative of the received view of depression in Canadian and American psychology. Confidence in this narrative is achieved through its tidy components, its objectivist and authoritative stance, and its declarative language. For the most part, the story is clear, unambiguous, and certain. There is little of substance in dispute.

One significant, although short-lived, rupture in the narrative, however, is the way in which the conjunction of women and depression is managed. Women are mentioned only twice in this fact sheet: once in regard to their being at twice the risk of men to experience depression, and once in regard to their experiencing of depression after childbirth. The first reference occurs in the paragraph on the incidence and prevalence of depression for Canadian men and women, and looks and reads as follows: "**Women are at twice the risk of men** to experience depression, but regardless of gender, once a person has had one experience of clinical depression, they are at risk for repeated experiences." There is a curious ambivalence here. Although the phrase "**Women are at twice the risk of men**" is in bold, presumably as a way of attracting the reader's eye and signifying its importance (as with other key phrases in the document), the remainder of the sentence precipitously takes the focus off gender. As such, the reader is back to an ungendered presentation of who is at risk for becoming depressed. Gender (as a statistic) is important enough to draw attention to, but not important enough to warrant serious focus. In essence, then, a key part of the story is glossed over and remains undeveloped.

The second reference to gender in this fact sheet occurs at the end of the paragraph on the causes of clinical depression. After a listing of the risk factors, the final sentence reads: "Further, some individuals experience depression in a regular seasonal pattern, or in the case of women, after childbirth." Although the previous reference to gender being a risk factor was silent as to how such information might be understood, this reference to depression after childbirth activates a popular lay belief in the link between women's depression and changing hormonal levels. Again, there is a curious ambivalence in how Canadian psychology, through the CPA website, presents the conjunction of women and depression to the public. On the one hand, a reference to postpartum depression occurs not in the primary list of risk factors, but in a separate sentence and in conjunction with seasonally related depression, a condition about which there is still some controversy. Being set apart in this manner suggests an "otherness" to depression following childbirth, suggests that it is to be distinguished from that which is caused by primary risk factors, such as major negative life events. On the other hand, postpartum depression is considered important enough to warrant its own summary (as I detail further on), despite there being little support for it as a condition separate from major depression disorder.[17]

Psychology Works for Postpartum Depression (PPD)

The CPA fact sheet on postpartum depression, like its counterpart on depression, establishes its credibility as an expert narrative through a variety of devices, including the display of the CPA logo, references to research findings, and the provision of links to another website on postpartum depression and to lists of clinical psychologists across Canada. However, unlike the linear, uncomplicated, and singular story line in the fact sheet on depression, this summary contains two competing story lines: one based in a model of illness coupled with personal responsibility and one in a gender-based, social model of health that takes the context of motherhood and women's lives into account, albeit in a fairly conventional way.

This fact sheet begins with a description of postpartum depression that is formatted as text and box charts. The box charts comprise traditional components of an illness-based conception of a phenomenon, specifically, symptoms and risk factors. As with the fact sheet on depression, the symptoms of postpartum depression that are listed include affective (for example, "sadness and/or anger"), behavioral (for example, "increased or decreased appetite"), and psychological features (for example, "cannot think clearly"). Similarly, the list of risk factors includes characteristics both of the mother (for example, "depressed or anxious during pregnancy") and of the baby (for example, "baby is 'difficult'"), as well as social problems (for example, "lack of support from husband and/or family," "financial problems"). The graphic structure and bolded headings of these box charts draw the (presumably female) reader's eye to them, thereby highlighting the significance of their content.

While the salience of the box charts privileges an illness model of postpartum depression, some of the text that surrounds these charts is consistent with positions that have been emphasized by those who adopt a gender-based, social model of health. For example, in presenting risk factors for postpartum depression, misconceptions about the causes of this experience are dispelled. The fact sheet states that "there is little scientific evidence to support [the] view" that depression is caused by childbirth, and that "PPD does not necessarily reflect a mother's negative feelings about her baby," and "may not even begin after childbirth." In addition, postpartum depression may not, in fact, actually be an experience distinct from depression ("[R]esearch shows that the symptoms of PPD are common to both postpartum and non-postpartum depression"). A further challenge to a strict biologically based understanding also occurs with the statement that "[a]lthough some professionals blame PPD on hormones, there is little scientific evidence to support this view." What is concluded is that "[t]he vast majority of women with PPD become depressed because of psychological and social risk factors."

In addition to dispelling misconceptions about the causes of postpartum depression, this fact sheet includes a conceptualization of the costs of motherhood that is consistent with accounts by women who have experienced postpartum depression. Specifically, in the opening paragraph, there is an acknowledgment that "[t]he birth of a child creates many changes in a woman's life." For example:

> A new mother may give up paid work or she may no longer have time for her own activities about which she can feel sad and isolated. Some women are unprepared for these losses and for the amount and type of work involved in caring for an infant. They may feel resentful of the baby and ashamed that they are not living up to the image of the perfect mother—feelings which can sometimes spiral into postpartum depression.

Themes of loss and of the burden of cultural expectations to be the perfect mother have been found to be central in studies that seek to understand postpartum depression from the standpoint of women.[18]

However, despite this recognition of the social and cultural contexts in which PPD is located, women continue to be conventionally inscribed in the opening paragraph as individual persons, rather than as members of a social category. Use of singular adjectives, nouns, and pronouns ("a woman's life," "a new mother," "her relationships," "she may no longer have time") places the attention on an individual woman as the locus of PPD; further, the separation of "some women" into the category of those who are unprepared for the losses associated with motherhood creates the potential for person-based attributes regarding readiness for motherhood. From the opening paragraph of this fact sheet, then, there is a tension between a story line that implicates and is directed toward an individual woman as mother, and one that hints that gendered expectations and constructions of motherhood figure into what is understood as PPD.

While the first half of this fact sheet can be read as interweaving two competing story lines, there is a clear shift to a single story line of personal responsibility beginning with a cryptic, two-sentence, stand-alone paragraph at the end of the section on causes of postpartum depression: "Men also can experience PPD. Research shows that when a woman has PPD, often her husband is depressed and anxious as well." Although the sentences do not explicitly contain a statement of directional causality, the use of "when" in the second sentence implies such a relationship. In addition, postpartum depression is said to have "a dramatic impact on the parents and the baby." Husbands are characterized as "often feel[ing] burdened by their wives' depression and unable to help, which can have a negative effect on the marriage for years afterward." This subtle blaming is also present with regard to the impact of postpartum depression on babies. The references to babies of mothers with postpartum depression being "more irritable" and "difficult to soothe," "tend[ing] not to develop as well" and being "at risk for emotional and behavioural problems" when they are older could be read as a recognition of the interactional role of "difficult" babies in women's experience of postpartum depression and, as such, as an acknowledgment of the multiple conditions that contribute to PPD. However, when these references are combined with the sentence "Women with PPD can be impatient, distant or insensitive with their babies, which may affect the mother-child bond and have consequences for their future relationship," the implication that the experience of postpartum depression may be permanently damaging is clear. The subtext here is that it is a woman's duty to her family to get treatment if she is experiencing PPD.

As with the fact sheet on depression, a personal illness model of PPD is reinforced in a section on psychological treatments that follows the characterization of PPD. Psychologically based approaches, specifically interpersonal therapy and cognitive-behavioral therapy, are presented as effective evidence-based treatments for PPD: for example, "Research clearly shows that **Interpersonal therapy (IPT)** is effective." Again, the focus of treatment is on helping the individual woman to change aspects of herself, including learning how to "make changes within important relationships so that [she] get[s] the emotional support, help, and understanding [she] need[s]," and to "identify and change those beliefs and expectations that make [her] feel depressed." In other words, it is the responsibility of the woman who is experiencing PPD to work toward engineering change in herself or in others who are significant persons in her life. While the language of the effectiveness of individual therapy is definitive, the only other treatment option is presented in qualified terms ("Some women may find **postpartum support groups** to be helpful. Although the evidence for the effectiveness of these groups is mixed, groups may help women to overcome feelings of guilt and isolation"). Creating uncertainty as to the effectiveness of these groups and delimiting the scope of their influence serves to further enhance the appeal of individually based psychological treatments.

Unlike the obligatory, either terse or stereotyped, inclusion of women in the CPA fact sheet on depression, women as mothers are front and center in the PPD fact sheet. And unlike the unambiguous story line in the former, the competing story lines in the latter create an unresolved tension. If the term "postpartum depression" is misleading, why is it still used? Given that guilt about the baby and feelings of inadequacy are likely to be a part of a woman's experience of PPD, why is personal responsibility for the impact and alleviation of PPD further reinforced rather than downplayed? If the losses and high expectations associated with motherhood are part of the context in which PPD is experienced, why are institutional and cultural changes in the practices and meanings of motherhood not privileged in the same way that individual behavior change is?

Women and Mental Health

A fact sheet on women and mental health on the website of the World Health Organization (WHO) serves as a foil to the CPA-endorsed fact sheets and further brings into relief how women are implicated and positioned in these psychological narratives of depression. As with the CPA fact sheet on postpartum depression, this WHO fact sheet places women front and center in its narrative, and as with the CPA fact sheet on depression, it has a single story line. However, rather than treating women as individual persons, it relies on a conception of women as a social category; and rather than adopting an illness-based narrative, it employs a gender-based, social model of health as the organizing frame for its narrative.

It begins with a statement on the place of women in society, which is presented as necessary background for understanding women's mental health:

> Women are integral to all aspects of society. However, the multiple roles that they fulfill in society render them at greater risk of experiencing mental problems than others in the community. Women bear the burden of responsibility associated with being wives, mothers and carers of others. Increasingly, women are becoming an essential part of the labour force and in one-quarter to one-third of households they are the prime source of income.

Gender discrimination, "poverty, hunger, malnutrition, and overwork," and sexual and domestic violence are cited as factors contributing to mental health problems experienced by women, and in explaining the higher rates of depression for women, social causes, such as "living in poor social and environmental circumstances with associated low education, low income and difficult family and marital relationships," are singled out as the most important determinants.

Having presented a context for understanding women's mental health, cited the higher prevalence of problems such as depression for women, and highlighted a specific set of social causes as an explanation for the gender difference in the rate of depression, the narrative in this fact sheet shifts to a final section on actions that need to be taken. Ways of "**promoting women's mental health**" are, for example, (1) distinguishing between risk factors that can be addressed through "individual action and individual behaviour change and those that are dependent on factors outside the control of the individual woman," and (2) augmenting findings from quantitative research with those from qualitative research focused on firsthand accounts of depression from the standpoint of women. In contrast to the declarative style of the CPA fact sheets (for example, "Like any other depression . . . PPD can be treated psychologically"), the tone of the final section of the WHO fact sheet is imperative (for example, "Women's views and the meanings they attach to their experiences have to be heeded").

This statement from the WHO brings absences in the CPA-endorsed fact sheets on depression into sharp focus. Nowhere in the latter is there an explicit reference to the place of women in society and to the many pressures placed on women. There is no mention of the consequences of gender discrimination or violence; no listing of routes to alleviating depression other than through individual behavior change; no reference to the importance of women-centered accounts in fashioning new responses to women's distress. And, in the end, there is no advocacy for societal change and prevention. Rather, in these brief, "official" narratives, women's depression is either cursorily mentioned and effectively ignored, or taken up separately as a category that is historically tied to women's reproductive biology and of dubious validity.

Lay Women's Narratives of Depression

As referenced in the WHO fact sheet, the burgeoning literature on lay women's narratives of depression serves as a powerful counterpoint to the impoverished and ambivalent ways in which women are inscribed in the fact sheets on the CPA website. In a volume of work comprised of eight studies on a diverse collection of women from countries such as Canada, England, Ghana, Wales, and the United States,[19] a common way in which women constructed accounts of their depression was in terms of their everyday lives as *women*. For example, in a set of interviews with seven urban Canadian women who had symptoms of depression but who had not sought treatment, themes of being betrayed by significant others—typically through being abused, being disrespected, or being abandoned—figured prominently in the analysis of their narratives of depression.[20] In comparable interviews with fifteen women living in a rural part of Canada, with thirty-five women from an industrial town in south Wales, and with seventy-five women from a town in a farming region of Ghana, explanations anchored in social "stressors" such as financial problems, child-care responsibilities, and abusive relationships with partners were drawn upon to account for experiences of depression.[21]

Cultural meanings of motherhood as well as everyday experiences of mothering were similarly prominent in the narratives of women who were identified by themselves or others as having experienced postpartum depression. In a study of eighteen women from England, a central conflict was highlighted between the kind of mother the women wanted to be and the kind of mother they perceived themselves to be. Although what constituted a "good" mother differed across these women's accounts, they nevertheless constructed themselves as falling short of their image of the ideal mother.[22] This discrepancy between the expected and the actually experienced was also paramount in another set of interviews with twenty-four British women conducted during and after their pregnancies. In their narratives, themes of unexpected loss—of autonomy, time, appearance, femininity, sexuality, and occupational identity—were central to the distress that the women experienced following childbirth.[23] These studies suggest that postpartum depression is understood by many women as intricately tied to the constraints imposed by normative constructions of motherhood and by the everyday tasks of caring for infants.

In addition to containing understandings about etiology, these women's narratives of depression included statements on forms of intervention. Consistent with accounts of depression that are couched in social determinants, many women stressed the need for access to support, leisure, or recreational groups, more accessible daycare services, better paying jobs, education, and assistance from male partners.[24] At the same time, they recognized that these socio-structural changes would be unlikely to occur to any significant extent. In the absence of such prospects for change, women often resorted to citing individual-based ways of managing depression. However, rather than referring to professional intervention (which was often not available or even desired), women typically told about how they relied on empathic family members (when available), friends, and sometimes strangers for support, how they just tried to carry on, or in keeping with a preference not to disclose one's troubles, how they managed their experiences on their own.

A reliance on narratives that implicate social determinants (such as major life changes, family problems, economic hardship) as causes of mental distress, and that focus on personal agency as the primary and most realistic means of dealing with such distress, is common in lay accounts of mental health.[25] As well, the narratives of many women implicate or directly draw upon a gendered understanding of such distress.[26]

Conclusion

As the popularity of distributing and accessing web-based health information increases, assessments of the quality of this information grow.[27] A not-uncommon conclusion from such assessments is that the quality of online information varies considerably and is often poor. A typical remedy for such deficiencies in quality is the promotion of evidence-based information on professional websites. As seen in the present analysis, however, what counts as evidence also varies. The failure to include story lines from lay women's accounts in "official" psychological narratives of depression suggests that the former have not achieved the status of evidence in the judgment of many experts. One consequence of this omission is that women may have to go to less "official" online venues, such as depression blog sites and health boards, to read women's narratives of depression.

Notes

1. Kline, *From Sad to Glad*, 220.
2. Goldberg and Lecrubier, "Form and Frequency of Mental Disorders across Centres," cited in World Health Organization, *The World Health Report 2001*, 24.
3. IMS Health Canada, Press Release.
4. Statistics Canada, *Canadian Community Health Survey*.
5. General population studies are summarized in Piccinelli and Homen, *Gender Differences*. See also Mazure et al., *Summit on Women and Depression*; Mood Disorders Society of Canada, *A Report on Mental Illnesses in Canada*; WHO, *Women's Mental Health*; WHO, *The World Health Report 2001*.
6. Kessler et al., "Lifetime and 12-Month Prevalence of DSM-III-R Psychiatric Disorders in the United States"; Gater et al., "Sex Differences"; WHO, International Consortium of Psychiatric Epidemiology, "Cross-National Comparisons."
7. See for example Patel et al., "Women, Poverty and Common Mental Disorders"; Weissman et al., "Cross-National Epidemiology."
8. WHO, *The World Health Report 2001*, 27.
9. Nolen-Hoeksema, "The Role of Rumination."
10. Brown and Harris, *Social Origins of Depression*; Brown and Harris, "Depression"; Blue et al., "The Mental Health of Low-Income Urban Women."
11. Morahan-Martin and Anderson, "Information and Misinformation Online," 732.
12. Morahan-Martin, "How Internet Users Find, Evaluate, and Use Online Health Information," 497–98.
13. Morahan-Martin and Anderson, 736–37.
14. Valente, "Research Dissemination and Utilization," 116–18.
15. Portions of the following analysis of the CPA fact sheets also appear in McMullen and Stoppard, "Women and Depression: A Case Study of the Influence of Feminism in Canadian Psychology," *Feminism & Psychology* 16.3 (2006): 273–88.
16. Woody and Sanderson, "Manuals for Empirically Supported Treatments."
17. Support for the claim that postpartum depression is not distinct from non-postpartum depression can be found in Whiffen, "Is Post Partum Depression a Distinct Diagnosis?"
18. See, for example, Mauthner, "'Imprisoned in My Own Prison'"; Nicolson, "Postpartum Depression."
19. Stoppard and McMullen, *Situating Sadness*.
20. Hurst, "Legacy of Betrayal."
21. Scattolon, "'I Just Went On. . . .'"; Walters et al., "'Your Heart Is Never Free'."
22. Mauthner, "'Feeling Low,'" 152–53.
23. Nicolson.
24. Mauthner, "'Imprisoned in My Own Prison'"; Scatollon; Walters et al.
25. Rogers and Pilgrim, "The Contribution of Lay Knowledge."
26. See also Laitinen and Ettorre, "The Women and Depression Project."
27. See, for example, Griffiths and Christensen, "Quality of Web-Based Information on Treatment of Depression"; Eysenbach et al., "Empirical Studies."

Bibliography

Blue, I., M. E. Ducci, A. Jaswal, B. Ludermir, and T. Harpham. "The Mental Health of Low-Income Urban Women: Case Studies from Bombay, India; Olinda, Brazil; and Santiago, Chile." In *Urbanization and Mental Health in Developing Countries*, edited by T. Harpham and I. Blue, 75–102. Aldershot, UK: Avebury, 1995.

Brown, G. W., and T. O. Harris. *Social Origins of Depression: A Study of Psychiatric Disorder in Women*. London: Tavistock, 1978.

———. "Depression." In *Life Events and Illness*, edited by G. W. Brown and T. O. Harris, 49–93. London: Unwin Hyman, 1989.

Canadian Psychological Association. *Psychology Works for Depression*. http://www.cpa.ca/publications/yourhealthpsychologyworksfactsheets/depression/ (accessed November 1, 2005).

———. *Psychology Works for Postpartum Depression (PPD)*. http://www.cpa.ca/publications/yourhealthpsychologyworksfactsheets/postpartumdepressionppd/ (accessed November 1, 2005).

Eysenbach, G., J. Powell, O. Kuss, and E.-R. Sa. "Empirical Studies Assessing the Quality of Health Information for Consumers on the World Wide Web: A Systematic Review." *Journal of the American Medical Association* 287 (2002): 2691–2700.

Gater, R., et al. "Sex Differences in the Prevalence and Detection of Depressive and Anxiety Disorders in General Health Care Settings." *Archives of General Psychiatry* 55 (1998): 405–13.

Goldberg, D. P., and Y. Lecrubier. "Form and Frequency of Mental Disorders across Centres." In *Mental Illness in General Health Care: An International Study*, edited by T. B. Üstün and N. Sartorius, 323–34. Chichester: John Wiley, 1995.

Griffiths, K. M., and H. Christensen. "Quality of Web-Based Information on Treatment of Depression: Cross-Sectional Survey." *British Medical Journal* 321 (2000):1511–15. http://bmj.com/cgi/content/full/321/7275/1511 (accessed July 24, 2005).

Hurst, S. "Legacy of Betrayal: A Theory of Demoralization from the Perspective of Women Who Have Been Depressed." In Stoppard and McMullen, *Situating Sadness*, 139–61.

IMS Health Canada. *Press Release: Retail Prescriptions Grow at Record Level in 2003*. March 25, 2004. http://www.imshealthcanada.com/web/content/0,3148,77303623_63872702_77770096_77809465,00.html (accessed March 29, 2008).

Kessler, R. C., et al. "Lifetime and 12-Month Prevalence of DSM-III-R Psychiatric Disorders in the United States." *Archives of General Psychiatry* 51 (1994): 8–19.

Kline, N. S. *From Sad to Glad: Kline on Depression*. New York: Putnam, 1974.

Laitinen, I., and E. Ettorre. "The Women and Depression Project: Feminist Action Research and Guided Self-Help Groups Emerging from the Finnish Women's Movement." *Women's Studies International Forum* 27 (2004): 203–21.

Mauthner, N. S. "'Feeling Low and Feeling Really Bad About Feeling Low': Women's Experiences of Motherhood and Postpartum Depression." *Canadian Psychology* 40, no. 2 (1999): 143–61.

————. "'Imprisoned in My Own Prison': A Relational Understanding of Sonya's Story of Postpartum Depression." In Stoppard and McMullen, *Situating Sadness*, 88–112.

Mazure, C. M., G. P. Keita, and M. C. Blehar. *Summit on Women and Depression: Proceedings and Recommendations*. Washington, DC: American Psychological Association, 2002. www.apa.org/pi/wpo/women&depression.pdf (accessed March 29, 2008).

Mood Disorders Society of Canada. *A Report on Mental Illnesses in Canada*. October, 2002. http://www.mooddisorderscanada.ca/report/english/index.htm (accessed April 23, 2003).

Morahan-Martin, J. M. "How Internet Users Find, Evaluate, and Use Online Health Information: A Cross-Cultural Review." *CyberPsychology & Behavior* 7, no. 5 (2004): 497–510.

Morahan-Martin, J. M., and C. D. Anderson. "Information and Misinformation Online: Recommendations for Facilitating Accurate Mental Health Information Retrieval and Evaluation." *CyberPsychology & Behavior* 3, no. 5 (2000): 731–46.

Nicolson, P. "Postpartum Depression: Women's Accounts of Loss and Change." In Stoppard and McMullen, *Situating Sadness*, 113–38.

Nolen-Hoeksema, S. "The Role of Rumination in Depressive Disorders and Mixed Anxiety/Depressive Symptoms." *Journal of Abnormal Psychology* 109, no. 3 (2000): 504–11.

Patel, V., R. Araya, M. de Lima, A. Ludermir, and C. Todd. "Women, Poverty and Common Mental Disorders in Four Restructuring Societies." *Social Science & Medicine* 49, no. 11 (1999): 1461–71.

Piccinelli, M., and F. G. Homen. *Gender Differences in the Epidemiology of Affective Disorders and Schizophrenia*. Geneva: World Health Organization, 1997.

Rogers, A., and D. Pilgrim. "The Contribution of Lay Knowledge to the Understanding and Promotion of Mental Health." *Journal of Mental Health* 6, no.1 (1997): 23–35.

Scattolon, Y. "'I Just Went On. . . . There Was No Feeling Better, There Was No Feeling Worse': Rural Women's Experiences of Living with and Managing 'Depression.'" In Stoppard and McMullen, *Situating Sadness*, 162–82.

Statistics Canada. *Canadian Community Health Survey: Mental Health and Well-Being, 2002*. Catalogue 82-617-XIE, 2002. http://www.statcan.ca/Daily/English/030903/d030903a.htm (accessed June 1, 2005).

Stoppard, J. M., and L. M. McMullen, eds. *Situating Sadness: Women and Depression in Social Context*. New York: New York University Press, 2003.

Valente, S. M. "Research Dissemination and Utilization: Improving Care at the Bedside." *Journal of Nursing Care Quality* 18, no. 2 (2003): 114–21.

Walters, V., J. Y. Avotri, and N. Charles. "'Your Heart Is Never Free': Women in Wales and Ghana Talking about Distress." In Stoppard and McMullen, *Situating Sadness*, 183–206.

Weissman, M. M., R. C. Bland, G. J. Canino, C. Faravelli, S. Greenwald, H. G. Hwu, P. R. Joyce, et al. "Cross-National Epidemiology of Major Depression and Bipolar Disorder." *Journal of the American Medical Association* 276, no. 4 (1996): 293–99.

Whiffen, V. E. "Is Post Partum Depression a Distinct Diagnosis?" *Clinical Psychology Review* 12 (1992): 485–508.

Woody, S. R., and W. C. Sanderson. "Manuals for Empirically Supported Treatments: 1998 Update." *The Clinical Psychologist* 51 (1998): 17–21.

World Bank. *World Development Report 1993: Investing in Health.* New York: Oxford University Press, 1993.

World Health Organization (WHO). *Women and Mental Health.* http://www.who.int/ mediacentre/factsheets/ fs248/en/index.html (accessed November 5, 2004).

———. *Women's Mental Health: An Evidence Based Review.* Geneva: World Health Organization, 2000. http://whqlibdoc.who.int/hq/2000/WHO_MSD_MDP_00.1.pdf (accessed March 29, 2008).

———. *The World Health Report 2001: Mental Health: New Understanding, New Hope.* Geneva: World Health Organization, 2001.

———. International Consortium of Psychiatric Epidemiology. "Cross-National Comparisons of Mental Disorders." *Bulletin of the World Health Organization* 78 (2000): 413–26.

III

Depression across the Media

Chapter 10

A Dark Web

Depression, Writing, and the Internet

Kiki Benzon

The term "depression," when used in the context of mental health discourse, is a regrettably misleading one. While low mood and dysphoria form part of the diagnostic criteria for this debilitating condition, depression affects more than an individual's emotional state and interpersonal conduct. The condition is, crucially, characterized by concentration difficulties, cognitive impairment, confusion, and a general retardation of psychomotor functioning[1]—in some cases, to be likened more to dementia than to the milder "sadness" the word "depression" connotes. When not viewed as antisocial, weak-willed, or narcissistic, depressed persons are often ostracized to another (more respectable but equally isolating) margin, where uni- and bipolar illnesses are seen to be part of a creative disposition and therefore acceptable. In this rather romantic view, the "unquiet mind"[2] is also an inventive, perspicacious, idiosyncratic mind, whose psychic anguish is the inevitable flip side of artistic genius. While it is true that many artists have been clinically depressed, it is perhaps more accurate to say (as one would of the deaf Beethoven or the blind Milton) that remarkable work was produced in spite of—and not because of—a disabling affliction.

Given the cognitive impediments and distortions associated with depression, most literature on the subject is generated either by clinicians, who can document only what they observe, or by patients in remission, who must reconfigure their experiences, through the transformative lens of memory, to fit the particular stylistic codes of conventional narrative, journalistic or autobiographical. Although writers like Andrew Solomon, William Styron, and Lewis Wolpert have produced beautifully cogent and illustrative accounts of depression, their work is

145

essentially (albeit powerfully) *descriptive.*[3] Recent fictional work featuring
affective disorders has helped to bring such illnesses into the public consciousness, but it is a rare narrative whose evocation of psychological distress is more than a sentimental or parodic device.[4] I am interested
in textual enactments of depression, rather, where flows and fissures
of thought are represented by the structural dynamics of the textual
environment itself. In what follows, I examine the ways in which the
internet—pliable, immediate, and democratic—is a particularly apt
space for expressing and rendering the stasis and convolution of depressed cognition. In trying to understand these renderings, I will explore individual and collective narratives that emerge from online chat
forums, health discussion boards, and personal websites. These web-
based patterns, I submit, constitute an ongoing, multitudinous narrative
of depression—a disease whose "anarchic disconnections," "bifurcation
of mood," and "murky distractedness"[5] make it incompatible with the
causal systems and linear teleology imposed by the print medium and
conventional publishing. This effort to map out and analyze the perpetually shifting patterns of depression, as they occur in web-based writing,
constitutes part of a larger project on the generative and stultifying role
of mood disorders (and their myriad treatments) in contemporary literary production. My ultimate hope is to redirect psychiatric disability discourse away from anecdotal and clinical interpretations that highlight
affect, toward a structural and broadly cultural conception of the disease.

As existent literature is put online and new creative works are written for electronic environments, the internet has become a valuable publication venue.[6] This venue is particularly amenable to works dealing with
mental health issues because, for one thing, it is largely free from the economic pressures that require printing houses to factor celebrity and scholarly saleability into publication decisions. While candid accounts of
depression by famous figures such as Jane Pauley, Mike Wallace, and
Marie Osmond have helped to bring the disease "out of the closet" and
into public discourse,[7] a reader's identification with these accounts is inevitably receptive rather than participatory, binary rather than multiple.
As George P. Landow says in his discussion of hypertext[8]—which "permits
readers to choose their own path through a set of possibilities"—a networked text "offers liberation, idiosyncrasy, and even anarchy, obviat[ing]
the kind of control feared by Lyotard and other culture prophets who
confused old-fashioned centralized mainframe computing with the new
information technologies as a whole."[9] Furthermore, the internet allows
authors—should they desire it—a degree of anonymity in revealing what
stigmatization so often compels them to keep hidden; the pressure to
conceal depressive illness is, indeed, a common refrain among sufferers.
Austrian composer Hugo Wolf lamented having to sustain a public per-

sona that would hide his condition: "I appear at times merry and in good heart, talk, too, before others quite reasonably . . . yet the soul maintains its deathly sleep and the heart bleeds from a thousand wounds."[10] On a recent episode of *Larry King Live*, former talk-show host Dick Cavett expressed a similar predicament, recalling Marlon Brando's advice to keep the depression invisible by way of "automatic pilot"; "I use it all the time," Brando confessed to Cavett.

These problems of confidentiality and the resulting sense of social disconnection are potentially ameliorated in an online environment, which is conducive to anonymous interaction and disclosure. In *Another*, a web page dedicated to depression, the site owner, "Nathalie C.," writes:

> My hope is that, in assembling an honest account of my depression and by providing relevant excerpts from writers' autobiographies and psychiatric literature, I can offer readers moments of identification that undermine the loneliness and shame of mental illness. And I suspect that blogs can contribute to the public discourse on depression in ways that more traditional representations of depression can't; since a blog is continually updated, its representation of depression is less likely to hide or mitigate contradictions and ambiguities, and more likely to challenge practiced wisdom and "pop psychology" simplifications.[11]

While many websites concerning depression offer clinical guidance or personal exchange, *Another*—a coalescence of writings from paper- and web-based fiction—is unique in its specifically literary concerns. Though currently edited by one person, the venue will be "open to other authors" (according to the site owner), creating a node through which multiple related but discrete experiences and texts may permeate.

The internet is a particularly apt space through which to read depression because its formal variability corresponds to the fluctuating nature of the disease itself; the "dispersed, multiply centered network organization of electronic linking"[12] is able to accommodate the cognitive shifts and fissures of depressed or manic discourse. To illustrate this, I present here extracts from an e-conversation taking place in the discussion stream "Depression and the Pen" at the writers' website *Speculations*. In jagged prose, one young person describes his/her depressive isolation:

> I, just, sometimes go insane, when im alone at night shut in my room, its like, a sanctuary, when I look out the window its just black. there might as well be nothing else in the universe as far as im concerned. A couple of my friends say im too self

deprocating, but thats because ive never known anything better, except for relatives, ive never had a friend thats been really nice and understang to me. Well, except for one. But, I just get so frustrated with the people in the world, the way theyre so bliss-fully ignorant, I hate theway religious people can be brought up like sheep and believe in a scam like god, i know im only 14 and I dont know all the answers but at least I can see what is true and what isnt. Every time I close my eyes the world dissapears but when I open them again the worldis still there, I just wish I could close my eyes and go a deep, eternal sleep, lost in the unreality of dreams. . . . . .

The naive candor and slipshod typography here would normally exclude this kind of text from critical appraisal. But in the polyvocal space of the discussion stream, these unselfconsciously disjointed comments work to supply an important subjective dimension to the representation of depression emerging on the web page. The series contains some question-and-response entries, but on occasion the personal cedes to the prescriptive; for instance, another e-locuter submits:

> I think I'm going to hijack this topic and link it to Nancy Etchemendy's "Writers and Depression" article, on view in our Sample Articles section. There's also some good stuff online from Poets & Writers, Silja J.A. Talvi's "The Price Of Great-ness", and Ilana Stanger's "Still Crazy After All These Years: Art and Mental Illness", from theartbiz.com's Notes on the Artist's Life. Both articles quote Dr. Arnold Ludwig's 1992 sur-vey of a thousand famous 20th-century artists and writers, and compare their mental health with people in other professions. (Hint: poets should be kept away from sharp objects.)

Perhaps inadvertently, the tenor of these comments evinces the fine line between advice and aggression in this interactive context; although an entry may contain ostensibly "useful" references, terms like "hijack" add to a hierarchical dynamic among discussion board contributors.[13] Frac-tures in tone and topic are borne out (with fewer nefarious conse-quences) in the structural possibilities of the internet environment. With the previous remarks, the discussion stream is (potentially—dependent upon how it is read) bifurcated by points of yield that would draw the reader along new but related trajectories. Lines of thought span out rhi-zomatically, emulating the cognitive mechanics of depression itself, whose salient feature is impaired concentration, a tendency to shift er-ratically among logical strands and the contours of myriad emotional states. The multiply authored text at hand thus forms along multiple axes, where each interjection contains within itself a set of possibilities that may be explored or disregarded by writer and readers alike.

Whether what is wrought or emergent constitutes a "narrative" is bound up, of course, in philosophical questions of intentionality. But the narrative quality of many individual entries within the stream of linked, disparate texts is apparent. One man's description of his wife's illness illustrates this quality:

> My wife has been taking heavy doses of prozac and lithium for years. . . . It looks like [her drugs] had been prescribed based on an incorrect diagnosis. She has long had personal habits that are mistaken for depression—not socializing, lack of attention—and she had sought counceling for grief therapy when a grandmother died. She also had low energy levels that we now know is [due] to hypothyroidism. The doctor said "depression, take these pills". When her personal habits didn't go away, the doctor said "take higher doses". By this time, the doctor added lithium (which probably was called for—her emotions bounce around wildly). But the doses weren't monitored by regular blood workups. The doses were so high that she developed tremors in her hands and aggrivated the hypothyroidism. The high lithium levels befuddled her mind. Her doctor said, "still not enough prozac" . . . I think I have a case of malpractice. While the high lithium level was screwing up her hormones and thinking, the prozac was stealing her passions. Not just her libido, but her interest in almost everything—food, pets, writing; nothing mattered any more. She stayed that way for 4 years, then we moved and we got a new doctor. It's taken over a year, but now she's prozac-free. Her lithium dose is 1/4 of what it used to be. She's taking hormones to replace the thyroid hormone. Her hand tremors remain. She's a little more moody than before, but her brain works again. Last month, for the first time in over 5 years, she got out a notebook and started writing again.

A cultural narrative of depression thus emerges "organically" and collectively, irreducible to one specific text or official version. Formed within the polyvocal and stylistically variable parameters of the medium, internet expressions of depression may constitute uniquely accurate representations of the disease. As Kerry Kidd contends, "Mental health-type literature dealing with clinical depression in particular often falls into a trap of trying to say that which it precisely can't say by attempting to make meaning from the unmeanable or make sense of the unsayable."[14] Web renderings may be more "accurate" precisely because they permit inaccuracy.

The entry just quoted—a subject-based series of dramatic incidents and turns-of-events—confirms that depression is an illness of stories: of context, calamity, (ir)resolution, and conflict with both self and others. What might begin as web-based "research" into affective disorders thus often becomes an excavation of narratives that vary with successive readings and have no definitive conclusion or end (like hypertext fiction, another textual form with the potential to structurally emulate the chaotic cognition in psychological disorders).[15] In the *Underground Literary Alliance* chat forum, one contributor makes an insightful connection between depression and narrative:

> A main thing is that the, what, 9 symptoms of depression are also that of a good story. They all relate to potential change. They're about crisis. Which of course is opportunity. Except that true change or development is anathema to our society. (It may cause a hiccup in productivity. Oh no!) Hence the disease. In depression something is stirring in us. There's inner reaction against the way we are that wants to make it a way we were. It's happening to us whether we want it to or not. Old ways no longer work. Or the patches and fakery have given way. There's a chance for something good and new to come out of depression that the truly numb or clever can't see. Real cultures have rites of passage to handle this. We haven't found ours yet. How do cultures find new ways of living? Thru art. What's the art that covers development and growth the best?—Literature.

I quote this entry at length in order to illustrate a number of things. The reference to the professional writer's maxim—"crisis equals opportunity"—speaks to the universality of the depressed person's struggle; it is a struggle, furthermore, contained in all good stories. The adversity-compelled transformation (rather than defeat) of fictional characters and depressed persons alike is a means of bringing about a more robust status quo. The aforementioned remarks are interesting because even though depression would seem to epitomize fundamental patterns of individual and social growth—being one of many "rites of passage" all citizens must inevitably endure—*art* rather than *life* here is cited as the space for acknowledging such growth; "true change," to reiterate the author's assertion, "is anathema to our society." Thus depression and its implicit summons to change are, in the West, shunted to the margins (to the space of the antisocial, the unemployable, the disabled) with other subversive or otherwise irregular phenomena, which have the capacity, as the contributor to the *Underground Literary Alliance* says, to "cause a hiccup in productivity."[16]

As with a good deal of writing found on the internet—literary, anecdotal, epistolary, analytic—online depictions of depression do not necessarily accord with the grammatical codes or stylistic tenor typical in academic writing. In part, this can be attributed to the fundamental nature of the disease, where "energy is profoundly dissipated, the ability to think is clearly eroded, and the capacity to actively engage in the efforts and pleasures of life is fundamentally altered."[17] This stylistic variability is, of course, also a function of the medium itself; internet publishing often sets itself in opposition to the rhetorical and polemical conventions of print publication. Thus, some internet prose we find on depression (and all topics, generally) is more lucid than others. *Melancholia*, a website owned by someone who is self-professedly "not a shrink, preacher, or Scientologist, so fear not," contains an essay called "What It's Like," which uses similes and situational examples to convey the inexpressible:

> Depression is walking the neighborhood in the night, relieved there are no streetlights because if someone sees you and asks what's wrong, you won't be able to understand them. It's forgetting how to speak, when all you can do is feel. It's walking like a drunk, but not being drunk, just dizzy with despair that nothing short of a miracle can change. It's knowing miracles aren't real.
>   . . . Depression is obsession, but knowing that the one great fix will always be out of reach. It is being separated from the herd, trapped behind a fence created by self-doubt, self-loathing, and the absolute conviction that there's nothing between you and the black sky, not even air.

However, remarks made by a "Senior Veteran" contributor to the depression stream of *Health Boards*, written apparently in the midst of distress, are characterized by a verbal difficulty apparent even in its subject line— "I just . . . just . . . I don't know"—which alone tells the story:

> I just keep drawing blanks. . . . I can never find the right words anymore. . . . *Sigh* I'm a mess. I can't begin to explain my overwhelming sadness. <Sad laugh.> It's so hard to explain, that I've erased and re-typed this paragraph about 7 times. I really don't even know what I'm trying to say. I just . . . I guess . . . I'm hoping somebbody might understand me.

It must be stressed: not all valuable texts are beautifully written. While the first text quoted offers an evocative and imaginative description of the ailment, the second one enacts the ailment. Moreover, a web reader would not assume the same levels of objectivity and empiricism in online discourse that one would expect from edited or peer-reviewed work (unless such controls are demonstrably practiced in, for example, an MLA- or APA-affiliated web journal). But rather than dismiss informal or testimonial web writing as an illegitimate source of information, a reader must interpret such texts as one would a cultural artifact, whose meanings are embedded in fractured dialogue, *leitmotif*, contradiction, hyperbole, and the like.

Although its potential as a discursive and creative medium is still largely unmined, the internet has become perhaps the dominant means of transmitting diverse information. With information, however, comes misinformation—and this can be a significant problem when it comes to understanding issues of psychiatric consequence.[18] One study reveals a correlation between internet use itself and depression, where surfing the web is practiced in lieu of other social activities in the same manner as one succumbs to an addiction.[19] But while a number of similar investigations have indicated that internet use can exacerbate depression, others have found that sufferers find relief through interacting with online communities.[20] This latter finding is corroborated by Houston et al., who found that "[h]eavy users of the Internet groups [are] more likely to have resolution of depression . . . than less frequent users."[21] In a dissertation, Andrew Campbell provides some explanation for this web-induced amelioration of symptoms:

> [It was hypothesized] that the Internet increases the chance of meaningful relationships and can help to improve self-confidence, social abilities and social support. The test hypotheses [were] based on the researchers [*sic*] model of Escapist Behaviour, which claims that individuals tested as having low level mood disorders, such as depression, anxiety and social fearfulness, who spend large amounts of time using specific Internet resources, do so as a means of "escape" from reality. It [was] also theorised that time spent using the specific function of "chat" on the Internet enables these users to explore facets of their cognitive processes and general social behaviour. When offline, reflection of their social experience online may lead these users to perceive coping with their mood disorder. . . . No evidence was attained in the data to suggest that time spent online correlates with contributing to depression, anxiety or social phobic disorders. . . . Chat users believed that the Internet is psychologically beneficial to them but also believed that frequent Internet users are lonely and that the Internet can be addictive.[22]

Empirically determining any causal relationship between internet use and depression is difficult because, for one thing, sources of depression are themselves overdetermined: varying widely in severity and symptomology, depression may be linked to biochemical, genetic, cognitive, traumatic, circumstantial and nutritional factors. Campbell's notion of internet use as an "Escapist Behavior," however, is interesting because, as Alice Flaherty maintains, writing may offer a means of fleeing all types of confinement—whether they are internally or externally imposed: "What do prisoners do?" Flaherty asks. "Write, of course; even if they have to use blood as ink, as the Marquis de Sade did. The reasons they write, the exquisitely frustrating restrictions of their autonomy and the fact that no one listens to their cries, are also the reasons that mentally ill people, and even many normal people, write. We write to escape our prisons."[23] Escape to the internet thus generates narratives, whose writers provide the substance and whose readers, in determining which paths within the network to pursue, produce the structure.

Notes

1. As stipulated in the American Psychiatric Association's *Diagnostic and Statistical Manual—IV*, "Major Depressive Disorder" is defined by the presence of least five of the following nine elements within the same two-week period, where either 1) or 2) is present: 1) depressed mood, 2) loss of interest or pleasure in activities, 3) significant weight loss or gain, 4) insomnia or hypersomnia, 5) psychomotor retardation, 6) fatigue or loss of energy, 7) feelings of worthlessness, 8) diminished ability to think or concentrate, and 9) recurrent thoughts of death.

2. I draw this phrase from Kay Jamison's *An Unquiet Mind* (1995), an autobiographical account of bipolar disorder. Professor of Psychiatry at Johns Hopkins University and diagnosed manic depressive, Jamison has worked to synthesize subjective, historical, and biological conceptions of affective disorders in *Touched by Fire: Manic-Depressive Illness and the Artistic Temperament* (1993) and *Night Falls Fast: Understanding Suicide* (New York: Knopf, 1999), as well as (with Frederick K. Goodwin) *Manic-Depressive Illness* (New York: Oxford University Press, 1990), the standard medical textbook on the disease.

3. Andrew Solomon, *The Noonday Demon: An Atlas of Depression* (New York: Scribner, 2001); William Styron, *Darkness Visible* (1990); and Lewis Wolpert, *Malignant Sadness: The Anatomy of Depression* (New York: Faber, 1999). Other books of this genre include A. Alvarez's *The Savage God: A Study of Suicide* (New York: Random House, 1971), Lauren Slater's *Prozac Diary* (New York: Random House, 1998), Susanna Kaysen's *Girl, Interrupted* (New York: Vintage, 1993), Martha Manning's *Undercurrents: A Life Beneath the Surface* (San Francisco: HarperCollins, 1994), and Nell Casey's edited collection *Unholy Ghost: Writers on Depression* (New York: William Morrow, 2001).

4. David Foster Wallace's "The Depressed Person"—in his short story collection, *Brief Interviews with Hideous Men* (Boston: Little, Brown, 1999)—is one of the best fictional representations I have encountered of the illness. Depression here is formally enacted by parasitic footnotes that encroach exponentially upon the text proper.

5. Styron, *Darkness Invisible*, 12.

6. The emergence of online literary journals and writing workshops/collectives such as *Writing.com*, *Underground Literary Alliance*, and *McSweeney's* (http://www.mcsweeneys.net) suggests the increasing momentum of this trend.

7. Other celebrities who have spoken openly about mental illness are actresses Margot Kidder, Linda Dano, and Mariette Hartley (who is honorary director of the American Foundation for Suicide Prevention). In her recent memoir, *Down Came the Rain: My Journey Through Postpartum Depression* (New York: Hyperion, 2005), Brooke Shields wrote of her use of medication to ameliorate postpartum depression and was consequently condemned for doing so by actor and Scientologist Tom Cruise.

8. Hypertext, as defined by N. Katherine Hayles in *Writing Machines*, "has at a minimum the three characteristics of <u>MULTIPLE READING PATHS</u>, <u>CHUNKED TEXT</u> and some kind of <u>LINKING MECHANISM</u>. The World Wide Web, with its links, millions of pages, and multiple reading paths, is a vast hypertext of global proportions" (26).

9. Landow, "What's a Critic to Do?" 33.

10. Walker, *Hugo Wolf*, 361.

11. In *The Midnight Disease*, Alice Flaherty explains the blog's particular allure to depressed persons who, she argues, are particularly susceptible to hypergraphia, "the overpowering desire to write" (2): "Perhaps the compulsive memoirism of the mentally ill can help explain an age so memoir-mad that most young novelists present their thinly veiled autobiographies as fiction. . . . Thanks to the Internet . . . [t]housands of authors simply write their diaries directly onto Web pages for the rest of the world to read" (37). This public form of memoir is useful in understanding both the experience and evolution of depressive illness. One blog, for example, includes a timeline of key developments in a particular "narrative" of depression: cessation of "ineffective psychoanalysis," commencement with a psychiatrist, antidepressant treatment ("finally after 30 years I was being treated for the disease I suffered from"), and various points of turbulence ("I've been feeling physically ill, and my mood is sometimes stable, and sometimes very low. Added to this, I have been feeling a constant level of anxiety").

12. Landow, 23.

13. On *Health Boards* (http://www.healthboards.com), contributors are assigned an icon, which appears beside their user names to indicate the total number of comments respectively made—"veteran," "newbie," or some intermediary status—and potentially conditions perception (perhaps, intimating relative legitimacy) of the remarks.

14. Kidd, "Styron Leaves Las Vegas," 292.

15. Psychological ambiguity is enacted in the structural turbulence (reiteration, multiple reading paths) in, for example, Kathryn Cramer's *In Small and Large Pieces* and Rich Holeton's *Figurski at Findhorn on Acid* (Watertown, MA: Eastgate, 1994 and 2002).

16. Michel Foucault's *Madness and Civilization* comes to mind here: our current propensities to segregate mentally ill persons from "normal" society, Foucault argues, stems from a seventeenth-century culture of "reason" that saw confinement of the "mad" as "an economic measure and social precaution": madness was "perceived on the social horizon of poverty, of incapacity for work, of inability to integrate with the group" (59).

17. Jamison, *Touched With Fire*, 18.

18. This danger is implied by Howard Rheingold in his discussion of misinformation and the internet: "While a few people will get better information . . . the majority of the population, if history is any guide, are likely to become more precisely befuddled, more exactly manipulated. Hyper-reality is what you get when a Panopticon evolves to the point where it can convince everyone that it doesn't exist; people continue to believe they are free, although their power has disappeared" (*The Virtual Community*).

19. This study, which emerged from Carnegie Mellon University, was presented by Robert Kraut et al. in "Internet Paradox." Interestingly, the same author four years later published "Internet Paradox Revisited": "This follow-up research," states Kraut, "reports dissipated negative effects. The article also offers results from another sample, new computers and television purchasers, which show general positive social and psychological effect of Internet use" (49).

20. See Eysenbach et al., "Health Related Virtual Communities and Electronic Support Groups," 1–6.

21. Houston et al., 2062.

22. Campbell, "An Investigation," 16–17.

23. Flaherty, 36.

Bibliography

Campbell, Andrew J. "An Investigation into the Theory of Escapist Behaviour and the Relationship between the Internet and Depression, Anxiety and Social Phobia." Ph.D. diss., University of Sydney, 2003.

"Depression and the Pen." July 16, 1998; August 10, 2002. *Speculations.* http://www.speculations.com/rumormill/?z=123025&f=123075 (accessed October 13, 2005).

Diagnostic and Statistical Manual of Mental Disorders: Fourth Edition. Washington, DC: American Psychiatric Association, 1994.

Eysenbach, G., et al. "Health Related Virtual Communities and Electronic Support Groups: Systematic Review of the Effects of Online Peer to Peer Interactions." *British Medical Journal* 328 (May 15, 2004): 1166.

Flaherty, Alice W. *The Midnight Disease: The Drive to Write, Writer's Block, and the Creative Brain.* New York: Houghton Mifflin, 2004.

Foucault, Michel. *Madness and Civilization: A History of Insanity in the Age of Reason.* Translated by Richard Howard. 1965. New York: Vintage, 1988.

Hayles, N. Katherine. *Writing Machines.* Cambridge, MA: MIT Press, 2002.

Houston, T. K., et al. "Internet Support Groups for Depression: A 1-Year Prospective Cohort Study." *American Journal of Psychiatry* 159 (December 2002): 2062–68.

Jamison, Kay Redfield. *An Unquiet Mind: A Memoir of Moods and Madness.* 1995. New York: Picador, 1997.

———. *Touched With Fire: Manic-Depressive Illness and the Artistic Temperament.* New York: Free Press, 1993.

Kidd, Kerry. "Styron Leaves Las Vegas: Philosophy, Alcohol and the Addictions of Experience." *Janus Head* 6, no. 2 (Winter 2003): 284–97.

Kraut, Robert, et al. "Internet Paradox: A Social Technology That Reduces Social Involvement and Psychological Well-Being?" *American Psychologist* 53, no. 9 (September 1998): 1017–31.

———. "Internet Paradox Revisited." *Journal of Social Issues* 58, no. 1 (2002): 49–74.

Landow, George P. "What's a Critic to Do? Critical Theory in the Age of Hypertext." In *Hyper/Text/Theory*, edited by George P. Landow, 1–50. Baltimore: Johns Hopkins University Press, 1994.

Larry King Live. "Panel Discusses Depression." CNN, June 12, 2005.

"Nathalie C." *Another.* http://nchicha.com/other (accessed July 20, 2005).

Rheingold, Howard. "Chapter 10." *The Virtual Community*, April 12, 2005. http://www.well.com/user/hlr/vcbook/vcbook10.html (accessed July 17, 2005).

"Senior Veteran," "EoR." *Health Boards.* http://www.healthboards.com/boards/showthread.php?t=308514 (accessed July 23, 2005).

Styron, William. *Darkness Visible: A Memoir of Madness.* 1990. New York: Vintage, 1992.

Underground Literary Alliance. May 16, 2005. http://www.literaryrevolution.com (accessed July 2, 2005).

Walker, Frank. *Hugo Wolf: A Biography.* 1951. London: J. M. Dent, 1968.

"What It's Like." *Melancholia.* http://www.geocities.com/melancholia (accessed August 10, 2005).

Chapter 11

A Meditation on Depression, Time, and Narrative Peregrination in the Film T𝐻ℰ 𝐻ℴ𝓊𝓇𝓈

Diane R. Wiener

I begin to have what happened to me.

—Muriel Rukeyser, "Children's Elegy"

Narrative is the vehicle through which individual and collective voices, identities, and enactments of agency are emplotted—or not. The term "emplotment" was developed by philosopher Paul Ricoeur[1] and has been adapted by numerous writers from a range of disciplines to describe the processes by which subjects are repeatedly placed, place themselves, and may resist placement in relation to specific identities, stories, images, histories, events, meanings, and so on. In addition to its obvious reference to literary and cinematic plots, and to the ways that a life is like a literary or filmic world that is variously molded by oneself and others, emplotment can be metaphorically considered in terms of plots of land, plots on a graph, plots of time, or any related process of creating schemes, negotiating spaces, and making plans that may or may not be difficult to alter.

The question of how identities, stories, and cinematic images of depression are realized and could be said to realize themselves through narrative acts is central to my discussion of narrative in relation to structures of time. In *Time and Narrative*, Ricoeur asserts that the nonlinear or nonchronological is not equivalent to the atemporal. Time can be understood to be circular, layered, spectral, multiplicitous, and processual. He notes, "Peregrination and narration are grounded in time's approximation of eternity, which, far from abolishing their difference, never stops contributing to it."[2] Ricoeur's references to peregrination in relation to narration are compelling when one considers that peregrination—a journey from one place to another that involves migration, wandering, or roving—can be understood to occur in nonlinear ways.

Although there are potentially parallels and convergences between peregrination and narration, practitioners in the social sciences, cultural theory, and psychotherapy frequently identify narration as a process which renders coherent, cohesive, and linear a set of temporal experiences or variables that are often initially more disparate and nonlinear than orderly. Thus it might seem that peregrination and chronological narration are wholly different: peregrination is typically nomadic whereas narration is typically serial and linear. However, rather than seeing peregrination and narration as separate and different processes, I believe that peregrination can be used as a metaphor to describe nonlinear narration. In this essay, I am interested in reading two recent cinematic narratives of depression and "madness"[3]—and the social messages that these films carry, forward, deny, and refuse—as narrative peregrinations, rather than as merely "coherent" or "incoherent" narratives.[4]

A uniquely layered portrait of women's depression and "madness," *The Hours* presents its audience with myriad opportunities to consider narrative in relation to temporality and themes of coherence. Expressions of identity that are or can be socially coded as deviant or incoherent have long been experimented with and critiqued by filmmakers, visual and musical artists, and poets. In its representations of depression and "mental illness," and in its special use of nonlinear time, *The Hours* joins other creative endeavors that complicate culturally widespread definitions of coherence and competence.

Like a brilliantly colored sample from an origami instructional manual, *The Hours* folds and refolds the interconnected stories of three women living at different times, from the 1920s through the 1950s to the present: Virginia Woolf, Laura Brown, and Clarissa Vaughan. Each character is affected by profound emotional anguish, by her own suicidality or that of someone very close to her, and by Virginia Woolf's novel *Mrs. Dalloway*. Film critic Peter Travers summarizes the film as follows:

> In the 1920s, Woolf lives in the London suburbs with her protective husband (the superb Stephen Dillane) and battles demons of the mind as she writes *Mrs. Dalloway*. That novel will affect the lives of Laura Brown (Julianne Moore), a housewife and mother living in 1950s Los Angeles, and Clarissa Vaughan (Meryl Streep), a modern New Yorker planning a party for a former lover (an off-key Ed Harris), a poet dying of AIDS. Director Stephen Daldry interweaves these stories with uncanny skill.[5]

I would argue that Woolf's novel does much more than cleverly bridge the three narratives: it acts as a catalyst for each woman's pained self-awareness and complicated interpersonal alliances. *Mrs. Dalloway* strongly influences the relationships between the women and the characters around them within their respective temporal landscapes. Even more interestingly, like Michael Cunningham's novel upon which it was based,[6] the film uses the novel *Mrs. Dalloway* to create relationships between the three women themselves, sometimes in a brave and overt dismissal of linear time.[7]

Laura Brown's adult son Richard (Ed Harris), who calls Clarissa Vaughan "Mrs. Dalloway" because of her party-hostess role, says good-bye to Clarissa before killing himself, leaping to his death from the window in front of her. Richard tells Clarissa shortly before his death that she is "always giving parties to cover the silence." Clarissa has been planning a party for Richard on the occasion of his being awarded a literary prize and, as she tells him, has invited "a group of people who want to tell you your work is going to live."

After Richard dies, Laura comes to New York and meets Clarissa, who is destroying all of the special food dishes that she prepared for the party in a symbolic act of resignation, anger, and relief in the wake of her friend and ex-lover's tragic death. Laura had been estranged from Richard because she left him when he was a child, but she is treated with courtesy upon her arrival by Clarissa, her lover Sally (Allison Janney), and Clarissa's daughter Julia (Claire Danes). In the overlap between these characters in this section of the film, linear time is preserved rather than questioned, since Laura is elderly in the present time that is Clarissa's. This is not the strongest or most interesting part of the film narrative, however. More interesting is the idea that throughout the film Laura Brown and Clarissa Vaughan are already linked through themes of grief and sexuality that extend beyond their relationships with Richard and their eventual meeting.

Lesbian intimacy—and the frequent inability to express it freely— is a dominant theme in this film, but the intriguing lesbian characters are not Clarissa and Sally, the "out" yuppies with a great New York brownstone who live comfortably in the early twenty-first century. Clarissa and Sally seem to have it all, yet Clarissa is aggrieved by Richard (while he is still alive and later), for whom she is and has been a primary caretaker and with whom she may still be in love. Clarissa seems trapped in the past, emotionally dead inside herself and, from all appearances, to her lover. She is depressed despite her frenetic preparations for the party. Aware of the deep trouble she is in, Clarissa makes comments such as, "I seem to be unraveling." Richard also has an awkward relationship with time and memory, in part because of all the medications he is taking for AIDS. Moreover, he experiences lingering grief over the loss of his mother at a young age, as he seems to have felt abandoned by her. At one point he thinks that he has already received the literary prize, and when Clarissa gently corrects him, he says, "I seem to have fallen out of time."

In my reading, the first homoerotic intrigue in the film is between Laura Brown and her friend Kitty (Toni Collette), who awkwardly and passionately kiss in Laura's suburban kitchen while her young son Richie (Jack Rovello) waits for his mother in a nearby room. Kitty has just tearily told Laura that she has to have a "procedure" and needs Laura to feed her pet, and in sharing comfort their lips meet. In fact, Laura kisses Kitty full on the mouth. Kitty's desire is vivid and obvious, but her response when the kiss is over is to say, "You're sweet," thus denying that anything really significant has happened beyond the bounds of what occurs in a caring friendship. In a parallel scene, Virginia kisses her sister Vanessa (Miranda Richardson) on the mouth at the end of an awkward family visit, and asks Vanessa if she (Virginia) seems better, emotionally speaking. The depression from which Laura and Virginia obviously suffer creates a cross-temporal connection between these two passionate kisses and the two women who initiate them. In this and in other ways, *The Hours* reckons with simultaneity and points to the possibility of concurrent emotional universes that transcend apparently separated times, spaces, and other dimensions. Moreover, the film may be suggesting that unfulfilled lesbian yearning, or unfulfilled desire more generally—desire for escape from a dull life, in both cases—can lie behind depression. It seems to me that the freedom as well as the ability to follow one's desires and meet one's needs may be, in part, a way out of depression. For some, however, such a path may not be realistic or possible as an actual choice to make, or if selected may still not be enough to move away from great pain and suffering.

In one of the film's most troubling and effective scenes, the train station scene, Leonard (Stephen Dillane) tells Virginia that she has "an obligation to [her] own sanity," as they debate the merits of psychiatric expertise and medical treatments for her "illness." She says that her life has been "stolen" from her, and that she is "living a life [she has] no wish to live." She wants to leave their country house and go back to London, where it is vital and busy. Virginia tells Leonard, "You cannot find peace by avoiding life." This is essentially the same sentiment that Richard expresses to Clarissa. Richard consistently asks Clarissa to stop living her life for him, and he is keenly aware that his death will free her, a fact that she resents. He asks her, "Who's this party for?" and says, "I think I'm only staying alive to satisfy you." Unsurprisingly, after Richard dies, Clarissa's passion for life indeed reignites, and she embraces Sally with warmth and feeling, probably for the first time in many years.

In a dimly lit room, shortly after Richard's death, Laura narrates her life choices to Clarissa, including her decision to leave her children, although she does not overtly make mention of her sexual orientation: "It would be wonderful to say you regretted it. It would be easy. But what does it mean to regret when you have no choice? It's what you can bear. There it is. No one's going to forgive me. It was death. I chose life." It is implied that Clarissa somehow knows what Laura has endured, in terms of Laura's sexuality, difficult choices, and attendant losses. Laura's admissions help Clarissa to come into contact with her own desires for freedom, which she then expresses to Sally.

In the 1950s thread of the film narrative, Laura is barely functioning and suicidal. Trapped in suburbia, she is a woman who cannot freely express her sexuality. Pregnant and miserable, Laura does not want to abandon her family, but she considers ending her life by taking an overdose of pills. Instead of committing suicide in a hotel room alone, however, she chooses life; waiting until her second child is born, she then leaves her family and moves to Canada. As viewers we do not find out this information until Laura enters Clarissa's life. We do know that Richard has somehow lost his mother, and some viewers may guess early in the film that Laura is Richard's mother, but it is quite possible that this crucial detail is not completely clear until, shortly before his death, we see Richard crying as he admires a picture of the mother who eventually left him. The sensual black-and-white photograph of Laura in her wedding dress is a chilling moment of well-placed melodramatic excess in the film. Because of his age, it is not clear if Richie knew as a little boy that when his mother was reading *Mrs. Dalloway*, she was thinking of leaving him and of killing herself.

Despite the poignant and often disturbing tone of the film, some reviewers joked about its content, perhaps because of its sometimes heavy-handed dramatic flourishes, or perhaps because depression and the larger topic of suicide make some people very uncomfortable. Other reviewers found the film to be an important contribution to discussions of depression among women.[8] While *The Hours* received mixed reviews, I am interested in its promise as a text that speaks volumes about temporality and narrative structure. Whatever its critical reception, this film is a sophisticated piece of cinema that merits analysis, and also highlights the importance of including women's own "voices" in cinematic narratives of "mentally ill" women. I will draw some comparisons with *Girl, Interrupted* (1999), another recent film on women and "mental illness," in order to highlight further the unique visual features and peregrinating narrative structure of *The Hours*.

Based upon the memoir of the same title,[9] the film *Girl, Interrupted* uses creative temporal manipulations, moving between present moments and memories as protagonist Susanna Kaysen experienced these temporal shifts while she was institutionalized in a psychiatric hospital during the late 1960s. In ways that are different but parallel to those of *The Hours*, *Girl, Interrupted* uses nonlinear time sequencing and flashbacks in order to reenact Susanna's emotional perspective while in the asylum. Susanna's confusion, sadness, and anger, particularly in relation to her family, and her at times defiant resistance to a changing American society at war, are depicted through a variety of crosscuts between periods and scenarios in her life. For example, an early scene shows Susanna (Winona Ryder) in an ambulance immediately after her suicide attempt, but the viewer soon discovers that this event has already happened in the overall film narrative, and the cut to this scene can be read as a comment on Susanna's experiences of displacement.

Addressing the memoir, Susan Hubert notes, "Kaysen employs several 'postmodern' narrative techniques in *Girl, Interrupted*. The novel is a pastiche of sorts, containing Kaysen's personal narrative, various documents associated with her hospitalization and diagnosis, and stories about other patients."[10] Although I would not call the book a novel, as Hubert does, there are clear correspondences between the written text and its film adaptation in terms of the use of pastiche. The film's narrative structure in some ways echoes the book's design.

Temporal manipulation in the film *Girl, Interrupted* is often accomplished with the use of "checks." The psychiatric nursing staff does routine checks in each of the rooms in the women's psychiatric ward to make sure everyone is stable and safely sleeping in bed at night. Susanna dreams of—or awake, perhaps actually sees—people (not the nurses) at the door of her asylum room, but these are really at the doorway(s) in her past. She sees events literally open and close with the movement of her door, events often associated with the time when she lived with her difficult parents. As Susanna's condition improves, and she gets closer to being discharged from the hospital, the number of scenes of her writing increases, and these scenes are faster in tempo than other scenes. The frequency of flashbacks and dreamy temporal crosscutting lessens, implying that Susanna's improved mood and lessening depression accompany a progressive developmental movement into her own future and away from her fraught past.

The "checks" are used in *Girl, Interrupted* to move back and forth in time and to create empathy with Susanna's pain and disorientation, but these shots and scenes do not overtly encourage viewers to question the existence of flat, linear time itself, as *The Hours* does. Rather, *Girl, Interrupted* manipulates time to show how Susanna can be and is "cured"; once she has become reoriented to the expectations of a normative daily life, normative (linear) time is restored.

In contrast, *The Hours* creates webs of time that layer upon each other, and while some characters from different temporal layers eventually meet and interact in a shared present, the aftermath of a suicide, temporal resolution is not a primary goal of the film. By the end of the film, I was left with the impression that the three narratives are tangled together like the single string in a game of cat's cradle, and that perhaps there is no past, or future, either for the characters or for the film audience who might care for them in "real" life. Rather time, whatever it is, exists in the experiences of trauma, sadness, and pleasure, in the present—the here-and-now. As depicted in the film, Woolf shows within *Mrs. Dalloway* that a woman's entire life can be said to happen in a single day. In watching the film, viewers understand the adage of carpe diem ("seize the day"). The here-and-now also has its own changing shapes, and tributaries in *The Hours*—like the river pictured at the outset and at the end—seductively draw the viewer into an undertow of pain and curiosity.

At the end of the film, Virginia Woolf, with stones in her pockets, again walks into the deep water of the River Ouse as she does at the beginning. A visual palimpsest is invoked; the traces of Woolf's death and life have been remarked upon and thus seem to linger in perpetuity. Due to the ways in which Woolf and her peer characters are depicted, film viewers are encouraged to bear witness to their suffering, to call into question how as members of a society and as individuals we address (or do not address) the ethics surrounding suicide, suicidality, and depression. *The Hours* creates visual-emotive and temporal landscapes that one can repeatedly visit, as Woolf's death and life are and have been repeatedly "visited."[11] When we watch, assess, talk, and write about the film, we create and retrace palimpsests in a seemingly infinite regress of linked memories and interactive, peregrinating experiences, which problematize the idea that time, human responsibility, trauma, and suffering are ever limited to a single life.

Notes

This essay is a tribute to my beloved aunt, Joan Fallert, and is also in memory of my recently departed friend, Tommy Jarmiolowski, both of whose experiences of *The Hours* affected my own, immeasurably.

1. As Ricoeur explains in *Time and Narrative*, Volume 1, his idea of emplotment is an extension of Aristotle's concept *muthos* as described in the *Poetics*. While Ricoeur says that he "borrows" the concept from Aristotle, he also expands it in new directions (31). After unpacking Aristotle's usage of *muthos*, Ricoeur explains, "Aristotle . . . ignored the temporal aspects of emplotment" (Volume 1, 54). In the *Time and Narrative* trilogy, Ricoeur in part sees his project of helping readers "apprehen[d] [the] correspondence between narrative and time" as accomplished by a "confrontation between the Augustinian theory of time and the Aristotelian theory of the plot" (Volume 3, 241). One of his goals, among many others, is to think through "the configuration of time by narrative" (Ibid.).

2. Ricoeur, *Time and Narrative*, Volume 1, 29.

3. I use quotation marks around the terms "madness" and "mental ill-ness" to indicate that the definitions of these terms are contested and variable.

4. My theory of narrative (in)coherence is discussed at greater length in my Ph.D. dissertation, "Narrativity, Emplotment, and Voice in Autobiographical and Cinematic Representations of 'Mentally Ill' Women, 1942–2003."

5. Travers, review of *The Hours* in *Rolling Stone*, January 23, 2003, 76.

6. *The Hours* (1998).

7. In the second volume of *Time and Narrative*, Ricoeur discusses *Mrs. Dalloway* and remarks, "Overall, may we speak of a single experience of time in *Mrs. Dalloway?* No, insofar as the destinies of the characters and their worldviews remain juxtaposed." He refers to a "monumental time" in the novel "resulting from all the complicities between clock time and the figures of authority" (112).

8. See, in particular, the reviews of *The Hours* by Dana in *Rolling Stone*, July 10, 2003, 79; Giles in *Newsweek*, September 16, 2002, 55; Schickel in *Time*, December 23, 2002, 72; and Rozen in *People*, January 27, 2003, 29.

9. Kaysen, *Girl, Interrupted* (1993).

10. Hubert, *Questions of Power*, 99.

11. In a special "filmmaker's introduction" to the 2003 DVD release of the film, director Stephen Daldry invites his viewers to watch *The Hours* again and again, now that it is available on DVD. He says that he knows that they will find new and intriguing things to consider with each viewing. (For what it's worth, I agree with him.)

Bibliography

Cunningham, Michael. *The Hours.* New York: Farrar, Straus and Giroux, 1998.

Dana, Will. Review of *The Hours. Rolling Stone*, July 10, 2003.

Giles, Jeff. Review of *The Hours. Newsweek*, September 16, 2002.

Girl, Interrupted. Dir. James Mangold. Screenplay by James Mangold and others. Perf. Winona Ryder, Angelina Jolie, Clea DuVall. Red Wagon and Columbia Pictures, 1999.

The Hours. Dir. Stephen Daldry. Screenplay by David Hare. Perf. Nicole Kidman, Julianne Moore, Meryl Streep, Stephen Dillane. Miramax Films, 2002.

Hubert, Susan. *Questions of Power: The Politics of Women's Madness Narratives.* Newark: University of Delaware Press, 2002.

Kaysen, Susanna. *Girl, Interrupted.* New York: Turtle Bay Books, 1993.

Ricoeur, Paul. *Time and Narrative.* Volumes 1–3. Translated by Kathleen McLaughlin and David Pellauer. Chicago: University of Chicago Press, 1984, 1985, 1990.

Rozen, Leah. Review of *The Hours. People*, January 27, 2003.

Rukeyser, Muriel. "Children's Elegy." In *Out of Silence: Selected Poems*, edited by Kate Daniels, 97–100. Evanston, IL: Northwestern University Press, 1994.

Schickel, Richard. Review of *The Hours. Time*, December 23, 2002.

Travers, Peter. Review of *The Hours. Rolling Stone*, January 23, 2003.

Wiener, Diane. "Narrativity, Emplotment, and Voice in Autobiographical and Cinematic Representations of 'Mentally Ill' Women, 1942–2003." Ph.D. diss., University of Arizona, 2005.

Chapter 12

Therapy Culture and TV

The Sopranos as a Depression Narrative

Deborah Staines

Tony Soprano—big man—crashes to the ground beside his BBQ. This collapse seems precipitous, but only that morning he saw the young family of ducks that were nesting in the Soprano family *jardin* take to the air for the first time, take flight into new horizons. Witnessing this, mobster Tony Soprano (James Gandolfini) falls into unconsciousness.[1] And we begin our witnessing of Soprano family life.

The Sopranos (HBO, 1999–2007) has occasioned critical interest since it began broadcasting. Half a dozen books and any number of feature articles specifically on *The Sopranos* appeared within its first five years.[2] In the United States, it drove an unprecedented uptake of cable television, and garnered accolades from the broadsheet press and multiple Emmy Awards. The story of a hardwired mobster turning to therapy to resolve his anxieties, and the convolutions of his two families (Mob and kin), drew impressive ratings and a level of academic interest that has crossed the disciplines. In Australia, *The Sopranos* was critically well received although it could not claim high audience numbers; in an increasingly niche-oriented market, it retained a dedicated late-night audience averaging just under 500,000.[3] It appears that they appreciated its myriad intertextual ploys: a knowing reading of the "television text"[4] is anticipated by *Sopranos* scripts, in which the pleasure of the text derives in part from the reader's own agency in making it meaningful.[5] These scripts anticipate an audience whose relationship to the television medium has extended over many years; this audience is highly television literate, draws upon a large repertoire of popular media stories and images in its reception of the latest TV drama series, and is therefore productive rather than passive in the construction of televisual

165

meanings. What television means to this audience is vastly different from what it would have meant to audiences of a few decades ago, when "watching television" was first recognized as a complex cultural experience.[6]

Tony and his gang are therefore prime candidates for both psychoanalysis and textual analysis. One of the characters declares that Tony Soprano is a sociopath, and this claim is often repeated in critical appraisal of the series—usually in agreement.[7] At least one commentator has suggested that it is the audience who are depraved, for consuming *The Sopranos*.[8] Another finds it such a complex piece of popular culture that watching it must make people smarter.[9] What, then, does it mean to tell and consume this narrative of a depressed gangster through television? And, how does television travel when it starts performing psychotherapy? I argue that, aside from its mob narrative resonance, *The Sopranos* gains considerable audience recognition, at least in the West, from its intertextual connection with another, and even more prominent, Western text—the psychologized self.

Mob Narrative

The Sopranos builds on previous stories, and asks that its audience recognize the connections it is making. *The Godfather* (dir. Francis Ford Coppola, 1972) functions as the Ur-text of mob narrative. Or, put another way, "*The Godfather* . . . does not know itself as the object of cultural adulation,"[10] whereas in *The Sopranos*, key characters are constituted in relation to the *Godfather* trilogy, to *GoodFellas* (dir. Martin Scorsese, 1990), and a long history of gangster flicks. This "reified status of mob narrative" provides important reference points for intertextual scripting on *The Sopranos*.[11] Tony Soprano's mob family is thus always imagined in relation to the Corleone family, to the wiseguys of *GoodFellas*, to the gangster associates of *Casino* (dir. Scorsese, 1995) and *Donnie Brasco* (dir. Mike Newell, 1997). For example: when, in the closing scene of *GoodFellas*, gangster Henry Hill (Ray Liotta) nostalgically contemplates his past exploits from the quiet anonymity of FBI witness protection, he stands at the front of his bland suburban house wearing a bathrobe. The camera shot is from low—we view his legs. From the very same angle, the viewer of *The Sopranos* regularly sees Tony Soprano slouching down his paved suburban driveway to collect the morning paper and wearing a bathrobe. With this visual quotation, *The Sopranos* scriptwriters capture a diminished mob life, but demonstrate that Tony is far from being retrenched (literally or euphemistically) although business is not what it used to be. This kind of positioning locates *The Sopranos* within the history of mob narrative.

For a television product on the global market, genre hallmarks are an important part of the currency on exchange, perhaps especially when generic innovation is also part of the deal. *The Sopranos* astutely deploys its gangster genre credentials with convincing portrayals of contemporary organized crime. And then it plays around. One of the most cited episodes of Season One features a sharply written exchange around a dinner table that posits the centrality of lower-class gangsters to Italo-American identity, and those gangsters to narrative cinema, concluding that they are culturally iconic "just like Westerns."[12] This one exchange riffs on film theory, immigrant histories, and moral relativism. The same episode delivers a virtuoso performance from Tony's nephew, junior gangster Christopher Moltisanti (Michael Imperioli) articulating a paradoxical self-reflexivity: "It says in movie-writing books that every character has an arc, understand? . . . Where's my arc?" It is a classic example of *Sopranos* irony.

The status of television is also an important reference point. Although *The Godfather* is often mentioned, it is arguably Martin Scorsese's oeuvre that has had the greater influence on *Sopranos*' mise en scène.[13] Television barely existed in *The Godfather*. In *GoodFellas*, gangsters consume TV, but they are not its subject; instead, TV is sublimated as a typical Scorsese device for conveying subtext, era, and mood. In *The Sopranos*, television is finally given a prominent, plot-driving role, another example of the show's cultural reflexivity. In "The Legend of Tennessee Moltisanti," for example, television delivers the mobsters news of their impending arraignment for racketeering.

Another significant innovation of *The Sopranos* unwinds through the regular, story-rich sessions between depressed mobster Tony Soprano and his psychiatrist, and this is the main focus of my discussion. Tony's mental illness and subsequent therapy are recognizable to consumers as generic innovation, and the unpacking of his personal history has ramifications for all mob narrative to come.

Television and Psychotherapy Have Brought Us to This

Tony's faint leads him into therapy, with a diagnosis of "anxiety attacks" (Pilot, 1: 1). In therapy, Tony faces up to the emotions that surfaced when the ducks abandoned the hand-fed lifestyle he had provided, and took off on their own. He comes to understand that they signified a "family" to him, and that his attachments to family—his mother, father, wife and children, the mob—are also the source of his deepest fears and unresolved grief. Tony's faint slides him into treacherous terrain—not the dangers of mob killing and blood debts, but another secretive (yet related) domain: his unconscious and its armed gatekeepers. If you dreamt you were a murderer, you would probably want to wake up and find it isn't true. But if you were a murderer, perhaps you'd rather be left to sleep. Tony Soprano's particular rage and resistance to therapy is that of a murderer waking up to the effects of his pain, his savagery, and his criminal culpability. Tony's unconscious, eluding the gatekeepers, sends the first messages about his adult ambivalence to his current lifestyle; hence the physical collapse attributed to anxiety. It signals an impulse in Tony Soprano to undo some of his self-imposed blocks to self-knowledge. This criminal entity has been caught in his own prison, and now it appears he is unconsciously hoping for a new horizon. Enter Dr. Jennifer Melfi (Lorraine Bracco): professional, woman, psychiatrist.

The Sopranos gifts to us a view of the hidden working life of mobsters and their daily (meat) grind: assaults; labor racketeering; extortion; hijacking; bid-fixing; illegal gambling; tax evasion. Pornography. Kidnapping. Narcotics. Murder. Dr. Melfi's work is in a somewhat different register. Melfi borrows from such cinematic traditions as the female investigator and "the final girl" to discover and brave hidden horrors.[14] Melfi takes up a unique interrogatory position in the history of mob narrative. She asks the questions that have to be asked. She won't just go along with mob law, instead instituting the Law of Melfi: "Sad is good, unconscious isn't."[15] More specifically, unconsciousness as escapism and denial is not good, but the unconscious as source of knowledge is good.[16] On several occasions, Melfi clinically affirms the value of Tony's unconscious as a knowing state of mind. And she is not in the least indifferent to his interior landscape: it is a terrain that she becomes committed to exploring.

In another episode, after an accidental encounter between Tony and Jennifer Melfi at a restaurant, observed by Tony's dinner companions, gangster Big Pussy focuses on Melfi's lips; he thinks they would be "world class" for giving "blow jobs."[17] On the surface, this is just another round of misogynistic chit-chat among the fellas, insinuating that Melfi does the job on Tony. But this verbal spray is not so banal because Melfi does work with her mouth: as a psychiatrist, she does the job of the talking cure upon Tony. Furthermore, she is, in popular parlance, a *head*-doctor. If her work of therapy is ultimately designed to give "good head"—that is, address Tony's complaint of "feeling bad all the time" by making his head feel good again—then Melfi's mouth works for Tony even when she is saying "No" to him. If she could not make psychoanalytic interventions and articulate her refusal of his sexual advances, Melfi would be no different from many of the other characters seduced by Tony's charm. Moreover, unlike his mother Livia Soprano's (Nancy Marchand) refusals—to know, to remember, or to acknowledge—Melfi's refusals are accompanied by explanation, introducing Tony to a reasoning woman's boundaries.

In *The Sopranos*, therapy is integral to the emplotment of the central character's life story. Indeed, David Chase, the creator/director/producer of *The Sopranos*, has more than once asserted that the therapeutic dialogue established between Melfi and Tony Soprano was foundational to his concept of the show.[18] The techniques of serialized drama complement this depression narrative in a neat conjunction of medium and therapeutic message: the seriality of television is not unlike the seriality of sessions with a psychiatrist. In this stylish intersection of television culture and therapy culture, the cultural production (television serial) riffs on the therapeutic device (weekly visit). Serialized television drama enables a complex layering and point-counterpoint of narrative, across the duration of a broadcast season—just as the practice of analytical therapy can reveal and locate an individual's experience of episodic depression within the context of a lifetime. Tony's journey is rendered televisually via dream sequences, Freudian slips, and the weekly dialogue with Melfi.

The vagaries of interpersonal relationships are as much the substance of *The Sopranos* as of other television drama. Although unexpected in the gangster genre, these preoccupations enable a more complex mob narrative, enriched by a medium renowned for its capacity for intimacy. As one newspaper critic observed: "At its heart, *The Sopranos* is an exploration of relationships. . . . The life presented here is an uneasy equilibrium, always threatening to come apart as adversarial relationships dominate both families."[19] Nothing looms larger for the audience, who can treat as mere stage props the dirty politics and corrupt construction sites, the outcome of racketeering trials, and Tony's progress as capo, boss, and bidder for the New York family's failing empire—what they want is the theater of Tony Soprano and his dealings with people. For the audience tuning in, it is not coincidental that Tony and Melfi encounter each other over a glass-topped coffee table, in a low-light room, to transact a dialogue about feelings. This décor is typical of television soap opera, which in turn reflects the domestic setting of television viewing, enabling viewer identification. And Tony does talk. Despite many histrionics (which all derive from the conventions of feminine melodrama, especially TV soap operas—walking out, slamming doors, upsetting the coffee table, being coy on the phone), Tony talks about his feelings. Thus, the mob narrative's relocation from film to television enables a move from Hollywood's action-man mode of a diegesis-controlling hero/anti-hero to the more intimate relations of television.

But the therapeutic journey is complex. Tony demands something more linear from these sessions, like a path to coherent subjectivity, habitually asking, "Where is this getting me?" Tony's refrain is all about refusing to become a subject (the reconstructed male, the law-abiding citizen) he is reluctant to embody. Perhaps because waking up is hard to do: in the episode when Tony is shot as a result of his mother and uncle learning about his therapy, he jokes around in the hospital bed, still in denial; but his wife Carmella Soprano (Edie Falco) is not buying it:

TONY. Nothing's gonna happen.
CARMELLA. Wake up Tony—it already did.[20]

The analysand emerging from the therapist's office, searching for external signs of change that might reflect inner changes, is likely to be disappointed. Sessions are performed at a remove from the relational world they dissect. They may be fraught with tension and revelation. Then, after leaving therapy in a state of heightened perceptions (awakened), the analysand may reencounter his or her daily life with a level of dissonance. In Tony's case, the relationship between therapy and the rest of his life is depicted by associative visuals and montage—a life in which the red and white–checked tablecloths of the mob café, and the red meats and white-frosted fridges of Satriale's Pork Store, presage the red blood–splattered, pasty white skin of his murdered victims. Melfi's office is the fulcrum of Tony's individual journey and *The Sopranos'* meditation on human violence. There, in its restrained setting, Tony's physical ferocity can be, at least to himself, placed under scrutiny.

For the audience, too, *The Sopranos* represents a glimpse into a dangerous domain of volatile masculinity, violent confrontation, and unconscious desire. Watching the first episode, I commit a bit of my own intertextual play, recalling the chorus of an old Cold Chisel song, "Standing on the Outside." Chisel, an Australian pub-rock band, was always hypermasculine, yet also capable of baring the psychic wounds veiled by that macho discourse. "Standing on the Outside" is a song that would not be out of place on a *Sopranos* soundtrack, giving voice to an outsider on the edges of society tempted to "buy a .22 and cut the whole thing down."[21] In this context, the song's refrain also speaks to the position of a curious audience: standing on the outside looking in describes both Tony's relationship to his unconscious and our relationship to him. His epiphany with the ducks is our entrée into the disconcerting privilege of watching a criminal psyche turning itself inside out. Only time will tell how effective the therapeutic undoing of Tony's accreted ways of thinking and feeling will be. Despite Melfi's strenuous attempts to redefine choices for Tony, the audience is often given the message that there is no way out. As Tony fatalistically observes at one point: "There's only two ends for me—in prison, or dead." We, the audience, are standing on the outside, looking in on that self-destruction.

The Sopranos' success in the marketplace follows from this raw point of view. It embraces the gendered exchanges that, for example, see Melfi erupt into swearing or dress Tony down at a diner even as Tony removes the cutlery from her hands, unconsciously complimenting Melfi's discovery of one of his childhood traumas around his mother.[22] Or, in another example much later in the series, when he comes around the corner of the country house and blasts his cousin Little Tony with a shotgun, just one shot, end of story, and his victim's eyes seems to follow him with an accusation from all of the colleagues, friends, and relatives he has killed over the years.[23] These are scenes of tragedy and reveal some of the contortions of Tony's psyche. His escape from the law in the latter episode, through seasonal snow leading to wet socks and the banality of Carmella's wifely scolding, summarizes *Sopranos'* play on existential absurdity, even as it signals that the hegemony of masculine violence is "to be continued . . ."

Watching Therapy

Viewing the series in Australia, I relish the narrative innovation of the opening sequence, which takes us out of New York City. Driving through the New Jersey turnpike, Tony leaves this city of so many American dreamings, and the genuine historical location of celebrity mob lairs like the Bergen Hunt and Fish Club.[24] He's driving in his SUV, and the narrative is driven too—into the low-rise suburban drift of New Jersey. There is little glamour here. The camera casually trails past Pizzaland and Satriale's Pork Store, vital sites to the show, but set in a landscape of seeming indifference. So, how does this localized narrative travel in a globalized media market?

It says something about the broad accessibility of therapeutic discourse that Tony's story has such cogence with a commercial television audience. In today's Western societies, the central *Sopranos* narrative of mental illness and its accompanying tropes of anxiety, Prozac, unconscious denial and weekly therapy do not go unrecognized. *The Sopranos* is spinning a myth to initiates. Its intertextual plying of the discourses of psychotherapy and psychopharmacology are one of the main reasons, I argue, that it travels so well to audiences in North America, Europe, and Australia[25]—it's *our* thing to be talking therapy. If television sets up its own reading relations with the audience,[26] then mob narrative is not the only backstory that *The Sopranos* assumes of its viewers; a certain familiarity with therapy discourse is also useful. As Ellen Willis observed, *The Sopranos* meditates on the legacy of Freud for contemporary Western culture.[27] There are many dream sequences—indeed, it sometimes seems that Tony and Melfi's story cannot be told without Freud's *The Interpretation of Dreams* running in the background. Similarly, the narcissistic subtexts of personal growth, of grappling with desire, and failing to control the body and its appetites, situate viewers squarely in the *affluenza*-prone West.[28]

The Sopranos therefore raises and addresses questions about subjectivity in contemporary Western society, particularly how it is psychologized and medicalized. The scripts are informed by the genre of psychological literature and its array of descriptors for unconscious desires, conflicted socialization, and psychic wounds. This psychologizing of the subject is generally not under critique within the show.[29] Instead, the scripts use them to characterize Tony. Psychoanalytic terms are offered up to an audience who, while geographically distant, is anticipated to have a shared cultural exposure to the language of therapy. The modern Western experience of a psychologized existence is the cultural frame of reference that situates this narrative and its popular reception.

That the "public" medium of broadcast television is a site for the mediation of "private" subjectivity is argued by Frank Furedi in *Therapy Culture*, in which he criticizes the dissolution of private and public boundaries through "self-disclosure television."[30] Relying on British data, Furedi argues that contemporary Western society accommodates, validates, and encourages a therapeutic sensibility.[31] Similarly, Christina Hoff Sommers and Sally Satel in their polemical *One Nation Under Therapy* argue that this trend represents a commodification of suffering produced by "therapism" in the United States.[32] In Australia, *The Sopranos* made its debut at the same time as *beyondblue*, a federally funded initiative to address a statistical rise in clinical depression in Australian society, which received wide media coverage.[33] The interpretability of *The Sopranos* in the West supports the notion of a pervasive therapy culture; indeed, if the show did not successfully tap into a present identification and desire, why would it continue to be broadcast? The economics of television dictate that only the popular will survive.

Modern Western existence is bound by definitions of the normal and the pathological, definitions that utterly depend on each other, according to the foundational work by Georges Canguilhem: "Every conception of pathology must be based on prior knowledge of the corresponding normal state, but conversely, the scientific study of pathological cases becomes an indispensable phase in the overall search for laws of the normal state."[34] Further, according to Michel Foucault, the concepts of health and well-being are subject to epistemic shifts, suggesting that culture dictates the supposedly natural body.[35] The pathologizing of some mental states and not others, in other words, is given a normative force by culture. In today's context, Sommers and Satel call this a tendency toward "emotional correctness" and argue against a social imperative or cultural coercion into therapy.[36] Similarly, Furedi concludes that, far from fulfilling the liberatory narrative it is promoted as, therapy simply "teaches people to know their place."[37]

It is difficult to peg the exact parameters of Tony's clinical condition. He has been told by his general practitioner that he has panic attacks; Tony reports these as anxiety attacks, not panic attacks, to Melfi in the pilot episode (and the audience is invited to note this minor deception); but Melfi decides that Tony is suffering from depression, and puts him on Prozac. The ambiguity of his state is not uncommon; the border between anxiety and depression can be ill-defined.[38] In any case, Tony suffers, and deploys whatever defenses he can muster. Fortunately, his clinical status does not have to be determined here; my interest is in where the Western text of the self and the text of Tony Soprano intersect, and how these texts carry our cultural concerns. The idea that criminality be placed in relationship to therapy is not new. No doubt the *Sopranos* scriptwriters are cognizant of the industry of forensic psychological assessments of criminal behavior, and the contemporary literatures on wounded masculinity and anxiety. The nameless dread that Tony feels and that Melfi attempts to guide him toward exploring is closely linked to his brutal families. Familial dread is a recognized theme in late twentieth-century screen texts such as *Cape Fear* (dir. Scorsese, 1991) and the television series *Twin Peaks* (dir. David Lynch, 1990), and the traumatic afterlife of abuse is boldly claimed in the more recent *Mystic River* (dir. Clint Eastwood, 2003). So it is not surprising to find abuse and analysis as objects of a television narrative. Rather than asking why, we might be wondering why not sooner?

Western culture is not necessarily more obsessed with health at this point in time than ever before, but it has new tools with which to articulate this interest and give it cultural visibility, of which television is a prime example with its extensive range of medically themed dramas and reality shows. Through such television scripts, a contemporary emphasis on a subject's mental health is articulated in both the *techné* of psychology and the technology of digital media. Whether *The Sopranos* actually performs therapy is another matter; it displays, it portrays, it narrates—but is it therapeutic? And what would it mean for a TV show to do therapy? This must be an issue of increasing relevance to new media industries and to therapists, raising the possibility that television could redefine therapy.

Conclusion

American Mafia tales have often been the site for thinking through social discontent. Mob narrative has portrayed social conflicts associated with ethnicity, class, and gender, and *The Sopranos* too takes on issues of difference. When Tony's son Anthony Jr. (Robert Iler) reads and responds to Albert Camus' *The Outsider*, he acts as the mouthpiece for some of the existential questions that the show sifts through. While A. J. does not note that Existentialism peaked in the same era as the Mafia ruled the U.S. wharves, the audience can certainly speculate on its textual influence. Tony's confrontations with his inner dread, Melfi's analytical reflections on mortality, and Carmella's religiosity articulate a range of existential quandaries. Tony's life is an entanglement of forces he commits to both peaceable and violent actions, in which uncertainty constantly hovers.

Notes

For Dr. Jane Connell.

1. The real-life American Mafia, to which the fictional Tony Soprano belongs, was dominated by Italo-Americans and also known by the Sicilian phrase La Cosa Nostra or "this thing of ours."

2. See Lavery, *This Thing of Ours*; Gabbard, *The Psychology of the Sopranos*; and Barreca, ed., *A Sitdown with the Sopranos*.

3. The show attracted a middle-age grouping, possibly because its recurrent themes of mortality, divorce, moral ambivalence, and unremitting struggle are less palatable to those in younger demographics: "*The Sopranos* doesn't reach the top 100 for either the general audience or the groovers. Insofar as AC Nielsen can identify any viewers, they tend to be men 40 to 54 and women 25 to 39." See "Never Mind the Quality, Feel the Niche," *Sydney Morning Herald News Review,* May 5, 2001.

4. See Williams, *Television*.

5. Barthes, *The Pleasure of the Text,* 27.

6. Fiske, *Television Culture,* 99; Williams, *Television*.

7. Buchanan, "All the World Loves a Sociopath."

8. Cited in Lavery, *This Thing of Ours,* xii.

9. Johnson, *Everything Bad Is Good for You*.

10. Messenger, *The Godfather and American Culture,* 257–61.

11. Ibid.

12. "The Legend of Tennessee Moltisanti," *Sopranos* 1:8.

13. See Stern, *The Scorsese Connection*.

14. See Clover, *Men, Women, and Chainsaws*. The "final girl" is a proud convention of horror films, as the one who endures the worst but survives to slay the monster. For a reading of the female investigator as a final girl, see Tasker, *The Silence of the Lambs*.

15. "46 Long," *Sopranos* 1:2.

16. Quite a few of the Sopranos injured end up in comas—symbolizing, perhaps, a tendency toward denial that ultimately catches up with them.

17. "Toodle-fucking-oo," *Sopranos* 2:3.

18. Lavery, *This Thing of Ours*; also see Lavery and Thompson, "David Chase, *The Sopranos,* and Television Creativity," 21.

19. Casimir, "Don't Miss This."

20. "Isabella," *Sopranos* 1:12.

21. Words and music by Don Walker, Rondor Music, 1980.

22. "Guy Walks into a Psychiatrist's Office," *Sopranos* 2:1.

23. "All Due Respect," *Sopranos* 5:13.

24. A hangout of the real-life New York gangster John Gotti. See Cummings and Volkman, *Goombata*.

25. The markets highlighted by Lavery in his introduction, xi.

26. Fiske, 84–127.

27. Willis, "Our Mobsters, Ourselves," 2.

28. See De Graaf et al., *Affluenza*.

29. Nor are they under critique in the literature that focuses on the therapy, generally applauding its realism; see Gabbard, *The Psychology of the Sopranos*.

30. *Therapy Culture*, 40.

31. Ibid., 49.

32. *One Nation Under Therapy*, 6.

33. *beyondblue: the national depression initiative.*

34. Canguilhem, *The Normal and the Pathological*, 51.

35. Foucault, *Madness and Civilization*; *The History of Sexuality*, Volume 1.

36. *One Nation Under Therapy*, 110.

37. *Therapy Culture*, 204.

38. The lack of distinction between anxiety and depression coincides rather too neatly, some say, with the commercialization of the selective serotonin reuptake inhibitor class of medications. See Healy, *Let Them Eat Prozac*, 19.

Bibliography

Barreca, Regina, ed. *A Sitdown with the Sopranos: Watching Italian American Culture on TV's Most Talked-About Series.* New York: Palgrave Macmillan, 2002.

Barthes, Roland. *The Pleasure of the Text.* Translated by Richard Miller. New York: Hill and Wang, 1975.

beyondblue: the national depression initiative. http://www.beyondblue.org.au

Buchanan, Matt. "All the World Loves a Sociopath." *Sydney Morning Herald*, Spectrum, July 7, 2001.

Camus, Albert. *The Outsider.* 1946. Translated by Joseph Laredo. Harmondsworth, UK: Penguin, 1983.

Canguilhem, Georges. *The Normal and the Pathological.* New York: Zone Books, 1989.

Casimir, Jon. "Don't Miss This." *Sydney Morning Herald, Guide*, November 15, 1999.

Clover, Carol. *Men, Women, and Chainsaws: Gender in the Modern Horror Film.* Princeton, NJ: Princeton University Press, 1992.

Cummings, John, and Ernest Volkman. *Goombata: The Improbable Rise and Fall of John Gotti and His Gang.* Boston: Little, Brown, 1990.

De Graaf, John, David Wann, and Thomas H. Naylor. *Affluenza: The All-Consuming Epidemic.* San Francisco, CA: Berrett-Koehler, 2001.

Fiske, John. *Television Culture.* London and New York: Routledge, 1997.

Foucault, Michel. *The History of Sexuality, Volume 1: An Introduction.* Translated by Robert Hurley. Harmondsworth, UK: Peregrine (Penguin), 1984.

———. *Madness and Civilization: A History of Insanity in the Age of Reason.* Translated by Richard Howard. 1965. London: Routledge, 1993.

Freud, Sigmund. *The Interpretation of Dreams.* Translated and edited by James Strachey. 1899. Harmondsworth, UK: Penguin, 1978.

Furedi, Frank. *Therapy Culture.* London: Routledge, 2004.

Gabbard, Glen O. *The Psychology of the Sopranos: Love, Death, Desire and Betrayal in America's Favorite Gangster Family.* New York: Basic Books, 2002.

Healy, David. *Let Them Eat Prozac: The Unhealthy Relationship between the Pharmaceutical Industry and Depression.* New York: New York University Press, 2004.

Johnson, Steven. *Everything Bad Is Good for You: How Today's Popular Culture Is Actually Making Us Smarter.* London: Allen Lane, 2005.

Lavery, David, ed. *This Thing of Ours: Investigating the Sopranos.* New York: Columbia University Press, 2002.

———, and Robert J. Thompson. "David Chase, *The Sopranos,* and Television Creativity." In Lavery, *This Thing of Ours,* 18–25.

Messenger, Chris. *The Godfather and American Culture: How the Corleones Became "Our Gang."* Albany: State University of New York Press, 2002.

Sommers, Christina Hoff, and Sally Satel. *One Nation Under Therapy: How the Helping Culture is Eroding Self-Reliance.* New York: St. Martin's Press, 2005.

Stern, Lesley. *The Scorsese Connection.* Bloomington: BFI/ Indiana University Press, 1995.

Tasker, Yvonne. *The Silence of the Lambs.* London: BFI Modern Classics, 2002.

United States Congress. Racketeer Influenced and Corrupt Organizations (RICO) Act. Title 18, United States Code, Sections 1961–1968.

Williams, Raymond. *Television: Technology and Cultural Form.* London: Fontana, 1974.

Willis, Ellen. "Our Mobsters, Ourselves." In Lavery, *This Thing of Ours,* 2–9.

Films

Cape Fear. Dir. Martin Scorsese. Universal, 1991.

Casino. Dir. Martin Scorsese. Universal, 1995.

Donnie Brasco. Dir. Mike Newell. Baltimore, 1997.

The Godfather. Dir. Francis Ford Coppola. Paramount, 1972.

GoodFellas. Dir. Martin Scorsese. Warner Bros., 1990.

Mystic River. Dir. Clint Eastwood. Warner Bros., 2003.

Television

The Sopranos. Writ. David Chase and others. HBO, 1999–2007.

Twin Peaks. Dir. David Lynch. ABC, 1990.

Music

Cold Chisel. "Standing on the Outside." *Cold Chisel.* Words and music by Don Walker. Sydney: Rondor Music, 1980.

IV

Literary Therapies

Chapter 13

For the Relief of Melancholy

The Early Chinese Novel as Antidepressant

Andrew Schonebaum

A world of change faced literate men in late imperial China. It was harder to gain official employment than it ever had been before. The civil service examinations that determined the amount of official responsibility and compensation had become so crowded with candidates that success was virtually impossible. Odds were also reduced by increasing graft and the practice of purchasing office by those rich merchants who, despite their wealth, were otherwise looked down upon. Literati had been turning to other professions, such as tutor, doctor, editor, or author, for a few centuries, in greater numbers near the end of the Ming dynasty (1368–1644) and in still greater numbers during the Qing dynasty (1644–1911) when Manchu rulers were even less inclined to appoint Chinese to office.[1] It was a tough time to be a man of letters.

This was the time that the novel began to establish itself as a new and important genre in China. The situation of literati, turning their esteemed hobbies into mundane, practical professions, is likely why the Chinese novel has a particularly encyclopedic nature. After spending their youth memorizing philosophical and historical texts, literati who failed the official exams and turned to writing were often simultaneously learning to practice a trade. The late imperial Chinese novel, identified by unity of plot, structural coherence, and single authorship, in contradistinction to folk novels with their patchwork of traditional stories, incorporated a broad range of practical knowledge. It seems that early novelists in China turned to vernacular literature in part to display their knowledge of medicine, science, architecture, design, and poetry; the new genre accommodated (and later served as) encyclopedic texts, portrayed quotidian life, entertained the reader with complex plots, and enabled literati to criticize the system that turned them into novelists.

One of the first, if not *the* first, of these late imperial novels, published in 1618 or shortly thereafter, is the *Jin Ping Mei* or *Plum in the Golden Vase*, the original title of which carries the designation *cihua*, a new term in the last half of the sixteenth century loosely applied to works of vernacular fiction that contain examples of verse.[2] Along with later novels such as *Honglou Meng* (*The Story of the Stone* or *Dream of the Red Chamber*), *Jin Ping Mei* is aware of its divergence from the previously established form of the vernacular "folk" novel that developed from traditions of oral storytellers, in its more detailed mode of literary representation and in its shift from the epic to the mundane and domestic, more developed characterization, and more sustained plots. *Jin Ping Mei* incorporates an almost encyclopedic range of texts and genres such as jokes, popular songs, comic skits, and short stories and verse, all made available to a wider audience than ever before because of the contemporary boom in commercial publishing. These varieties of texts are incorporated into the narrative in a highly reflexive way, constantly drawing attention to the structure of the novel. In addition to these varied texts that constituted the author's work, novels circulated in popular commentary editions laden with paratexts before, after, above, and actually within the lines of narrative themselves. While the novel was written in lines of single characters, commentary was added in a smaller typeset, surrounding the text, bookending the page, chapters, and the entire novel. Often, double lines of commentary were printed within a line of the novel text at the end of sentences, like a long parenthetical comment. This multiplicity of texts creates a discourse about the novel itself, its literary uses, and its production of knowledge all within the covers of the book held in the reader's hands.

The early Chinese novel needed to be defended against accusations of pornography, baseness, moral depravity, and corruption of the literary tradition, especially in the Qing dynasty with its official sponsorship of strict neo-Confucian mores and frequent banning and sometimes burning of books.[3] Since most novels were published in (often illustrated) commentary editions, which were much more popular than unadorned editions of the same work, readers found in the prefaces and commentary explicit and implicit apologies for the novel genre in general and each work in particular. These justifications often used medical discourse not just to defend the novel, but to prescribe it.

The Chinese novel incorporated discussions of medical theory and practice among other topics. The apologetic prefaces and commentaries often borrowed medical rhetoric and did their part to create a medical knowledge of the novel and to portray the novel as having medicinal qualities. Plots were described as being as complex as the conduits of the circulatory system, and the author was described as an able doctor who could elucidate hidden complications in the body of the text. The rise of the novel in China also coincided with the rise of the medical case history genre. There are clear links between the two forms, in borrowed critical terminology, in publishing history, and in the sympathetic and detailed portrayal of the patient.[4] The Chinese novel focuses more than any of its fictional predecessors and more than most of its contemporary medical texts on the centrality of medical practice in the actual lives of the literati. The novel was innovative in its focus on the character as patient, on his or her experience of disease, on the details of his or her treatment and convalescence. Not only is the patient described lovingly within the narrative, but the reader of the novel is also described as a sufferer of these illnesses by the novel paratexts. Literati wrote about literati. The diseases of characters were the diseases of readers, and with regard to certain maladies, prefaces to novels made that connection explicit. This stance was useful, because not only did the reader relate to character and author, but the novel, as it claimed of itself, could serve as preventative medicine and palliative, and further, if used correctly, as cure.

Claims defending the novel usually argued that the novel and its characters served as a negative role model for readers, that if they realized how risky it is to behave in such a manner, they would avoid illnesses of depletion and congestion that accompany excessive intercourse or excessive emotionality. In tandem with this argument—that the novel served an important purpose in its implied warning—was another claim: that the novel was actually medicine for a particular type of person predisposed to suffering from melancholy, depression, and neurasthenia.[5] This person is likely the type of literatus who would read or write a novel. As expressed in the preface to the *Jin Ping Mei cihua*:

> Of the seven feelings (*qing*) natural to mankind, melancholy (*youyu*) is the most intractable. For such men of superior wisdom as may occasionally appear in the natural course of evolution, the fogs and ice that melancholy engenders disperse and splinter of their own accord, so there is no need to speak of such as these. Even those of lesser endowment know how to dispel melancholy with the aid of reason. . . . Among the many who fall short of this, however, who have been unable to achieve enlightenment in their hearts, and who do not have access to the riches of the classic tradition to alleviate their melancholy, those who do not fall ill are few. It is in consideration of this fact that my friend . . . has poured the accumulated wisdom of a lifetime into the composition of this work.[6]

It was common enough to defend the novel genre by citing tribulations of the unemployed literati, the official outsiders of the influential elite, but to claim that the novel exists for the purpose of warding off melancholy was something new. Late imperial literati were often interested in emotions, putting a primacy on feeling as the basis of aesthetics: this interest is often discussed in scholarship as "the cult of *qing*" that emerged in seventeenth and eighteenth centuries. *Qing*, having evolved over time from feelings, came to mean something more like "passion" and "desire," and their accompanying sadness, anxiety, and melancholy when unfulfilled. This, in turn, led to a refiguring of the beautiful, feminine body as something more frail and weak, more subject to extreme fluctuations of passion and sadness. The literati aesthetic ideal was a weak and fragile maiden and, in turn, to be one having the sensibilities to be attracted to such beauty. Depression, then, was something that should affect men and women at the same rate.[7] The fad of literati culture at the time was both to feel the vicissitudes of passion and to be one who admires that quality in others, despite, or perhaps due to, its potential health hazards. Yet the preface to *Jin Ping Mei* claims that it does not harm its readers, but that it merely brings them to the threshold:

> It is scarcely to be denied that in this work the language encroaches on the vulgar and the atmosphere is redolent of rouge and powder. But I would assert that such allegations miss the point. [It is like] the first song in the *Shijing* [*The Book of Songs*] that has been characterized by Confucius as expressing "pleasure that does not lead to wantonness and sorrow that does not lead to injury."[8]

That is, *Jin Ping Mei* was written to help readers avoid the dangers of melancholy. To this end, it claimed to be careful not to elicit extremes of emotion from them.

Chronic illness is new in the late Ming and early Qing dynasty fictional narrative, and so is depression.[9] Before *Jin Ping Mei* (and frequently after), excessive emotion was described as dangerous to one's health, but in a very potent, sudden, and often fatal way. It was not uncommon in the Chinese literary tradition to see characters dying of frustrated rage, shock, or a sudden onset of sadness or laughter. But the representation of the long-term accommodation to melancholy and other illnesses was innovative. The cult of *qing*, the incorporation of medical texts and rhetoric into the novel and novel commentary, the need to justify the novel against accusations that it elicits harmful extremes of emotion, all contributed to the late imperial Chinese novel's claim to be an antidepressant.[10]

The preface to the *cihua* edition of *Jin Ping Mei* claims that the novel cures melancholy, or rather, it prevents melancholy-related illnesses common among a certain kind of reader. Those who are usually free from such worries are the very intelligent and very educated. That means that *Jin Ping Mei* at once admits to being less literary than the great, instructive literature of the Confucian canon and also claims to be of equal value in keeping its particular readers healthy. The preface makes a claim for the novel as popular, literati medicine. It goes on to say that the novel instructs the reader on how to observe the correct human relationships and how to avoid excesses, and while it may be its teachings that prevent illness in the long run, the clever construction of the story and the charming rhetoric are the sugar on the pill.[11]

The reader will be so enticed by the structure and language of the novel, says the author of the preface, that he may be "beguiled into forgetting his melancholy."[12] This is preventative medicine. By giving the reader a certain amount of licentiousness to consider, the author intrigues him enough to forget his melancholy and illness caused by excessive worry, sadness, or desire. On the other hand, the author does not exceed prescribed amounts of risqué subject matter, as to do so would lead to injury. This concern—not about the text and its direct influence on the health of the reader, but about the ability of the reader to control his delight in the novel, to read for the moral significance and not to imitate or admire the characters—is made explicit in a preface to the 1695 Zhang Zhupo commentary edition.[13] Certainly, if the reader were to try to emulate the characters, not only would he be putting himself in a great deal of danger but also he would be showing himself to be a poor reader, unable to understand the significance of what the author is saying, and thus deserving the sort of illnesses brought on by uncontrolled emotional excess.

The preface claims that *Jin Ping Mei* is a kind of surrogate for the classics, and that its instruction, which focuses on the benefits and dangers of particular behaviors, can heal readers. The novel is not only formally structured like the circulatory system but also healing for its readers because its medical discourse is medicine. In an instance that might serve as an example of the influence of paratexts on the reader, Zhang Zhupo writes in his prefatory essay, "Zhupo Xianhua":

> More recently, oppressed by poverty and grief, and goaded by "heat and cold," when time weighed heavily on my hands, I came to regret that I had not myself composed a book about the way of the world in order to relieve my depression. Several times I was on the point of setting pen to paper but was deterred by the amount of planning which the overall structure required.

And so I laid aside my pen and said to myself, "Why don't I carefully work out the means by which this predecessor of mine constructed his book on 'heat and cold.' In the first place this task
will relieve my depression; and, in the second place, my elucidation of the work of my predecessor can count as an equivalent
for my own planning of a book in the present."[14]

Zhang goes along with the notion that *Jin Ping Mei* can cure melancholy,
just as stated in the earlier *cihua* preface, and he also accepts the preface's implication that one text can substitute for another as a means to
curb excessive emotion, in particular that of melancholy. Instead of writing his own novel, Zhang will elucidate his favorite theme in *Jin Ping Mei*,
which will serve as his creation. Writing commentary, a record of his
reading of *Jin Ping Mei*, is therapy. In line with the implication that this
novel serves in the stead of the classics as a curative for idle or underemployed literati, Zhang uses *Jin Ping Mei* as a proxy for his creation
in order to doctor his own melancholy.

The use of fictional text as medicine was a new idea in the late
Ming, with the rise of private reading and the spread of literacy. Just a
few decades after the early publications of *Jin Ping Mei*, Li Yu writes in his
Xianqing Ouji (*Casual Expressions of Idle Feeling*):

That which was never before seen in one's life can be taken as
medicine. To want what one has never possessed is a desire all
men have. This is like [the feeling of] men of letters toward
marvelous and strange books. . . . To allow these persons to
see these objects, to find these especially under difficult conditions, this is the technique whereby to manage and control
the patient. . . . What I mean by "men of letters" does not necessarily refer only to those with talent [but] rather all who are
literate, who can read, who can use books as medicine.[15]

It is clear that among literati, there was a feeling that they were particularly
susceptible to depression because of their sensibilities and that books, particularly novels, could and should be used as treatment. Their literacy
made them candidates for melancholy, yet literature could cure them. All
of this cast literati without official employment as a sick class, below those
whose constitutions were sustained by the Confucian classics yet nobler in
their suffering and depression than those who could not read.

Positing novels as a cure for melancholy, whether reading or writing them, was a logical next step from the traditional kinds of therapies
invoked to deal with the illnesses brought on by excessive emotionality.
Wu Kun, writing in his *Yi Fang Kao* (*Researches on Medical Formulas*) of

1584, discusses the mode of treatment Nathan Sivin terms "emotional counter-therapy":

> When emotion is overwhelmingly excessive, no drug can cure [the resulting disorder]; it must be overcome by emotion. Thus it is said that "anger damages the hepatic system, but sorrow overcomes anger; joy damages the cardiac system, but apprehension overcomes joy; worry damages the splenetic system, but anger overcomes worry; sorrow damages the pulmonary system, but joy overcomes sorrow; apprehension damages the renal system, but worry overcomes apprehension." A single saying from the Inner Canon, and a hundred generations have venerated it! These are immaterial medicines.[16]

This kind of therapy, the belief that illnesses are caused by forces and treated with their complimentary opposite force, was nothing new in medicine, but the focus specifically on emotion and on emotional manipulations emerged only in the late imperial period.[17] Sorrow cures Anger, Anger cures Worry, Worry cures Apprehension, Apprehension cures Joy, Joy cures Sorrow, and Sorrow cures Anger, all neatly in accord with five-phases theory medicine dating back to the *Huangdi Neijing* (*Yellow Emperor's Classic of Internal Medicine*).[18] That a lascivious novel, or any novel, with its base vernacular and intricate tales could provide the kind of controlled joy that would cure a reader or writer of his sorrow, ennui, or melancholy was a claim consistent with contemporary medical thinking. The novel is emotional counter-therapy for melancholy.[19]

As for the representation of "depression" in the Chinese novel, the most notable accounts begin in 1792, with the publication of what is generally agreed to be the greatest of all Chinese novels. In order to appreciate the position of *Honglou Meng* (*The Story of the Stone* or *Dream of the Red Chamber*) in Chinese culture, we must, as Dore Levy writes, "imagine a work with the critical cachet of James Joyce's *Ulysses* and the popular appeal of Margaret Mitchell's *Gone with the Wind*—and twice as long as both combined."[20] Twenty chapters longer than *Jin Ping Mei*, but demonstrably indebted to it, *Honglou Meng* also chronicles the moral and financial decline of a once-noble house. In addition to the structural and thematic borrowings, both novels suggest a similar culture of reading, one of using novels as encyclopedias and as medicine.

One of the major plots of *Honglou Meng* follows the effeminate hero, Jia Baoyu, through adolescence and the ultimate thwarting of his seemingly karmic relationship with Lin Daiyu. The reader witnesses Baoyu's first sexual encounters, his constant concern for the welfare and feelings of the many women in his household, the awakening of his romantic feelings for

Daiyu, his eventual marriage to another woman, and his ultimate enlightenment and escape from the attachment of human relationships.

The author, Cao Xueqin, on whom it has often been argued the character of Baoyu is based, is quoted by his brother in a preface[21] to the novel that recounts its writing:

> Having made an utter failure of my life, I found myself one day, in the midst of my poverty and wretchedness, thinking about the female companions of my youth. As I went over them one by one, examining and comparing them in my mind's eye, it suddenly came over me that those slips of girls—which is all they were then—were in every way, both morally and intellectually, superior to the "grave and mustachioed signior" I am now supposed to have become. The realization brought with it an overpowering sense of shame and remorse, and for a while I was plunged into the deepest despair. There and then I resolved to make a record of all the recollections of those days I could muster—those golden days when I dressed in silk and ate delicately, when we still nestled in the protecting shadow of the Ancestors and Heaven still smiled on us. . . . In this way the memorial to my beloved girls could at one and the same time serve as a source of entertainment and as a warning to those who were in the same predicament as myself but who were still in need of awakening.[22]

Cao imagines a community of readers who are like himself: poor, outcast, filled with regret and nostalgia and in need of a palliative. Other prefaces (at least one of which is written by the author) prepare the reader to think of himself as a patient suffering from depression, and relate that experience to the condition of Jia Baoyu and Lin Daiyu. Baoyu is described as a sensitive boy prone to melancholy, depression, and, in two instances, insanity. Additionally, Baoyu is portrayed as being particularly effeminate. He says that "girls are made of water and boys are made of mud. When I am with girls I feel fresh and clean, but when I am with boys I feel stupid and nasty."[23] Baoyu surreptitiously eats lipstick on occasion and associates primarily with his female cousins and their maids. Daiyu, the other half of this pair of star-crossed lovers, is particularly afflicted by bouts of depression and "static congestion," and became among readers an archetype of the frail, wasting, beautiful young woman. Both characters are feminine and highly literate, with highly developed poetic sensibilities despite their youth. To some extent, *Honglou Meng* is about this relationship between two hypersensitive young people who are frequently making themselves sick with worry or sorrow.

Considering the emotional excess to which Baoyu and Daiyu are inclined, and the ultimate thwarting of their relationship, it might seem strange that the author believes that such a story can cure literati readers who suffer from similar ailments. Cao Xueqin writes in the first pages of *Honglou Meng*:

> My only wish is that men in the world below may sometimes pick up this tale when they are recovering from sleep or drunkenness, or when they wish to escape from business worries or a fit of the dumps, and in doing so find not only mental refreshment but even perhaps, if they will heed its lesson and abandon their vain and frivolous pursuits, some small arrest in the deterioration of their vital forces.[24]

This novel, like *Jin Ping Mei*, is both preventative medicine and palliative. It serves as a guidebook for identifying dangerous behaviors and extremes of emotion, and also removes the reader from his melancholy by engrossing him in a finely wrought work of fiction. It warns against the sort of excessive longing that can result in the loss of yang essence if matters are taken into the reader's own hands, and describes the dangers of excessive female emotion and desire that result in depression and "static congestion."

But the novel does not just distract the reader; it can cure him. It both presents examples of a late imperial belief in emotional counter-therapy and is a part of that therapy for the reader. The treatment of the ills brought on by excess of one emotion by bringing on its opposite emotion, or employing a drug that would have the same effect, became quite commonplace in medical texts of the mid-to-late Qing dynasty.[25] *Honglou Meng* suggests that this kind of counter-therapy is the only cure for depression and its attendant illnesses. One of the first things the reader learns about Lin Daiyu is that she is congenitally sick because of sadness. When she was very young, her mother became ill, and "she helped with the nursing throughout her mother's last illness and mourned for her bitterly after her death. The extra strain this placed on her always delicate constitution brought on a severe attack of a recurrent sickness, and for a long time she was unable to pursue her lessons."[26] When Daiyu first comes to live in the Jia household, she remarks of her illness:

> I have always been like this. . . . I have been taking medicine ever since I could eat and been looked at by ever so many well-known doctors, but it has never done me any good. Once, when I was only three, I can remember a scabby-headed old monk came and said he wanted to take me away and have me brought up as a nun; but of course Mother and Father wouldn't hear of

it. So he said, "Since you are not prepared to give her up, I am afraid her illness will never get better as long as she lives. The only way it might get better would be if she were never to hear the sound of weeping from this day onwards and never to see any relations other than her own mother and father."[27]

Daiyu suggests that the monk (who later cures Baoyu of his emotionally based illnesses) is crazy. The reader knows from the first episode in the novel, however, that Daiyu in a previous incarnation incurred a debt of life to Baoyu, and will have to repay that debt with her own tears. The reader knows the monk is right in saying that if Daiyu, who is predisposed to melancholy, could be prevented from having relationships outside of her immediate family, and could be sheltered from sorrow that would exacerbate her condition, her melancholy-related illness might remain latent. Yet, the reader also knows that she is fated to become depressed and thus repay her debt of tears.

The novel's claim that it will take the reader's mind off his worries is based on the same medical theory of emotional counter-therapy (and combines it in a complicated way with the notion of retribution, *bao*). The claims of the author and preface seem to contradict themselves since Daiyu comes to such a tragic end, suggesting that such therapy only works if one is not already fated to die. The men reading the novel, though, might have found inspiration in Baoyu who is able to break free of worldly attachments and concerns at the end of the novel, having overcome severe sickness brought on by excessive worry for the girls in his life. They would certainly find joy in the finely wrought novel and the beautiful poetry within.

Emotional counter-therapy in the Ming and Qing also included the use of herbal drugs. Further, the author of *Honglou Meng* makes the claim that it is the nature of the novel genre itself that enables its use as a drug. Such writing in the vernacular would entertain and warn a wider audience than scholarship, and it is able to *represent* a contemporary dilemma of aesthetics and health. Indeed, it is not the subject but the representation itself that makes the novel useful as medicine:

> Surely my "number of females," whom I spent half a lifetime studying with my own eyes and ears, are preferable to [unofficial histories, erotic novels, and talented-scholar-beautiful-maiden stories]. I do not claim that they are better people than the ones who appear in books written before my time; I am only saying that the contemplation of their actions and motives may prove a more effective antidote to depression and melancholy.[28]

There is a paradox here, that the contemplation of the melancholy, frail woman will cure the depressed and disenfranchised man. The resolution seems to lie in the mediating effects of representation, which moderates extremes of emotion and puts at a remove from the reader those characters that fall ill from harmful excesses of melancholy.

The inability of literate women to use literature as antidepressant, on the other hand, was celebrated by men as an extension of the aesthetics of the frail, melancholic woman. Even before the introduction of Western medicine and the popularization of Western literature that melodramatized the consumptive and beautiful young waif, China had developed a tradition that made similar illnesses quite desirable.[29] As David Hawkes says of the heroine of *Honglou Meng*, "Every languishing young lady imagined herself a Daiyu."[30] This trend in readership mirrored an earlier one that produced and consumed works such as the "three wives' commentary" on the Ming drama *Mu Dan Ting* (*The Peony Pavilion*) in which women readers, overly sympathizing with the plights of lovesick heroines, die from that overemotionality.[31] If the reader reception of the two texts is not identical, the fact that Lin Daiyu and Xue Baochai, the ailing, beautiful young women in *Honglou Meng*, both admit to having read or memorized passages from *The Peony Pavilion* indicates a shared pathology with the three wives and other female readers of such literature. The heroine of *The Peony Pavilion*, Du Liniang, dies from lovesickness and melancholy brought on by desire conceived in a dream. The figure of Du Liniang "sparked a rage that one modern Chinese critic [Wang Yongjian] has likened to the vogue for young Werther that seized Europe in the late eighteenth century"; such a vogue contributed, in particular, to the fact that *The Peony Pavilion* had repeatedly found "discerning and sympathetic readers among the fair sex, who intensely identified with Du Liniang."[32] Judith Zeitlin remarks that "the recurrent cultural myths about the deaths of the readers, commentators and actresses who come in contact with *The Peony Pavilion* point to an infectious danger emanating from the play—the allure of women dying young and the exquisite pleasure and pain produced in contemplating those deaths."[33] That is, desire and depression were dangerous and contagious— transmitted through literature and culture. Women were less able to use literature as medicine, apparently, having their desire and depression exacerbated by reading tragic romances and consequently falling ill themselves. The popularity of such myths among male readers suggests that they found such emotional attachment alluring and endearing. As well, they could have felt confident in their superiority as readers who were able to appreciate aesthetic representation more dispassionately, to engage in emotional counter-therapy, and to use novels as medicine.

The fact that both female protagonists and the male protagonist of *Honglou Meng* are drawn to *The Peony Pavilion* is another extratextual indicator of the characters' melancholy and romantic sensibilities. The second line of a title couplet to chapter 23 of *Honglou Meng* reads, "Songs from *The Peony Pavilion* move a tender heart to anguish," and in three other chapters the play is mentioned by name. The lexicon of forbidden and dangerous texts becomes the language through which these melancholy and passionate young characters communicate. Understandings and misunderstandings in the courtship of Baoyu and Daiyu are based on references to *The Peony Pavilion*.[34] That is, their desire is expressed through texts of desire, resulting inevitably in misreading, melancholy, and heartbreak. The reader of *Honglou Meng* continues this tradition of reading and sympathizing with lovesick and depressed characters. He reads of characters that read *The Peony Pavilion* and is reminded by the prefaces that he is also engaging in a culturally and historically specific practice of treating himself with texts that represent frail and melancholic characters. The reader heals himself, but if he engages in misreading, in sympathizing too much, that very therapy can exacerbate his condition.

Honglou Meng paradoxically serves as a watershed moment in the history of depression and narrative in China. On the one hand, it develops the archetype of the beautiful young girl, depressed because she has internalized too much passion and desire, and consumptive from the resulting static congestion. She now suffers from chronic depression rather than simply dying of unfulfilled desire like her predecessor, Du Liniang in *The Peony Pavilion*. On the other hand, *Honglou Meng* diverges from tradition in presenting the illness as something that afflicts male readers, and offers to cure them by presenting representations of extreme desire and melancholy, which will both warn them against, and cause them to forget, their own.

The novel fits in a complex way into existing beliefs about medical theory, retribution, gender, and the function of texts, particularly encyclopedic fictional texts. The practice of ingesting textual talismans was old, but that of going to the pharmacy and purchasing medicine taken by popular characters in novels was an innovation. The claim by prefaces and commentary that their novels could cure melancholy was not a simple metaphor; it incorporated, reflected, and advanced medical theory and practice. The ability to escape into a fictional world that was less epic and more domestic, something to which the reader could relate, was a palliative that immediately put a distance between the reader and his life concerns. The story itself and presentation of characters gave readers examples of what not to do when feeling depressed, namely to allow those emotions to become so excessive as to harm the body and cause physical illnesses. In this respect the novel was preventative medicine. Yet sympathizing or being repelled by these characters through the mediation of fiction could also provide the emotions of joy and anger that countered and cured those of sorrow or worry. Though it was widely believed that women were prone to dangerous excesses of emotion and were less able to control their feelings, the novel claimed that it was an antidepressant— emotional counter-therapy for those who knew how to use it.

Notes

1. In premodern China, the vast majority of literate people were men, and those who failed the examinations for official employment were exclusively men. Although some women (invariably of wealthy families) were literate, the literati class primarily designates men, and increasingly those men who had to find alternate professions.

2. This work has long been known in the west as "Golden Lotus" but is now becoming available in a complete, annotated, scholarly translation by David Roy, published as *Plum in the Golden Vase*. Translations of the *Jin Ping Mei* in this chapter follow his.

3. The "literary inquisition" of Qianlong (1736–1795) in the late 1770s and early 1780s is the most notorious of these, though lists of banned books were not uncommon before then.

4. See my article "The Medical Casebook of *Honglou Meng*."

5. Psychiatry is an invention of nineteenth-century Europe and, as such, it is not really accurate to speak of "depression" and "neurasthenia" in premodern China. Yet the basis of Chinese medicine is that psyche and soma are intimately connected; any major fluctuations in emotionality would have dangerous consequences for the body and vice versa. In Chinese medical texts we find terms that translate as "sadness," "melancholy," "depression," "lassitude," "neurasthenia," or a combination of these, and most were considered serious conditions, or conditions that if left unchecked could develop into serious physical illnesses.

6. Preface to the *Jin Ping Mei cihua*, 1a–b. I follow David Roy's translation in *Plum in the Golden Vase* or *Chin P'ing Mei*, 3. The seven feelings, as defined in the Confucian classic *The Book of Rites* (*Li Ji*), are joy, anger, sadness, fear, love, liking, and disliking. Medical texts in the Ming and Qing disagree as to the number of emotions tied to health: some say five, some say seven. The medical textbook *Golden Mirror of the Medical Tradition* (*Yizong Jinjian*) of 1742 adopts a classification of seven emotions under the title of "spiritual disorders" or "disorders of consciousness," notably distinguishing between "sadness" *bei* and "worry" *si* (Sivin, "Emotional Counter-Therapy," 5). The word in the *Jin Ping Mei* preface being translated as "melancholy" or depression is *youyu*, which is usually a Buddhist substitution for "sadness" *bei*—likely emphasizing the karmic or retributory inevitability of too much passion. In medical texts, it also seems to be the result of prolonged worry or concern for others.

7. According to Charlotte Furth, women were more likely to suffer from "static congestion" (*yujia*), "a kind of melancholy syndrome of congealed blood associated with spleen system dysfunction . . . experienced as feelings of oppression

and suffocation, pressure or tightness in the chest, languor and loss of appetite, all linked to pent-up resentments and repressed desires" ("Blood, Body and Gender," 305). Women were considered more emotional than men, and since they were unable to control feelings of compassion, love, aversion, melancholy, and grief, their illnesses were considered more deeply rooted and more difficult to cure than those of men (Furth, 297). But literati men suffered from depression and from their attraction to depressed women, since they had refined their sensibilities through study of poetic and philosophical works. In Jiang Guan's *Mingyi Leian* (*Classified Case Histories of Famous Physicians*) of 1591, five of the nine cases categorized under *yu* static congestion/depression are men, more than would be expected based on medical texts that discuss women's disorders.

8. Preface to the *Jin Ping Mei cihua*, 2a–b.

9. A condition that prefigured representations of depression, at least among women, was possession by or sexual interaction with ghosts and fox spirits, resulting in *yin* depletion, emaciation, and madness. This condition is common in literati fiction and novels of the Ming, especially that in which retribution is the structuring notion. Such fiction posits girls as particularly susceptible to possession by avenging ghosts (and by extension as worthy targets for such retribution) or as particularly susceptible to seduction by such ghosts while in overly melancholic or lovesick states.

10. The term "antidepressant" is useful for the discussion of treating melancholy in late imperial China. While not at all exclusive to China, in the late Ming and early Qing dynasties it became common in medical texts not only to see the prescription to battle one extreme of emotion with its opposite, but to prescribe medicine that will do so. Sivin refers to this practice as "emotional counter-therapy," which, with respect to the novel's claims to be able to relieve or curb melancholy, sounds quite like a method or prescription for "antidepression." Some medical texts, beginning with *Yi Fang Kao* of 1584, list a collection of anecdotes under the category of "Emotions" (*qingzhi*) featuring the use of emotions to treat disorders caused by emotion (Sivin, 2–4).

11. A late-seventeenth-century text, *Shu Bencao* (*The Materia Medicia Librorum*), which classifies the medical qualities of various books in a taxonomy moving from those with the fewest side effects (the Confucian classics) to the most dangerous (novels and stories), makes similar claims: "The flavor of novels is sweet and their nature/effect is arid and highly toxic. This drug should be avoided because it induces insanity. It should be taken only during the summer months when suffering from a lassitude of spirits or stuffiness from overeating, when bad weather makes one feel awful. It also can help those suffering from diseases caused by external factors. Taking the drug can relieve anxiety and dispel melancholy. It can dissipate sluggishness and open up the chest. However, it ought not be taken on a prolonged basis" (Zhang Chao, 2a).

12. *Jin Ping Mei cihua* preface, 2a; Roy, 3.

13. Zhang Zhupo's (1670?–1698?) commentary edition of *Jin Ping Mei*, first printed most likely in 1695, was by far the most widely read edition of the novel.

14. "Zhupo Xianhua," 4b–5a. He uses "depression" (*menhuai*) in contrast to the *cihua* preface's "melancholy" (*youyu*). One of the ways in which *Jin Ping Mei* was

traditionally discussed was in its employment of the binary of heat and cold and yang and yin as these pertained to characters and the illnesses associated with them.

15. Li Yu, "Yi Sheng Weijian zhi Yao," 304.

16. Sivin, "Emotional Counter-Therapy," 6.

17. Ibid., 3.

18. Many scholars put the first compilations in the Han dynasty (206 BC–220 AD).

19. Emotional counter-therapy might usefully be compared with the notion of "emotional contagion" developed in Hatfield, Cacioppo, and Rapson.

20. Levy, *Ideal and Actual in "The Story of the Stone,"* 1.

21. Many editions of the novel, including the most popular premodern and modern printed editions, publish this preface as the first part of chapter 1 in the novel proper.

22. *Jin Yu Yuan* 1.1a; translated by David Hawkes, Cao Xueqin, *The Story of the Stone*, 20–21. I use the *Jin Yu Yuan* edition of *Honglou Meng*, because it has polymeniscous commentary and was widely available to readers at the end of the Qing dynasty.

23. *Jin Yu Yuan*, 2.4b; *Story of the Stone*, 76.

24. *Jin Yu Yuan*, 1.2b; *Story of the Stone*, 50.

25. See notes 6 and 10. *Honglou Meng* was first published in 1792, about fifty years after the *Yizong Jinjian*.

26. *Jin Yu Yuan* 2.2a, *Story of the Stone*, 70.

27. *Jin Yu Yuan*, 3.3a; *Story of the Stone*, 90.

28. Literally, *xiao chou po men*, "relieve depression and disperse [the haze of] melancholy." *Jin Yu Yuan*, 1.2b; *Story of the Stone*, 50.

29. The relation of consumption and depression is very old in China. The emotion of "sorrow" was linked to the pulmonary system as early as the first century BC.

30. One of two female protagonists in *Honglou Meng*. She dies of consumption resulting from static congestion brought on by desire and depression. Hawkes, introduction to Cao Xueqin, *Story of the Stone*, 16.

31. The *Wu Wushan Sanfu he ping Mu Dan Ting Huanhun Ji*, a commentary edition of Tang Xianzu's enormously popular Ming dynasty drama *Mu Dan Ting*, *The Peony Pavilion*, was put together by one scholar's three successive wives, each commenting or completing the comments of her predecessor. The first of the three wives to comment on *The Peony Pavilion* was not the first woman to write a commentary on the play, nor the first to die, supposedly, from such intense sympathetic identification with Du Liniang. Indeed, she contributed only a tiny portion to the "sizable corpus of materials that document the play's near-cult status among seventeenth-century women." See Zeitlin, "Shared Dreams," 129. Zeitlin in "Shared Dreams" and Widmer in "Xiao Qing's Literary Legacy" both discuss a number of women who died prematurely because of their connection to *The Peony Pavilion*.

32. Zeitlin, 128.

33. Ibid., 130.

34. There is a similar use of another play featuring lovers who fall ill from longing, *Xi Xiang Ji*, which I will not discuss here.

Bibliography

Cao Xueqin. *The Story of the Stone*. Volume 1. Introduced and translated by David Hawkes. New York: Penguin, 1973.

———. *Zengping Buxiang Quantu Jin Yu Yuan*. 1884. Reprint, Taipei: Kuangwen Shuju, 1973.

Furth, Charlotte. "Blood, Body and Gender: Medical Images of the Female Condition in China, 1600–1850." In *Chinese Femininities / Chinese Masculinities*, edited by Susan Brownell and Jeffrey N. Wasserstrom, 291–314. Berkeley: University of California Press, 2002.

Hatfield, Elaine, John T. Cacioppo, and Richard L. Rapson. *Emotional Contagion*. New York: Cambridge University Press, 1994.

Lanling Xiaoxiao Sheng. *Jin Ping Mei Cihua*. 1618. Reprint, Tokyo: Taian, 1963.

———. *The Plum in the Golden Vase or Chin P'ing Mei*. Volume 1. Introduced and translated by David Tod Roy. Princeton: Princeton University Press, 1993.

Levy, Dore. *Ideal and Actual in "The Story of the Stone."* New York: Columbia University Press, 1999.

Li Yu. "Yi Sheng Weijian zhi Yao." In *Xianqing Ouji*. 1671. Reprint, Taipei: Mingwen Shuju, 2002.

Schonebaum, Andrew. "The Medical Casebook of *Honglou Meng*." *Tamkang Review* 36, nos.1–2 (Fall and Winter 2005): 229–51.

Sivin, Nathan. "Emotional Counter-Therapy." In *Medicine, Philosophy and Religion in Ancient China: Researches and Reflections*, 2–19. Brookfield, VT: Variorum, 1995.

Tang Xianzu. *Mudan Ting*. 1598. Ed. Xu Shufang. Taipei: Liren Shuju, 1995.

———. *The Peony Pavilion: Mudan Ting*. 2nd ed. Translated by Cyril Birch. Bloomington: Indiana University Press, 2002.

Widmer, Ellen. "Xiao Qing's Literary Legacy and the Place of the Woman Writer in Late Imperial China." *Late Imperial China* 13, no. 1 (1992): 111–55.

Zeitlin, Judith. "Shared Dreams: The Story of the Three Wives' Commentary on *The Peony Pavilion*." *Harvard Journal of Asiatic Studies* 54, no. 1 (June 1994): 127–79.

Zhang Chao. *Shu Bencao*. In *Xinzhai zazu*. Xia ju tang, Kangxi yi hai (1695). Volume 1, 1b–2a.

Zhang Zhupo. "Zhupo Xianhua." In *Gaohe Tang Piping Mingdai Diyi Qishu "Jin Ping Mei."* 1695. Reprint, Taipei: Kuangwen Shuju Yinxing, 1981.

Chapter 14

Manic-Depressive Narration and the Hermeneutics of Countertransference

The Rime of the Ancient Mariner

Mark A. Clark

In their exquisitely detailed description of the poet's lifelong struggles with misery and fear, Richard Holmes's biographical considerations of Coleridge[1] serve to corroborate Kay Redfield Jamison's clinical assessment that the Romantic writer was probably manic-depressive.[2] Holmes's work renders Jamison's argument sufficiently compelling, I think, to allow for one's taking Coleridge's manic-depressive affliction as at least a plausible given. And one is justified, consequently, in moving beyond the argument as to whether or not Coleridge was manic-depressive, and considering the poet's work in light of the poet's mental condition.

If one couples the plausibility of Coleridge's mental illness, for instance, with other, long-accepted assessments of the poet—that he was remarkably gifted verbally, that he was enormously sensitive, and that he was inclined if not compelled to engage in lyric disclosures of his psychic experience, in such works as the Conversation Poems—then one might consider that the poet's writing serves as a unique and valuable account of manic-depressive experience. The figures that Coleridge uses to convey this experience, of course, do not rely on those that we in this present era of psychiatric understanding have constructed in order to conceive of depression. Our reading of Coleridge's figures, consequently, presents us with a challenge: we must read with such generosity as to remain open to the possibility that the figures and narratives we have developed as a means of understanding manic-depression may be enriched or enlarged by Coleridge's account. We might, indeed, find these representations to be more revealing and astute than the ones we have constructed.

In exploring this possibility, I wish to consider *The Rime of the Ancient Mariner* as a narrative of manic-depressive experience, and specifically as an intrapsychic representation of interpersonal relations in the context of manic-depressive illness—a narrative drama, this is to say, within the mind, that anticipates what interpersonal relations are destined to become. I shall argue that as readers we are manipulated just as the Wedding Guest in the poem is, manipulated into being absorbed in this intrapsychic drama and thus into taking the manic-depressive perspective of the Mariner and Coleridge: indeed, we come to participate in manic-depressive thinking, particularly in the leaps of analogy characteristic of such thinking. Our absorption has benefits beyond our gaining a familiarity with the mental functioning of a manic-depressive, however. What we come to see, via the thinking we are encouraged to adopt, is the illusory nature—the "Life-in-Death"—of social custom in the absence of unconditional, inclusive love. We also come to look askance on the linguistic custom, the particular use of language I refer to as the "discourse of description,"[3] that seems to underpin this world of "Life-in-Death"— a world that casts out Mariners, homeless people, and mental patients.

What prompts my consideration of Coleridge's poem as a narrative of manic-depressive experience is, principally, the character of the Ancient Mariner, whose behaviors, characteristics, and relations with others resemble in striking ways the diagnostic criteria for Bipolar I disorder.[4] First of all, the bizarre character of the Mariner's tale and his account of claimed supernatural experience suggest a pronounced grandiosity. In addition, the Mariner's monopoly of the conversation, along with the sustained character of his marvelous speech, testify to a "pressure to keep talking"—particularly as the Mariner admits that his heart "burns" (l. 585)[5] until he can talk in such a fashion—and suggest a "flight of ideas or subjective experience that thoughts are racing." The apparently cyclical urge to tell his tale, which in the present has prompted him, with his "skinny hand" (line 9), to detain the Guest (an indication of psychomotor agitation, perhaps), to engage, compulsively, in the tale-telling once again, suggests an "increase in goal-oriented activity." The claimed influence of Life-in-Death and of the other spirits of the tale suggests that the Mariner suffers from psychotic, persecutory delusions of being controlled. His gaunt, frazzled appearance, coupled with his behavioral tendencies, has left the "grey-beard loon" (l. 11) on the fringe of society, looking and acting like a schizophrenic street person of our own day; he would hardly be welcome at the Wedding that the Guest hopes to attend. Finally, the manner in which the Mariner relates to the Wedding Guest is clinically typical of the interpersonal relations exhibited by the manic-depressive sufferer, relations marked by narcissistic control of conversation and audience manipulation.

We can explore this final point in detail momentarily. For now, let us recall only that the Mariner exerts a relational control over the Wedding Guest that is altogether striking. The former not only detains the latter, but transfixes him by means of a "glittering eye," and—even if this captivation means the Guest's failure to meet his social obligations—the Guest "*cannot choose but hear*" (l. 18, my emphasis) what the Mariner tells him. The entrancement gathers strength as the Mariner dominates the interchange by means of a rhapsodically rendered tale of claimed supernatural experience. At least one result of this absorption is that the Guest ultimately loses his identity, which derives from the Wedding that he never attends. Ultimately, the Guest seems destined to live out his life as an aimless wanderer and so to share, to a degree, in the identity of the Mariner: at the poem's end, the Guest departs "like one that hath been stunned, / And is of sense forlorn" (ll. 622–23). His fate sounds eerily like a perpetual countertransference.

I mention the diagnostic criteria for Bipolar I Disorder and the Mariner's control over the Wedding Guest to suggest that it is reasonable to consider that the poem serves as a dramatization or narrative, a figure—an allegory, essentially—of manic-depressive interpersonal dynamics. At this juncture, however, I do not wish to discuss in detail what the psychoanalytic tradition says about these dynamics, then reductively examine how Coleridge fits into this explanation. Instead, I would like to examine closely what occurs in Coleridge's representation, *then* consider the ways in which this authorial performance correlates with psychoanalytic accounts of manic-depressive interpersonal relations.

The poem relates the story of an interaction that occurs between a man who is supposed to be attending a wedding and an aged sailor who has been, according to his testimony, the sole survivor of a shipwreck of sorts. The Mariner detains the Wedding Guest and tells him a fantastic tale about the Mariner's ship having been driven by a storm to the polar regions of the south, where for no good reason and to his bitter regret, the old man shot an Albatross and incurred a curse upon the ship. The vessel was swept back north only to find itself becalmed in the equatorial regions. All the crew died there except for the Mariner, whose life was won in a game of chance by the female spirit Life-in-Death. The Mariner began to shake the curse upon him when he found himself blessing and finding beautiful some sea snakes that he had at first found repulsive. He remains doomed, however, to spend the rest of his life retelling his tale to people like the Guest.

The interaction between the Mariner and the Guest appears to be motivated by the fact that the Mariner sees the Guest going to the Wedding and wants to stop him from doing so. He dissuades the Guest from going to the ceremony by telling his tale and by following this tale up with a lesson, which appears to clarify for the Guest some relation between the Wedding and the experience of the Mariner recounted in the tale. In other words, the Mariner urges the Guest to discern some connection between the Wedding and the tale, the Mariner apparently understanding that, if the Guest can accomplish this task, he will refuse to attend the Wedding. What the connection is, however, the Mariner does not tell the Guest, nor does Coleridge tell his readers—which is to say that Coleridge invites us, on a secondary level of engagement, to guess at the connection just as the Guest does. The wonder that the narrative of the Mariner and Coleridge prompts in us urges us into identification with the Guest.

Thus, in reading the poem, we observe with Coleridge the drama that occurs between the Mariner and the Guest; further, as we are prompted to undertake the same interpretive labors that the Guest undertakes, we also *participate* in the drama, and we do so in relation to an apparently manic-depressive narrator (the Mariner) who is the projection of a manic-depressive poet. Coleridge's act of presenting the poem renders us silent, dumbfounded readers in relation to a poet who is urgent of speech and who would have us, ideally, be capable of a "willing suspension of disbelief."[6] We might conclude, consequently, that as we identify with the Guest, Coleridge identifies with the Mariner.[7]

To the degree that we truly devote ourselves to reading the poem, then—suspending our disbelief and becoming absorbed in the activity of reading—what we eventually discern is that the interchange between the Mariner and the Guest is a dramatic presentation and projected image of what is taking place between Coleridge and ourselves. Having this experience of a heightened sense of connections, as it turns out, is something like participating in the cognitive functions of the manic mind; and it is by means of our absorption in this function that we can come to a deepened understanding of the manic-depressive condition.

The narrative works to achieve this end. In it, the Wedding Guest serves as a kind of humanly textured space or relational perspective, potentially habitable, constructed by Coleridge to be embodied by the reader: the Guest is a prosopopoeic conjuration, a countertransferential agent and audience-ideal who can willingly suspend disbelief and cannot choose but hear the Mariner.[8]

The absorption of the reader that the narrative effects is every bit as manipulative as it sounds. Perhaps to our chagrin, however, it turns out to be beneficial for us; for by means of it, Coleridge wages a critique of language that is life-giving and rich *for us*. His illness, combined with his poetic vocation, rendered him acutely sensitive to problematic cultural conventions of language use spawned by Enlightenment thinking and reinforced by disciples of Locke—conventions grounded in an unquestioned allegiance to a discourse of description, and in a conviction that expressive discourse has negligible value in the quest for reason and understanding. The testimony of Coleridge's suffering, dramatized in the poem, presents in hyperbole the problems associated with conventional language use as championed by Locke and his followers—problems we share today but fail to recognize.

In order to appreciate the nature of this linguistic critique, we need to recognize, first, that the labor of analogy construction we are to share with the Wedding Guest is our key to understanding the nature and purpose of the narrative that Coleridge constructs for his readers. Consequently, we need to consider this labor closely. Coleridge prompts us to ask this two-part question: how is the Mariner's *lesson* related to the Wedding, and how is the Wedding, in turn, related to the *tale*?

The lesson appears to be trite, yet it is the decisive element in the interchange that persuades the Guest to turn his back on the Wedding. At the end of the tale, the Guest is ready to return to the ceremony, and it is only at this point that the Mariner preaches his lesson:

> Farewell, farewell! but this I tell
> To thee, thou Wedding-Guest!
> He prayeth well, who loveth well
> Both man and bird and beast.
>
> He prayeth best, who loveth best
> All things both great and small;
> For the dear God who loveth us,
> He made and loveth all. (ll. 610–17)

We are inclined to think that this passage is an admonition to love all of God's creatures, and that the Mariner is preaching the lesson in expiation for his killing of the Albatross; but why would this persuade the Guest to turn away from the Wedding? The crux of the lesson lies in the way that it points out the incompatibility of love and selectivity. The comparatives and superlatives in the passage do not make sense: how does one love best all creatures at once? The best love occurs, the Mariner suggests, when selectivity and hierarchy are dissolved: one loves best when he or she loves all equally.

The Wedding, which is presumably a ritual and a cultural sign that purports to be a celebration of love as well as a prayer that asks for God's blessing on this love, has in fact established a social hierarchy that ostracizes people like the Mariner. Certainly, a "grey-beard loon" who claims to have had supernatural experiences would be unwelcome at a social event like the Wedding. If it occurred to the Guest that this supposed celebration of love establishes a hierarchy that relegates the Mariner to the fringes of tolerability, then the Guest would be prompted to question his own status in the hierarchy. He is a "guest," after all; and he thus appears to be at least one step removed from the groom and bride. As far as we know, the only identity he has is that of fulfilling a role prescribed by the cultural ritual; and without even recognizing it, the Guest has, by living out this role, helped to perpetuate love's undoing. For that matter, marriage traditionally celebrates exclusive love, husband and wife "cleaving" to one another. A recognition such as this—an epiphanic comprehension of deluded faith—would be profound enough to warrant the Guest's reaction of turning away from the Wedding, thus relinquishing his identity, and wandering off, "stunned."

Clearly, as well, the lesson and Wedding are related to the *tale* in some fashion. The tale invites an analogy to be constructed, I would argue, between the Wedding and the Albatross, both of which the Mariner destroys.

The Albatross arrives on the scene, during the voyage, when the Mariner and his crew have been immured in ice. Through the fog the creature flies, "[a]s if it had been a Christian soul," and the crew greets the bird "in God's name" (ll. 65–66). Shortly after the arrival of the Albatross, the ice breaks apart and the crew receive a wind favorable enough to speed them along on their journey, whereupon they come to regard the bird as a good omen—a sign of divine care and concern (ll. 69–79). At this point, the Mariner shoots the Albatross. The crew, of course, are none too happy about this act; but when the fog blows off soon afterward, and the ship sails on, the crew members decide that the bird must have brought the curse of the fog and mist upon them and not, as they had supposed, delivered them from their predicament. Soon afterward, the ship speeds happily along to the equator, where the crew experience new suffering. They blame the Mariner again for this turn of events, and hang the dead Albatross on his neck.

Why the Mariner kills the Albatross remains one of the great mysteries in English literature, of course, and I don't propose to solve this mystery here. However, contemplating the killing in relation to the Wedding may provide us with some fresh insight, particularly if we also recall the Mariner's blessing of the sea snakes, which begins to reverse the curse that he has brought upon himself.

Just after all his shipmates die, the Mariner spies the sea snakes slithering along on the ocean surface, and he is repelled by the sight of them:

The many men, so beautiful!
And they all dead did lie:
And a thousand thousand slimy things
Lived on; and so did I. (ll. 236–39)

But "seven days, seven nights" (l. 261) later, the Mariner watches the snakes intently and sees in them something else:

> Beyond the shadow of the ship,
> I watched the water-snakes:
> They moved in tracks of shining white,
> And when they reared, the elfish light
> Fell off in hoary flakes.
>
> Within the shadow of the ship
> I watched their rich attire:
> Blue, glossy green, and velvet black,
> They coiled and swam; and every track
> Was a flash of golden fire.
>
> O happy living things! no tongue
> Their beauty might declare:
> A spring of love gushed from my heart,
> And I blessed them unaware . . . (ll. 272–85)

Immediately after he bestows this blessing, the Mariner finds that he is able to pray again, and the corpse of the Albatross falls from his neck, into the sea.

What the Mariner sees in the snakes is life—that is, life as independent of his attempts to interpret it in terms of his projected desires.[9] The way he sees and understands the snakes is shaped by his desires and needs, and so the meaning that the creatures have, in his eyes, changes. But the very lives of the creatures continually defy his capacity to fix their meaning—which in turn suggests that meaning should be unceasingly expansive and the meaning-maker perpetually generative. In retrospect, the Mariner knows that his killing of the Albatross was a violence misplaced. His animosity, which was of an unconscious, intuitive nature, was aimed at the reductive, self-interested nature of human knowing and understanding, not at the living creatures that are the objects of this knowing. What the Mariner was striking out at in killing the Albatross was really the inclination of the crew, and his own first inclination, to comprehend the bird as a messenger of God: the men were in truth projecting their own desires onto the bird.

In the Wedding, the Mariner sees the construction of a cultural ritual, which society assumes to be a celebration of love and an experience of communion with God. In fact, at least as it is practiced, the ritual is a cultural artifact constructed out of human desires aimed, unconsciously or not, at fostering hierarchies of social acceptance; and these desires are counter to the "best" love and God's love. Like the crew of the voyage, the Guest has devoted his life and being, his identity, to the cultural delusion. The Mariner, having had the experiences with the Albatross and the snakes, labors to kill not the Wedding itself but the Guest's illusions about what the Wedding is.

The Mariner has, furthermore, performed on numerous occasions, with respect to other people, the same labor of disillusionment. He first told his tale at the end of his voyage, in answer to the Hermit's question, "'What manner of man art thou?'" (l. 577); and since that time, he says,

> . . . at an uncertain hour,
> That agony returns:
> And till my ghastly tale is told,
> This heart within me burns.
>
> I pass, like night, from land to land;
> I have strange power of speech;
> That moment that his face I see,
> I know the man that must hear me:
> To him my tale I teach. (ll. 582–90)

This is to say that he has seen other people, presumably committed—but mindlessly so—to attending their various "Weddings," whose spiritual impoverishment is evident in their faces. The Mariner is able to draw an analogy between the Albatross of his experience and the social illusions that hold his various audiences captive. The problem lies not just in Weddings, of course, but in any cultural sign that people take to be more than the artifact of their projected desires. The telling of the tale prompts the audience to engage in the inverse of the Mariner's analogy construction—that is, linking the cultural rituals of the listener's experience to the dead weight of the Albatross.

The interchange, consequently, is one of mutual figural construction; and one ought to note the special status of the Albatross as sign in this process. As a figure that can contribute in very useful ways to the Guest's and the reader's understanding, the Albatross has substantial value *in spite of the fact* that it strikes one as the product of a deranged mind. No one could very easily believe the Mariner's claims to have had the experiences he has—unless, perhaps, these experiences all took place in the "grey-beard loon's" imagination. Yet, on the level of figure, the Albatross and all it signifies—faith and belief not in God, but in one's projected desires—make sense. The grandiose, perhaps psychotically fashioned tale seems to communicate an extraordinary insight and to clarify a useful lesson: namely, that what we human beings regard as truth, or as the incarnation of Divine being and care, is often nothing more than our own projected desire. And the Mariner, although he is described as a "loon," is worth listening to—worth accepting, perhaps, as a prophet or visionary—because of the insight he shares.

As I have suggested, readers of Coleridge's poem are led to undertake the same activity of analogy construction as the Guest. We are to ask, "What 'Wedding' do I dedicate my life to attending? What social customs do I unreflectively support; and do I recognize the ways in which these customs, these Towers of Babel, are fashioned from people's desires?" What Coleridge is probably encouraging us to explore—given the time in his life in which that he wrote the poem, and the trajectory of his intellectual interests—is the "custom" of *language* itself and specifically of the *word*. The figural activity, centered on the Albatross, that we share with the Mariner, the Guest, and Coleridge serves as a performative critique of the discourse of description championed by Locke and his nineteenth-century descendants—as well as a macabre celebration of the expressive discourse championed by the Romantics.[10]

This point deserves an essay of its own, but I am less interested here in the philosophical nature of this critique than in the way that the critique appears to be waged via the manipulation of the reader into sharing Coleridge's perspective. At this point, I would like to note the similarities between the interpersonal dynamics at work in the poem and those traditionally considered by the therapeutic community as typical of manic-depressives.[11] My sense is that Coleridge wages his critique precisely through a demonstration of his affliction—and the critique is all the more compelling because of his doing so.

Typically, manic-depressives are seen as highly narcissistic and manipulative.[12] As Frederick Goodwin and Kay Redfield Jamison note, "Psychoanalysts, with rare exceptions, [have] regarded the interpersonal lives of manic-depressive patients as unstable and chaotic, narcissistically based, bereft of empathic regard for the rights of others, too dependent or independent, singularly rigid, and full of rage."[13] Consequently, manic-depressives can arouse powerfully negative responses in others. However, they can also be tremendously appealing, particularly during the hypomanic phases of the mood swings. They may exhibit a charming vitality at these times, as well as talkativeness, wittiness, and an extraverted expansiveness. Their grandiose claims can make them appear to be prophetically insightful. They may exhibit increased sexual desires and accelerated mental functioning, as well as notoriously poor judgment. In the context of therapy, the seductive aspects of hypomania can prompt poor treatment

decisions on the part of the clinician, since the behavior seems quite positive; or they may generate countertransferential dynamics that can exacerbate the suffering of the patient. As Goodwin and Jamison point out:

> Moods are obviously contagious, and occasionally the loss of a
> patient's hypomania results in a corresponding, albeit lesser,
> loss reaction in the therapist. Some psychotherapists espouse a
> set of attitudes about psychosis that we term the Equus-Laingian
> view, which refers to a *romanticization of madness.* It can range
> from a tendency toward overvaluing the positive aspects of
> bipolar illness while minimizing the negative, painful ones to a
> conviction that psychopharmacological interventions in manic-
> depressive patients are oppressive and contraindicated.[14]

The conflicted yet rapt attention that the Mariner commands from the
Guest is a strikingly apt image of the spell that the manic-depressive can
cast over another; and one could imagine that, at some level, Coleridge's
presentation of the character is tantamount to his saying, "Observe: this
is the effect I can have on my listeners."

I do not mean to imply here that Coleridge feels himself to be a commanding influence in a wholly positive sense. We should recall how *unat-
tractive* the Mariner is in casting his spell—and how coerced the Guest feels
as the spell is cast. The dramatic interchange suggests some ambivalence,
in Coleridge, toward the spell-like effect he knows he can create. We may
get an even better sense of this ambivalence if we consider Thomas Carlyle's striking recollection of an encounter he once had with Coleridge,
who was, one suspects, in a hypomanic or manic phase at the time:

> I have heard Coleridge talk, with eager musical energy, two
> stricken hours, his face radiant and moist, and communicate
> no meaning whatsoever to any individual of his hearers,—
> certain of whom, I for one, still kept eagerly listening in hope;
> the most had long before given up, and formed (if the room
> were large enough) secondary humming groups of their own.
> He began anywhere: you put some question to him, made
> some suggestive observation: instead of answering this, or de-
> cidedly setting out toward answer of it, he would accumulate
> formidable apparatus, logical swim-bladders, transcendental
> life-preservers and other precautionary and vehiculatory gear,
> for setting out; perhaps did at last get underway,—but was
> swiftly solicited, turned aside by the glance of some radiant
> new game on this hand or that, into new courses; and ever

into new; and before long into all the Universe, where it was uncertain what game you would catch, or whether any.[15]

In reading this passage, I try to imagine the look on Carlyle's face and what it might have communicated to Coleridge—some mixture of horror and fascination, bafflement, discomfort, and compassionate anguish, perhaps—and then I wonder what effect this nonverbal feedback probably had on Coleridge, particularly as he saw so many others of this audience drifting away in discomfort. At least part of the rapidity and utterly stifling character of his speech must have derived from a panicked realization that the interpersonal connection he was trying to enjoy was unraveling, due to his participation in it. In some sense, Carlyle resembles the Wedding Guest, in that he lingers and remains fascinated, in spite of his moderate repulsion. But there is a difference between the two audiences as well: the Guest benefits somewhat from his absorption in a coherent if fantastic narrative, whereas Carlyle does not. This difference suggests that the Guest serves as the depiction of something approaching an audience ideal—or, as I say, a conjuring space into which flesh-and-blood ideal audiences are to step.

In any case, one must not assume that because manic-depressives can be manipulative, narcissistic, grandiose, and seductively charming, they lack beneficial, accurate insight. That one's extraordinary insights result from psychological compulsions or serve a pathological condition need not undermine the accuracy or usefulness of the perceptions. Indeed, D. S. Janowsky, M. Leff, and R. S. Epstein have concluded the following:

> Intimately related to the manic's ability to appeal to the self-esteem systems of others is his extraordinary perceptiveness. In interpersonal encounters, the manic possesses a highly refined talent for sensing an individual's vulnerability or a group's area of conflict, and exploiting this in a manipulative fashion. . . . [T]he manic patient is able to make covert conflicts overt, causing the person or group with whom he is dealing to feel discomfort. . . . What he says cannot be dismissed as untrue or unreal, for the areas attacked truly do exist and, indeed, are areas of vulnerability.[16]

If the manic person is "able to make covert conflicts overt," then I would argue that he may indeed fulfill the role of a prophet: he recognizes and points out to others those habits of living and belief that generate conflict. He does so not because he stands apart from and transcends these destructive customs but because he suffers so acutely from them.

My own sense is that, on a philosophical plane, Coleridge and his Mariner make overt that "covert conflict" that inheres in following the illusory desires generated by their culture's allegiance to a discourse of description. The narrative that Coleridge supplies accomplishes this revelation not by means of philosophical argument but by dramatically absorbing its audience into the dynamics of a manic mind—dynamics that are experienced through relational manipulation and conflicted entrancement.[17] Ideally, what we learn through our analogical labors is the ability to think in a divergent, dendritic manner with respect to a word, *Albatross*. Coleridge and his Mariner prompt the "fluency, rapidity, and flexibility of thought," the combinatory cognitive functions and creative syntheses, that characterize hypomanic thinking[18]—urging upon their audiences, in consequence, the emotional alienation that derives from thinking in such a manner when a culture has persuaded itself to profess and live in accordance with an unquestioned faith in a Lockean discourse of description. In accomplishing his language critique through the deeply empathic (if potentially conflicted and ambivalent) understanding that he forces upon us, Coleridge gives us some indication of the nature, power, and potential of the manic-depressive narrative; and he suggests what benefit may arise from our giving such narrative our dedicated—if not rapt—attentions.

Notes

1. Holmes, *Coleridge: Early Visions, 1772–1804* and *Coleridge: Darker Reflections, 1804–1834*.

2. Jamison, *Touched With Fire*, 67; 219–24.

3. In referring to a "discourse of description" and (later) to an "expressive discourse," I hope to situate my reflections in the genealogy of M. H. Abrams's thinking, in *The Mirror and the Lamp*, about the historical emergence of Romanticism, and to give this thinking the linguistic cast that A. C. Goodson does in his *Verbal Imagination*, by means of his own phrasing (123). A discourse of description, driven by a faith in empiricism, envisions words as mechanistically and reductively referential: words *name*, with specificity, the components of the natural world. In such a discourse, neither the subjective power of human imagination to produce meaning (and register that meaning in words) nor the polysemous nature of words that derives from that power is recognized as having much value or utility. In contrast to those descendants of the Enlightenment who adopted the discourse of description, the Romantics were inclined to envision the word as a site of meaning's propagation and generativity, quickened by the expressive imagination. Goodson writes that for Coleridge, words were living things that "represented the redemption of natural language through the expansion of a progressive reason. They were the stuff of thought, the material realization of the Logos" (89). However, Coleridge's ambition was not to assert, in the face of em-

piricism's rising tide, that expressive discourse is superior to descriptive—and thereby establish expressive poets as, say, the high priests of a unique, prophetic language different than any other language—but to seek acknowledgment that expressive discourse, together with the people whose minds were given to expressive thought, had a home forever in language and culture. My own sense is that the *Rime* constitutes precisely this seeking; it is the emotionally driven precursor to the philosophical explorations and argument regarding language that he would pursue in the nineteenth century.

4. See *DSM-IV*, criteria for Bipolar I Disorder, Most Recent Episode Manic (296.44). The phrases quoted in this paragraph are taken from the *DSM-IV* criteria for a Manic Episode.

5. Coleridge, *The Rime of the Ancient Mariner*, Volume 16, 1: 365–419. Citations in the text of this essay are to line numbers of the poem.

6. Coleridge, *Biographia Literaria*, Volume 7, 2: 6.

7. Numerous critics have noted this identification. See, for example, Coburn, "Poet into Public Servant," 1–11; Holmes, *Early Visions*, 172; and Holmes, *Darker Reflections*, 420.

8. Prosopopoeia is a "figure of speech in which an imaginary, absent, or deceased person is represented as speaking or acting" (*Random House Dictionary, Unabridged*). The "Dear Reader" address that one encounters in nineteenth-century novels, for example, is such a figure: it compresses a diverse audience with vast interpretive power into one imaginary person whose interpretive actions the author can control.

9. My reading of this passage parallels Goodson's, 180–98.

10. See Goodson, 198. The Mariner's experience "remains [for us readers] a potent reminder of the implications of life conceived in the mechanist manner of Locke and his followers, and of the will which, by an act of sympathetic imagination, is *free to expand the horizon of the real*" (my emphasis).

11. I wish to acknowledge, at this point, what may occur to my readers to be something of an irony: I appeal to the authority of psychiatric/psychological discourse, which most would regard as descendant from an Enlightenment discourse of description and therefore vulnerable to critique. What I am arguing, however, is that the psychiatric/psychological vision (here, of manic depression) *is*, generally, a helpful one *and* one that our ideologically influenced tradition of understanding encourages us to take—but that what occurs in our encounter with the Mariner and Coleridge is an experience of countertransference or something very much like it. And the outcome of this experience *can* be a heightened awareness of our own unacknowledged, unanalyzed conflicts, our ideologically fashioned modes of understanding. Ultimately, therefore, I regard Coleridge as something of an unwitting pioneer of the patient/sufferer discourse of very recent years, which has contested the medical/psychiatric understanding of and response to the experience of mental illness.

12. For an extended clinical consideration of manic-depressive interpersonal relations, see chapter 12 of Goodwin and Jamison, *Manic-Depressive Illness*, 281–317.

13. Ibid., 301. Goodwin and Jamison continue: "These conclusions are not surprising given that they have been based substantially on experiences with patients in the prepharmacotherapy era." These comments point to a difficulty that we need to acknowledge: living in a pharmacotherapy era, we are considering a narrative produced by a writer who, while known to be a self-medicator, lived in an era before pharmacotherapy. The psychoanalytic insights and research that Goodwin and Jamison cite are, though dated, still of value: "Manic-depressive illness—marked as it is by extraordinary and confusing fluctuations in mood, personality, thinking, and behavior—inevitably has powerful and often painful effects on relationships. Violence, poor judgment, and indiscreet financial and sexual behavior are almost always destructive and embarrassing to spouses, children, family members, and friends. Trust is not easily restored in the wake of mania, nor are goodwill and love always regenerated after months of severe, depleting, and unremitting depression" (301).

14. Ibid., 734 (my emphasis).

15. Carlyle, *The Works of Thomas Carlyle*, Volume 11, 56.

16. Janowsky, Leff, and Epstein, "Playing the Manic Game," 254.

17. This absorption approaches but is not equivalent to the sort sought by Romantic hermeneutics, in the tradition of Dilthey and Heidegger, where one assumes the being of another and acquires understanding as a result. In "Wordsworth at the Limits of Romantic Hermeneutics," Gerald Bruns writes, "[Romantic hermeneutics] is born of the impossible desire to possess the self-possession of the other, knowing the other from the inside out, with the self-certainty of Descartes's self-experience, not doubting the other as one not-doubts oneself" (403). In Coleridge's poem, one assumes the *relational* role defined by the manic's manipulations, and by one's absorption in this role one reaches an understanding of the manic's mind. But Coleridge, I emphasize, orchestrates this drama: the narrative is the means by which he garners understanding—the means by which he conveys the manic's "alienated" understanding of the illusion or constructedness of social and linguistic custom.

18. Jamison, 105.

Bibliography

Abrams, M. H. *The Mirror and the Lamp: Romantic Theory and the Critical Tradition.* London: Oxford University Press, 1957.

Bruns, Gerald L. "Wordsworth at the Limits of Romantic Hermeneutics." *The Centennial Review* 33, no. 4 (Fall 1989): 393–418.

Carlyle, Thomas. *The Works of Thomas Carlyle.* Volume 11. Centenary Edition. Edited by H. D. Traill. New York: Scribner's, 1896–1901.

Coburn, Kathleen. "Poet into Public Servant." *Proceedings & Transactions of the Royal Society of Canada* 54 (1960): 1–11.

Coleridge, Samuel Taylor. *Biographia Literaria.* Edited by James Engell and W. Jackson Bate. Volume 7 of *The Collected Works of Samuel Taylor Coleridge,* edited by Kathleen Coburn. Bollingen Edition. Princeton: Princeton University Press, 1983.

————. *The Rime of the Ancient Mariner*. 1834. Edited by J. C. C. Mays. Volume 16 of *The Collected Works of Samuel Taylor Coleridge*, edited by Kathleen Coburn. Bollingen Edition. Princeton: Princeton University Press, 2001.

Diagnostic and Statistical Manual of Mental Disorders: Fourth Edition. Washington, DC: American Psychiatric Association, 1994.

Goodson, A. C. *Verbal Imagination: Coleridge and the Language of Modern Criticism*. New York: Oxford University Press, 1988.

Goodwin, Frederick K., and Kay Redfield Jamison. *Manic-Depressive Illness*. New York: Oxford University Press, 1990.

Holmes, Richard. *Coleridge: Darker Reflections, 1804–1834*. New York: Pantheon, 1998.

————. *Coleridge: Early Visions, 1772–1804*. New York: Pantheon, 1989.

Jamison, Kay Redfield. *Touched With Fire: Manic-Depressive Illness and the Artistic Temperament*. New York: Free Press, 1993.

Janowsky, D. S., M. Leff, and R. S. Epstein. "Playing the Manic Game: Interpersonal Maneuvers of the Acutely Manic Patient." *Archives of General Psychiatry* 22 (1970): 252–61.

Locke, John. *An Essay Concerning Human Understanding*. Edited by P. H. Nidditch. Oxford: Clarendon Press, 1975.

V

*Depression and the
Limits of Narrative*

Chapter 15

Writing Self/Delusion

Subjectivity and Scriptotherapy
in Emily Holmes Coleman's
THE SHUTTER OF SNOW

Sophie Blanch

Following the death of Emily Holmes Coleman in 1974, her son accepted an invitation to donate his mother's extensive collection of diaries, manuscripts, and correspondence to the Special Collections Department at the University of Delaware. Among the holdings of the Coleman Papers is a letter in which the American poet and novelist writes to her father to announce the birth of her first and only child:

> Dearest of youthful and attractive grandfathers. . . . Regarding my part in this adventure, I am saying nothing for publication. Everything which ought to be said is unfit for publication. Let me remark to you in private, however, that from now on I favour the stork method of acquiring a family. I was much too blithe beforehand, but a good husband and a better doctor kept me from passing out entirely. Lest you take this too much to heart, I want to assure you that I have recovered my usual health and spirits today.[1]

Shortly after John Milton Holmes received the news of his first grandchild, Emily Holmes Coleman suffered a complete psychological breakdown. In 1924 Coleman was admitted to the Rochester State Hospital in New York, where, for a period of six months, she was confined and treated for acute postpartum depression. While Coleman remained convinced throughout her life that she was manifestly unfit for motherhood, she later retracted

213

her pledge that she would be "saying nothing for publication." In fact, upon her recovery—or, more arguably, in pursuit of a fully articulated recovery—Coleman encapsulated much of her experience in *The Shutter of Snow*, a partially fictionalized account of creative delusion and traumatized femininity. Written between 1924 and 1929, Coleman's only novel was finally accepted for publication by Routledge in 1930 after a series of disappointing rejections. It explores the breakdown and gradual rehabilitation of Marthe Gail, a woman who, like Coleman, experiences a series of psychotic delusions after the birth of her child, and is then forced to reconstruct herself as a capable wife and mother within the limits of the asylum in its disorder and often danger.

In its imaginative retelling of the author's own experience, the narrative of Marthe Gail and the Gorestown State Hospital tells the story of a woman caught between her identity as a writer and poet and her role as a young wife and mother. Even at the height of her traumatic delusions, Coleman's fictionalized alter ego seems able to acknowledge the discrepancy between the personal demands of her literary (pre)occupation and the public recognition of her feminine identity:

> Marthe sat down on the new patient's bed and began to write a letter to Dr Brainerd. She wrote several every day asking for things for herself and for the ward. Where did you get that pencil? said the new patient whose name was Luella. My husband said Marthe. You dont look old enough to be married. I am a mother said Marthe.
>
> Whats the matter with you? said Luella. Theres nothing the matter with me said Marthe, I am being kept here for a reason. She went on writing the letter.[2]

Throughout the course of the novel, language and the act of writing function as both symptom and therapy, even as a potential cure in the trajectory of Marthe's illness. As both a central characteristic of a shattered feminine identity and a necessary means of restoring that identity, the creative process comes to define the breakdown *and* potential recovery of both Marthe Gail and her literary creator. Amid the pain and confusion of severe depression, the privileged access to a pencil and paper signals to Marthe the possibility of release: "She held tightly to the pencil. She could write now, she could write two letters. They would know about it now because she would write."[3] Framed in these terms, the poignant account of a once-private trauma is opened up to express a wider narrative of conventional femininity, creative confinement, and the familiar conflicts between ambition and affection, delusion and definition.

Writing in her letters without the veil of fiction for protection, Coleman determined to articulate her own difficulty in resolving the internalized conflicts that disturbed her existence as a young, modern woman. In correspondence sent to her husband from Paris in 1929, Coleman revealed the extent of her inability to integrate motherhood with her choice of a literary career. As she worked in isolation on the final draft of her novel she wrote about the uncomfortable reality of being a writer first and a mother second:

> No use, these last months have finished me for motherhood—
> I might as well let the sentimental and rosy dreams go by the
> board and face the fact that the deeper my writing goes the
> farther behind I leave what is behind. I have been throwing
> things overboard in my usual ruthless fashion, now it is the
> maternal instinct.[4]

For Coleman, the nurturing and protective qualities attributed to the maternal relationship were given more instinctively to her writing than to motherhood itself. It is perhaps not surprising, therefore, that *The Shutter of Snow*, as an example of literary maternalism, was greeted more sympathetically by Coleman's fellow women modernists than by the father of her child. During the completion of Coleman's still-unpublished novel, *Tygon*, her close friend Djuna Barnes wrote to her about it, using terms more usually associated with the safe arrival of a new baby. As Barnes struggled to conclude work on her avant-garde novel *Nightwood*, she admitted to Coleman, "You sound divinely happy, that is so engrossed in your book, I wish I were with mine. . . . What do you mean you'll never show your book to me? . . . You'll feel less afraid when it's not so new, when as you say the umbilical is cut."[5]

At a meeting with her editors at Routledge in September 1929, Coleman received some much-needed encouragement of her writing style that began to transform her slow appreciation of the novel's literary worth. Writing to her father after the success of the meeting, Coleman reported that "they had obviously got all its implications, and regarded it not as a curiosity, but as a work of considerable talent. They seem to think the book will be a success, not only from a literary standpoint, but because of its originality."[6] This level of editorial approval seems to have provided Coleman with the critical distance to reevaluate the status of her novel beyond the limits of personal testimony. Later, in the same letter, her focus turns for the first time to the effectiveness of her writing style. Addressing her father in a newly confident and detached tone, Coleman considers the timely innovations of her use of language in *The Shutter of Snow*:

> It is the first time anyone has written an account of life in an
> insane asylum in any other way than to make propaganda—
> no-one has ever treated a subject of this kind in an imaginative,
> poetic way. Obviously such a subject lends itself gorgeously to
> the opportunities of modern writing—extravagant imagery and
> the dream forms that the Freud era has released for poetry and
> poetic prose.[7]

It is Coleman's skillful manipulation of the "dream forms" constructing the asylum experience that reveals the true extent of her modern-
ist imagination.

    As Marthe is first introduced to the psychiatric ward in the opening
pages of the novel, her sense of violent dislocation from herself, her sur-
roundings, and the other patients is expressed at the level of severe narrative disturbance. In addition to the strategic abandonment of apostrophes
already discussed, Coleman resists convention in another way by refusing
to attribute speech to specific characters. The effect of this in the early
stages of the novel is to simulate the chorus of seemingly disembodied
voices that Marthe senses around her but is unable to rationalize: "The
voice on the other side of her wall was shouting for someone. It never
stopped all night. It became entangled in the blankets and whistled the ice
prongs on the wind. The rest of the voices were not so distinct. It was very
still out in the hall when the voices stopped."[8] The nightmarish qualities associated with these auditory disturbances enable Coleman's reader to
identify, at least partially, with Marthe's fear and confusion. However, the
excess of sensory description surrounding this and other similar scenes returns the experience from the oddly familiar realm of dreams to the barely
recognizable realm of Marthe's psychic trauma. The use of the dream
form in the construction of Marthe's illness works particularly well at this
stage in the narrative simply because Coleman refuses her reader any alternative mode of perception. Rather than mediating Marthe's untamed,
frantic reactions through the controlled calm of an all-knowing narrator,
Coleman's reader is forced to inhabit the trauma itself. This arresting strategy can be seen working at the very start of the novel, as Marthe encounters the elderly and institutionalized Miss Ryan for the first time:

> When she came to the door she saw a groaning skeleton with
> wisps of hair and great yellow teeth, rubbing her hands on
> her nightgown. Her face was a lion coming forth to kill.
> Marthe put out her hand and drew back with a sharp scream.
> She screamed into her hands and tore at the woman's apron.
> She fled back to her room, the blanket dragging behind her
> cold feet. Whats the matter you arent afraid of that poor old

lady are you? The skeleton was coming into her room. She came slowly in, larger and larger. She approached the bed, chewing her horrid hands.[9]

It is only when the unacknowledged voice of the ward nurse intervenes in this scene that Marthe, and Coleman's reader, get a sense that what is actually taking place lacks the creeping malevolence that is being imagined.

Just as the language of *The Shutter of Snow* attempts to translate the displaced vocabulary of Marthe's experience of the asylum, the narrative also delivers a series of unpredictable changes in mood and linguistic intensity, once again replicating the structures of Marthe's psychosis. The violent terrors of her first encounters are soon replaced with the prospect of listlessness and bodily surrender in the bathing sequence: "Her arms long slender stems of pond lilies, and the water cress of her breasts floated and sank in the depth of the stream."[10] In a later moment, Marthe's detailed critique of Dr. Halloway's sense of style is immediately followed by the poetic but entirely strange observation, "That night was a steel helmet set on a mushroom head."[11] As Marthe's initial torment begins to lift, and she is again starting to contemplate an external reality beyond the confines of the hospital, these constantly shifting moods, images, tropes, and figures flood into the same psychic and narrative space:

> Marthe Gail looked out through the bars upon the blue glassy snow, ridged with the diamonds of the early sun. She could not see the evergreen trees that stood below to the right, that had been from her window a green pyramid of sparrows. Across the snow, across the closely meshed footprints of those who could walk in the snow, there was the sun, coming like an Oriental bride across the treetops and the cold brick walls of the outbuildings, coming with black braids and cobwebs sucked from the fire walls of the night.[12]

Examples like this of the vivid, starkly stylized language of *The Shutter of Snow* work to articulate much of the author's remembered experience of an acute and ultimately pathologized case of postpartum depression. In their biographical introduction to the Virago Press edition of *The Shutter of Snow*, Carmen Callil and Mary Siepmann emphasize Coleman's considerable ability in expressing the traumatic reality of becoming a mother: "Emily Coleman seems to have understood instinctively, through her madness, the conflicts experienced by so many women in relation to the process of birth: the powerlessness of the female body in this condition, the mixture of love and hatred felt for husband and child by a woman defenceless in the face of its mysteries and agonies."[13]

In *The Shutter of Snow*, Coleman clearly acknowledges the need for the female subject to script her own account of the conflict she experiences. Speaking through her fictional alter ego, Coleman articulates the pervasiveness of a patriarchal discourse that attempts to overwrite the experiences of femininity, and of maternity more specifically. Thus it is highly significant that at the peak of her psychotic delusions, Marthe Gail glimpses a vision of her husband as "[h]e leaned above the bed an elongated ribbon of ink."[14] In a moment of greater lucidity, Marthe is made similarly aware of her husband's authority as it relates to the power and ownership of language. Granted only temporary access to the necessary pencil and paper, Marthe must entrust the act of writing to her husband during an officially scheduled visit:

> She told him what she needed. He took out a pencil and wrote it all down. Not the scissors and the nail file he reminded her. Why not? Its against the rules he said. But Chris I wont do anything with them. You had better not have them he told her gently. I hate you she screamed at him, youre in league with all the rest of them.
>   . . . You must lie still he said, and let me do the talking. Will you let me talk a little? You have been very sick.[15]

In this partly remembered encounter, Coleman reveals the extent to which Marthe's husband is ultimately in league with the governing regime of an institution that asserts its authority by perpetuating the powerlessness of its inmates. It is only once Marthe has demonstrated that she can remain "ever so quiet" in compliance with asylum instruction, that she is granted supervised access to her own writing tools. Again, however, Marthe's ability to write for herself is shown to be possible only through the enabling presence of her husband:

> They went into her room, leaving the door ajar. You have to do that said Marthe. Marthe he said, youre so much better arent you? His eyes gleamed before her. You must be ever so quiet. . . . She gave him her pencil. He felt down in his pocket and brought out a knife which he opened and began neatly to sharpen her pencil. She was kissing his hands and his fingers. He looked at her as he pushed the knife.[16]

The violent portent that is captured in the phallic image of the knife suggests that while Marthe's husband does indeed facilitate her return to self-expression, his assistance is accompanied by an unspoken hostility toward his wife's increasing articulateness, which entails his own loss of absolute power in the symbolic sphere. This coded dynamic is revisited later as Christopher offers to use the knife once again to cut open the leaves of a new notebook that he has bought as a gift for Marthe. On this occasion Marthe attempts to resist her husband's intervention, insisting that she is soon to be allowed home. Again, however, Marthe's words are overpowered by her husband's symbolic actions: "I am well Christopher she said, I am going home. Plenty of time for that he said and slit the first page violently."[17] However, as Coleman reclaims ownership of Marthe's narrative—and her own—as the author of their shared experiences, she not only marks her own more determined resistance to this linguistic hierarchy but also identifies the act of writing the self as a potential mode of recovery and resolution.

In the context of life-writing, it is often suggested that the very process of self-articulation—of "writing the self"—functions as conflict resolution for the woman as subject of her own narrative.[18] It is this mode of personally inflected writing that best describes the literary output of Emily Holmes Coleman. Through her primary identification as a writer, it is clear that she engaged with many of the conflicts in her own life by exploring them on the page. Doubly bound within competing definitions of modern femininity and the always-shifting limits of mental illness, Coleman found in writing the possibility of recovering a recognizable and autonomous selfhood. In its ability to function as a form of mediation between disordered and conflicting states of being, the narrating of events, images, sensations, and emotions provided Coleman with a cathartic release in the subsequent period of rehabilitation and recovery. Further, as she describes in the context of her narrative and its heroine, writing can also deliver immediate relief to the female subject during the most unbearable moments of psychic trauma.

The distinguishing marks of honesty, interiority, and intensity of personal experience within Coleman's *The Shutter of Snow* have worked to identify the text as broadly autobiographical in its scope, if not in its experimental style. It is important to note, therefore, that Coleman established a self-imposed distance from her work once it had been accepted for publication; she remained determined that the intimate and disturbing nature of the novel's subject matter should be confined to the words on the page, that she should not become the subject of wider speculation or sympathy. In a letter written to her husband just six months before the publication date, Coleman insists that "the . . . thing is not to expect me to talk about my book to anyone. That I simply cannot do, and there is going to be all sorts of trouble if I am expected to."[19] Coleman's disavowal of the public status now afforded to her once-private experience goes some way to suggesting that the writing process took precedence over the product, which to some extent became a foreign object. Rather, the act of writing functioned primarily as a means of gaining a measure of control over an otherwise inassimilable episode in the narrative of her own identity.

This notion of the "writing out" of trauma or internal conflict is the focus of Suzette Henke's important book, *Shattered Subjects: Trauma and Testimony in Women's Life-Writing.* Henke's project is to explore the ideas of prominent trauma theorists and therapists, most notably Cathy Caruth and Judith Herman, and to apply key aspects of their theoretical insights and therapeutic approach to the study of twentieth-century women's writing. Henke's inclusive understanding of life-writing encourages an appreciation of a range of otherwise neglected literary modes; she advocates the effectiveness of the term within feminist literary criticism precisely because it challenges "the traditional limits of autobiography through the use of a category that encompasses memoirs, diaries, letters, and journals, as well as the *Bildungsroman* and other personally inflected fictional texts."[20] Within this "expanded genre," the "flux and discontinuity" of modern female experience can be expressed in a form that resists the imposition of fixed definitions and false certainties.[21] Her study forms part of a wider project of reclamation that has sought to recall the testimonies recorded in women's various "autofictive" narrative practices. However, what is potentially difficult about Henke's overarching argument is the suggestion that autobiography and scriptotherapy are in fact part of the same literary and/or therapeutic category. Henke positions her key terms in her introduction, writing, "What I would like to suggest in *Shattered Subjects* is that autobiography is, or at least has the potential to be, a powerful form of scriptotherapy—and that, as such, it lends itself particularly well to the evolution of twentieth-century women's life-writing."[22] Instead, I would argue from a closer investigation of the theoretical debates surrounding these discrete terms that autobiography and scriptotherapy propose very different solutions to the problem of feminine conflict and psychic trauma, and that in the context of this analysis, *The Shutter of Snow* emerges most powerfully as an example of the scriptotherapeutic project.

Much feminist work on women's autobiography has advanced a theory and practice of "integrated subjectivity" whereby, through autobiographical narrative, the female subject is somehow able to articulate an autonomous selfhood within a wider network of positive attachments and aspirations. In this view, initially overwhelming conflicts between ambition and affection, personal and social expectation are seemingly resolved through the intimate retelling of a coherent identity. It is important to emphasize here that this model of integration is not always to be found at the level of the autobiographical text itself. Rather, the privileging of an integrated subjectivity represents an established mode of reading among critics who are keen to claim these texts for their use in identity politics as much as for their contribution to literary culture. In particular, this has been a strategy employed to considerable effect by feminist critics working in the areas of race, class, and sexuality. In these contexts, the experiences, relationships, and scenes of adversity related in autobiographical terms are read not only as details in an individual life, but as elements in a broader narrative of resistance to established norms and social prejudices. In contrast to this politicized drive toward an autobiography of integration, scriptotherapy is concerned with making explicit the divisions within an internally conflicted identity. As the site at which the feminine subject's conflicts can be fully played or written out, the necessarily fractured narrative works to displace and resist the integration of such disturbances. A compelling feature of Coleman's *The Shutter of Snow* is that despite its primary reputation as an autobiographical text born out of personal anguish, its narrative strategies would seem to correspond more closely with the fractured dynamics of scriptotherapy.

Crucially, what has been posited under the banner of "feminist autobiography" is a narrative space modeled on the dynamics of an idealized maternal sphere. Thus, for critics drawing on French feminism and feminist object-relations theory, the pre-Oedipal realm of reciprocal mother-daughter identification functions as a site of enduring protection and reassurance. In *The Reproduction of Mothering*, Nancy Chodorow writes:

> Mothers tend to experience their daughters as more like, and continuous with, themselves. Correspondingly, girls tend to remain part of the dyadic primary mother-child relationship itself. This means that a girl continues to experience herself as involved in issues of merging and separation, and in an attachment characterized by primary identification and the fusion of identification and object choice.[23]

This construction can be seen to enable and to validate not only the previously overlooked category of women's life-writing, but also the increasingly public profile of a complex, fully functional, and wholly articulate female subject. However, this notion of self-determined feminine identity as an effect of an enabling and affectionate maternal dynamic is a model that bears little relation to the traumatized narrative development of Coleman's *The Shutter of Snow*. Here, the female subject's aversion to maternal affiliation structures both the development of the novel and, in terms of her delusional fixation on death and separation, the symptomatic nature of Marthe Gail's mental state. Even after her recovery and rehabilitation from her breakdown, Coleman continued to articulate the extent to which anxiety and guilt defined her experience of being a mother. In particular, it would seem that these feelings resulted from an ongoing resistance toward integrating the equally demanding spheres of motherhood and writing, ambition and affection, within a single and ultimately compromised existence. Despite the painful realities of this feminine conflict, Coleman expresses its persistence most effectively through the darkly witty asides recorded in her writer's diary. In an entry written during a working holiday in Paris during Christmas 1929, for example, Coleman comments lightly on her indignation at being asked to abandon her manuscript to look after another woman's child. She writes, "As sure as black is black and white is white if Dante's wife did not come in and ask me to mind the baby. I said, 'Madam, you perceive that I am writing. This is nothing to you, but it is my life. I have fled a far more attractive child than yours to do this.'"[24] Notwithstanding the wry humor of this remark, what is encoded in Coleman's diary entry and throughout both her public and private writing is an unresolved discomfort with her role as a mother, particularly as this discomfort relates to her guilt as a frequently absent figure in her child's life.

Thus Coleman's response to motherhood has little to do with the comforting, self-affirming and ultimately liberating realm of feminine experience that emerges from Chodorow's depiction of the pre-Oedipal maternal sphere. Rather, it has much more in common with an earlier theory of maternal relations put forward by the pioneering child analyst, Melanie Klein, for whom the psychic origins of selfhood predict a conflicted narrative of motherhood. In her 1928 paper, "Early Stages of the Oedipus Conflict," Klein offers an analysis that recognizes the conflicts, fears, and anxieties that govern the relationship between mother and child. In this seminal study of infantile development, Klein returns to the maternal realm to consider the consequences of castration anxiety for the child's subsequent relationship to the mother. In terms of the effect on the girl child, Klein is particularly interested in her overwhelming violence and hostility toward the mother figure, and attempts to reveal the disturbances that these resentments foster in the maternal dynamic:

> Because of the destructive tendencies once directed by her against the mother's body (or certain organs in it) and against the children in the womb, the girl anticipates retribution in the form of destruction of her own capacity for motherhood or of the organs connected with this function and of her own children. . . . It is this anxiety and sense of guilt which is the chief cause of the repression of feelings of pride and joy in the feminine *role*, which are originally very strong. This repression results in depreciation of the capacity for motherhood, at the outset so highly prized.[25]

This construction of a problematic and, in the context of future motherhood, ultimately disabling relationship is far removed from the affectionate bond imagined by Chodorow and put to the service of feminist autobiographical theory. Rather, Klein's analysis of a female subject attempting to reconcile motherhood with an already conflicted femininity provides an entirely more appropriate framework in which to read Coleman's narrative of maternal trauma. Indeed, Marthe Gail's reaction to her incarceration in *The Shutter of Snow* can itself be seen to chart the development from sadistic outbursts of violence and rage, toward the display of guilt and attempts at reparation; a narrative progression that has much in common with Klein's theoretical model. Marthe's narrative progression from sadistic rage to love, guilt, and reparation functions as a representation of her journey from madness to sanity, and also charts her equally traumatized response to the maternal relationship itself.

Like Marthe Gail's, Coleman's own experience of motherhood revolved around an initially traumatic relationship with her son and only child, John Coleman. In her role as a daughter, however, Coleman had already been forced to confront the pain and confusion of maternal detachment; when the writer was seven years old, her mother was permanently hospitalized for persistent episodes of severe depression, leaving her young daughter in the care of her loving but deeply traumatized father. Thus, it could be suggested that as Coleman/Marthe begins to create a narrative of her illness, her disconnection from her son and his imagined death come to assume the significance of unconscious inevitability. At the moment Marthe is being attacked by fellow inmate Mrs. Kemp, she believes that she has sacrificed the right to save herself because she was not able to sustain the life of her own child:

> Now she would reach down her throat now she would take from Marthe her blood and suck it into a slimy pipe to be delivered elsewhere. I must not stop it now, I must not make a sound, it is my baby, this is for me because my baby is dead and I could not give him sustenance.[26]

Underpinning this psychological inheritance is the author's own recollection of maternal loss which is structured in a similarly disquieting series of remembered images. As Coleman contemplates in the privacy of her diary:

> I do not know why I am so horrified at pictures of embryos. The thought of one of these gives me long shivers. I can think of nothing else that so makes me shudder. It must be collected with some childhood fear. . . . The bottled misfits in

the medical museum in Paris. These affect all people similarly, that is natural, but why should a healthy six-months
child frighten me?[27]

In her diary entry, Coleman attempts a Freudian analysis of her seemingly
irrational fear of the undeveloped fetus as the residue of a repressed childhood memory. However, fixed within the still image of the photograph,
or contained within the glass of the museum exhibit, the embryo also represents the impossibility of successful development in isolation from
the mother. For Coleman, this remembered image gains significance in its
anticipation of a similarly undeveloped and unsustainable maternal attachment. In the context of the novel, Marthe also struggles with the fragmented memory of a maternal bond that has been effectively disallowed. As
the lights on the ward go out, Marthe is left to recall the fact of her breasts
being pumped after the birth of her child: "Posy was tucking her in and
pumping her breasts with the small pump that hurt her breasts. Just a little
bit more. They were taking the baby away."[28] The remembered pain of this
encounter is not just associated with physical discomfort and indignity; for
Marthe, this brutal intervention signals the moment at which the intimate
bond with her baby is broken. This forced separation of mother and child
is revisited later in the novel as Marthe's husband brings her a lock of her
son's hair, but does not allow her contact with the whole child. Even this
small consolation does not remain in Marthe's hands for long, however, as
her husband takes it back to indulge his own observation: "She held the
hairs in her hand and stared upon them, yellow and soft. He took the little
bundle away from her and held it up against the light. Can you see? She
lifted her eyes and looked up to the light and some of the hairs glinted
bright against the dying sun. You see he said, another redhead."[29]

In the disturbed narrative of Marthe's self-construction, motherhood
is ultimately associated with her own childhood memory of absence and loss.
Following the early death of a mother afflicted with mental illness, Marthe
perceives her maternal legacy to be the inevitability of the same fate:

> And she rustled in and out in a carcass of black silk, that was
> her mother and her father would never see her again. Now
> she knew what had happened now she could see. It had been
> this it had been this very thing, and he was to stand it a second
> time. Her mother had rustled in and out of the silk and bars
> and had whispered into her coffin.[30]

In order to spare her father, husband, and child the pain of this second
maternal loss, Marthe is forced to reject the role of motherhood.[31] To

fuse with her mother in an imaginary relationship of mutual identity is for Marthe to accept a predetermined narrative of femininity. The fractured narrative affords the possibility of detachment from the maternal function, a way of writing herself out of an otherwise predictable conclusion.

What is perhaps most fascinating about Coleman's *The Shutter of Snow* is the fact of the writer's dual narrative presence within it. She is at once the patient writing herself out of an acute, specifically pathologized trauma, and the modern woman writer working to articulate a deeply felt psychic and social conflict within the female subject. For the critically informed reader of Coleman's novel, it is this sense of a fluid, formally undefined relationship between author and character that confirms an already unsettling reading experience. As a scriptotherapeutic project, the novel enables Coleman and her fictionalized self to write themselves out of the experience of mental illness, so that neither woman continues to be confined by the traumatic residue of unarticulated memory. It is this same prospect of linguistic release that is imagined by Marthe Gail in the first days of her incarceration: "She threw out her arms and her voice penetrated the bars and drew out their metal marrow."[32] Marthe's decision to remain fully vocal and literate throughout her illness, even as it assumes temporary residence in her delusional imaginings, ensures that she experiences its every development in her own terms. This level of agency would suggest that, as the patient attempts to recall the defining moments of her illness, she is no longer reliant upon the "official" record of the institution, or the guarded recollections of her concerned relatives.

However, even as Marthe's scriptotherapeutic narrative moves in the direction of recovery and restitution, the novel confronts its reader with a final, lingering difficulty. Concerned as it is with the frank articulation of fragmentation and psychic disturbance, scriptotherapy must finally remain resistant to fictions of complete and uncomplicated resolution. As a scriptotherapeutic text, *The Shutter of Snow* makes clear the impossibility of closure in the narrative of Marthe's breakdown, even as she prepares to leave the hospital for the last time. As she stands at the window anticipating the arrival of her husband the next morning, and the long-awaited reunion with her child, Marthe also senses a return of the freezing temperatures that had figured so strongly in the landscape of her illness: "It was the end of March and had turned cold again. And all the thumbs of ice began to whirl in shaking circles, keeping with the wind. I shall have snow on my glassy fingers she said, and a shutter of snow on my grave tonight."[33] Whether this unseasonable chill reflects Marthe's sudden fear at the prospect of going home, or signals the likely recurrence of depression and mental disturbance, as it did for Coleman herself, it is clear that her readers cannot expect an early thaw.

Notes

1. Coleman, letter to John Milton Holmes, January 8, 1924.

2. Coleman, *The Shutter of Snow* (Illinois: Dalkey Archive Press, 1997), 35. An earlier edition of the novel was published by Virago Press in 1981. Unless otherwise stated, all citations to the novel are to the Dalkey Archive Press edition. Throughout the novel, Coleman rejects the use of apostrophes in Marthe's and the other patients' speech. Although Coleman offers little direct commentary on the significance of this decision, its effect for the reader is to increase the immediacy of expression that is central to her communication of Marthe's illness. Identified at the level of grammar, the observations and conversations of the female patients appear unmediated by the expected codes and practices of the language itself. In a letter to her husband following the return of the first set of proofs, Coleman indicates that her treatment of punctuation is important to the self-conscious design of the text, and that this is in turn connected to the novel's ability to speak without restriction: "I am changing nothing, only making punctuation more regular. There still are 'inconsistencies.' The book is honest, it is written with a terrible intensity." Coleman, letter to Loyd Ring Coleman, February 15, 1930.

3. Coleman, *The Shutter of Snow*, 12.

4. Coleman, letter to Loyd Ring Coleman, April 20, 1929.

5. Barnes, letter to Coleman, May 17, 1935.

6. Coleman, letter to John Milton Holmes, September 16, 1929.

7. Ibid.

8. Coleman, *The Shutter of Snow*, 3.

9. Ibid., 4.

10. Ibid., 29.

11. Ibid., 38.

12. Ibid., 55.

13. Coleman, *The Shutter of Snow* (Virago Press edition), 3.

14. Coleman, *The Shutter of Snow* (Dalkey Press edition), 17.

15. Ibid., 26.

16. Ibid., 41–42.

17. Ibid., 90.

18. See Elizabeth Abel, Marianne Hirsch, and Elizabeth Langland, eds., *The Voyage In: Fictions of Female Development* (Hanover: University Press of New England, 1983); Shari Benstock, ed., *The Private Self: Theory and Practice of Women's Autobiographical Writings* (Chapel Hill: University of North Carolina Press, 1988); Bella Brodzki and Celeste Schenck, eds., *Life/Lines: Theorizing Women's Autobiography* (Ithaca: Cornell University Press, 1988); Mary Evans, *Missing Persons: The Impossibility of Auto/Biography* (New York: Routledge, 1999); Estelle Jelinek, ed., *Women's Autobiography: Essays in Criticism* (Bloomington: Indiana University Press, 1980); Laura Marcus, *Auto/biographical Discourses: Theory, Criticism, Practice* (Manchester: Manchester University Press, 1994); Janice Morgan and Colette T. Hall, *Redefining Autobiography in Twentieth-Century Women's Fiction* (New York: Garland Press, 1991); and Sidonie Smith, *Subjectivity, Identity and the Body: Women's Autobiographical Practices in the Twentieth Century* (Bloomington: Indiana University Press, 1993).

19. Coleman, letter to Loyd Ring Coleman, March 24, 1930.

20. Henke, xiii.

21. Ibid.

22. Ibid., xv.

23. Chodorow, *The Reproduction of Mothering*, 166.

24. Coleman, diary entry, December 26, 1929.

25. Klein, "Early Stages of the Oedipus Complex," 210–11.

26. Coleman, *The Shutter of Snow*, 65.

27. Coleman, diary entry, January 21, 1930.

28. Coleman, *The Shutter of Snow*, 16.

29. Ibid., 91.

30. Ibid., 18.

31. One can trace the markers of an incest narrative in Coleman's description of Marthe's relationship with her father. Certainly the moments at which Marthe recalls her childhood are overdetermined in their construction of an untouchable private idyll of father and daughter, in which Marthe is cast retrospectively as wife, mother, and daughter: "Her father must be taken care of first. . . . She would make him smile his whistling smile, he would whistle for her bright in the new morning, whistle the Mill Song and strop his razor. She loved his hands and his cuffs on which he had written the name of every lamb. . . . Her father, with chocolate almonds in the hay" (9). Mary Lynn Broe provides an excellent, biographically informed reading of *The Shutter of Snow* as incest narrative in her essay "My Art Belongs to Daddy: Incest as Exile—The Textual Economics of Hayford Hall," in *Women's Writing in Exile*, edited by Mary Lynn Broe and Angela Ingram (Chapel Hill: University of North Carolina Press, 1989), 41–86.

32. Coleman, *The Shutter of Snow*, 14.

33. Ibid., 124.

Bibliography

Benstock, Shari, ed. *The Private Self: Theory and Practice of Women's Autobiographical Writings*. Chapel Hill: University of North Carolina Press, 1988.

Caruth, Cathy. *Unclaimed Experience: Trauma, Narrative, and History*. Baltimore: Johns Hopkins University Press, 1996.

Chodorow, Nancy. *The Reproduction of Mothering: Psychoanalysis and the Sociology of Gender*. Berkeley: University of California Press, 1978.

Coleman, Emily Holmes. *The Shutter of Snow*. Introduced by Carmen Callil and Mary Siepmann. London: Virago Press, 1981.

———. *The Shutter of Snow*. Normal, IL: Dalkey Archive Press, 1997.

Emily Holmes Coleman Papers. Special Collections. University of Delaware Library, Newark, Delaware.

Henke, Suzette A. *Shattered Subjects: Trauma and Testimony in Women's Life-Writing*. Basingstoke: Macmillan Press, 2000.

Herman, Judith. *Trauma and Recovery*. New York: Basic Books, 1992.

Klein, Melanie. "Early Stages of the Oedipus Complex." In *Contributions to Psycho-Analysis, 1921–1945*, 202–14. London: Hogarth Press, 1948.

———. *Love, Guilt and Reparation and Other Works, 1921–1945*. London: Virago Press, 1991.

Chapter 16

Depressing Books

W. G. Sebald and the Narratives of History

Eluned Summers-Bremner

The enigmatic, hybrid narratives of W. G. Sebald are clearly recognizable as melancholy texts, if not always stories about depression. All four works of blended fact and fiction completed before the author's untimely death in 2001—*The Emigrants, The Rings of Saturn, Vertigo,* and *Austerlitz*—do, in fact, contain depressive incidents or characters, but the narratives' overall subject matter is more open to question. Prevalent in all, however, is a deep concern with history and its meaning, expressed through a muted longing for places and events now past. Each of the books concerns a solitary narrator whose travels, investigations, and encounters with other solitaries and eccentrics constitute the narrative. The narrator, who tends to bear the name and history of Sebald the writer so that we are never quite sure to what extent the two mesh, is often troubled in mood and demeanor, although we are given minimal explanation for this. The books have a circular, accretive structure and one of the most striking things about them is the way they build narrative suspense around a mood of portentous sadness that is without clear cause.

It is this structural aspect of the narratives, rather than their content, that is of most relevance to the experience of depression. For insofar as depression can give rise to narrative—usually belatedly, since writing requires mental alertness, equanimity, energy, the opposite of the depressed frame of mind—such narrative may be seen as an attempt to understand what was, at the time of greatest suffering, inexplicable. One of the most challenging aspects of suffering from depression is the difficulty in finding and making sense of causal explanations. Andrew Solomon's magisterial study indicates that depression is still commonly regarded less seriously than other kinds of illness by the public at large, and sometimes even among medical professionals.[1] And while it is certainly not always the case that to locate a cause is to alleviate mental suffering, a lack of general comprehension *of* the illness exacerbates the lack of meaning inherent in the illness itself, for depression is characterized by a flattening of mood and a diminishment of purpose and meaning.[2] In the relative absence of clear causal explanations medically speaking, then, heredity is given significant purchase, increasingly so in the era of applied genetics. And heredity, however it is understood genetically, is a narrative whose provision of meaning depends on placing a person within a comprehensible history.

Sebald's narratives, by contrast, complicate the relation of history to mental suffering. In both *Vertigo* and *The Rings of Saturn*, Sebald gives us first-person accounts of mental breakdown that are both searingly credible in their rendition of physical compulsion and diminished choices, and strongly, if obliquely, bound to an exploration of the nature of history. Instead of borrowing from history an element that stands for the enigma of the suffering human being—for instance, the relation named heredity— in Sebald the human's enigmatic suffering insists in combination with an obsession with history, so that history itself becomes a symptom or sign of suffering. In *Austerlitz*, the eponymous hero's interest in military and railway architecture centers on that which lies outside "architectural history proper" but which has historically motivated it, such as the railways' housing of "thoughts of . . . leave-taking and the fear of foreign places." In *The Emigrants*, the part-Jewish Paul Bereyter develops a fixation with the railways but only speaks of it "obliquely . . . as one talks of a quaint interest that belongs to the past."[3]

Each man's obsession has a relation to his own history that renders both overdetermined yet expresses a kind of truth. It is Jacques Austerlitz's own forgotten history of having been sent on a *Kindertransport* (rescue-transport of children) from Czechoslovakia to England at the outset of the Second World War, and Paul Bereyter's exile from his native region as a result of the Nuremburg laws, that motivates their respective preoccupations. But while Austerlitz's leave-taking belongs to the past, Paul's railway obsession enacts the future he, unlike many of his fellow Jews, escaped: at the age of seventy-four he lies down in front of a train near his hometown to end his life. Each man's obsession testifies to what historical accounts often exclude: the feelings that congregate in buildings, the yearning for a fate one has narrowly escaped. In this respect, the narratives display a psychoanalytic conception of history, in which history is the name not for the accessibility of the past but for the troubling combination of its inaccessible insistence.

Sebald's narratives signal a past that is not yet done with a subject or a culture. Real, living history is that which continues to inform and undermine lives in the present, and insofar as it continues to do this, it cannot be known directly but must be read through its persistent signs and traces. In both *Vertigo* and *The Rings of Saturn*—as in *The Emigrants* and *Austerlitz*, which contain third-person accounts—Sebald's narrators are shown to suffer to the precise extent that the past becomes both pressingly important to them and unmanageable. Whatever there might be in these narrators' and characters' pasts that is troubling them, it is inseparable from the larger question of how we come to know the past, any past, and to what extent we can measure or manage its impact on the present.

The first section of *Vertigo* sets up what will become familiar Sebaldian themes of war, trauma, and diminished or faulty perception. It is the second section, however, that presents depression as an act of pedestrian and narrative compulsion. It begins thus:

> In October 1980 I travelled from England, where I had then been living for nearly twenty-five years in a country which was almost always under grey skies, to Vienna, hoping that a change of place would help me get over a particularly difficult period of my life. In Vienna, however, I found that the days proved inordinately long, now they were not taken up by my customary routine of writing and gardening tasks, and I literally did not know where to turn.[4]

The narrator sets out to walk each day "without aim or purpose" through Vienna's streets and is astonished to find, at each day's end, that he has been covering exactly the same area. "My traversing of the city," he writes, "thus had very clear bounds, and yet at no point did my incomprehensible behaviour become apparent to me."[5]

This episode is a more extreme version of the state of mind of the narrator in each novel, who sets out to explore something scholastically or geographically not for any external reason but due to a personal motivation whose nature is withheld from the reader. Yet it also seems to be withheld from the narrator, so the experience of reading a Sebald work is akin to a controlled experience of depression in which we participate. Like the narrator, we are on a journey without clear end and without the usual markers of narrative progress: without plot but also without character in the developmental or achievement-oriented sense. We are also without that illusion of psychological depth provided by an articulated relation between character and context, or between outcome and underlying cause. The exact relation of narrator and characters to the places and times they inhabit or pursue is not always clear, either to them or to us, while at the same time they are clearly driven by something to the precise extent that it is not consciously identified, such as Jacques Austerlitz's past displacement and Paul Bereyter's displaced fate.

Nonetheless, the books have a cohesion and sense of purpose that keep them from being entirely depressing. Geoff Dyer notes how "the perpetual uncertainty, the hovering on the edge of infinitely tedious regress . . . generate[s] the peculiar suspense" of Sebald's writing.[6] The effectiveness of Sebald's portentous narrative method, however, also seems to me to derive from his own relation to the history of his homeland, Germany—what in Lacanian terms would be called subjective truth—which he has had to deal with retrospectively and which he has spoken of in a number of interviews.

To Carole Angier, Sebald describes his German education as the experience of encountering an impasse; to James Wood, he remarks on possible reasons. Chief of these is the presence of academic supervisors who had capitulated to the demands of the fascist regime and so were unable to comprehend certain questions, perhaps those that would undermine their own histories and achievements.[7] When Sebald is asked by Angier why he continues to write in German despite having been resident in England since the 1960s, he explains:

> I am attached to that language. And there's a further dimension. . . . If you have grown up in the kind of environment I grew up in, you can't put it aside just like that. In theory I could have had a British passport years ago. But I was born into a particular historical context, and I don't really have an option.[8]

The environment Sebald grew up in was one where matters of grave historical importance were not discussed, and accrued greater significance as a result. He cannot put this history aside, and it continues to haunt him. To Wood he confides: "Still, in England, I'm not at home. I consider myself a guest in that country."[9]

Unlike the explanation of depression in terms of heredity and gene variants, then, which simplifies the relation between individuals and the past from a position apparently outside it, Sebald places himself in his own life story as an instance of historical excess: neither his German nor his English contexts explain his melancholy concerns. As Cormac Gallagher's commentary on Jacques Lacan's eleventh seminar puts it, "it is around what has failed to achieve a representation," or what continues to be incomprehensible, "that your history revolves,"[10] a symptomatic structure played out clearly in *The Rings of Saturn*. There, the narrator begins his story with an account of breakdown that is then linked to similar episodes of loss and trauma in history. Meditation on these lost causes is the result, it emerges, of the narrator's year-long walking tour of Suffolk, a circular, repetitive journeying, and they have continued to circle in the narrator's mind until a central point of incomprehension has been reached.

At the opening of the book the narrator has come to the end of his tour, and, upon being admitted to hospital in Norwich one year after its completion "in a state of almost total immobility," he relates:

> It was then that I began in my thoughts to write these pages. I can remember precisely how, upon being admitted to that room on the eighth floor, I became overwhelmed by the feeling that the Suffolk expanses I had walked the previous summer had now shrunk once and for all to a single, blind, insensate spot. Indeed, all that could be seen of the world from my bed was the colourless patch of sky framed in the window.[11]

The text is accompanied by a picture of a patch of empty sky seen through a grid of wire mesh. The "blind, insensate spot" is an accurate rendition of the narrator's experience at this moment. He is no longer able to imagine history as a narrative stretching backward and forward in time; all has become meaningless or freighted with one single, unknowable meaning, underwritten by intimations of death. But there is a comment on ordinary, nondepressive experience here as well, a comment extended throughout the narrative. To see history as a narrative stretching backward and forward in time both gives priority to the position of the viewer imagining history thus and simultaneously hides his or her contribution. We are always at the center of our own imagination of history while this positioning is the one historical fact we are unable to see. Thus, while it is assumed that the person considering history adds nothing, by the fact of his or her looking, to the scene, this is not quite accurate. What we add to the scene of our imagination of history is what our own history contributes to this scene, for the history one lives is far richer than one's memory or consciousness allows. In the narrator's case his year-long walking tour has brought history's traumas repeatedly, incapacitatingly home. The blind spot of trauma within history that he comes to embody in his depressive breakdown—where an affectively registered reality exceeds narrative progression and imaginative understanding— demonstrates his centrality to his own narrative in a way that historical narratives more commonly suppress.

Sebald shows that the conception of history as a kind of linear narrative in which individuals can be simply inserted relies on a faulty dynamics of vision. Physiologically, the blind spot of the optic nerve within the human eye enables vision to the precise extent that we cannot see everything, including ourselves looking.[12] Something of this realization is conveyed to the reader of *The Rings of Saturn* by the way the narrative, with its absence of psychological explanation of the narrator's state of mind, places us in the reading scene. The photograph accompanying the

statement about the narrator's being "overwhelmed by the feeling" that
the Suffolk expanses, the external region that he had walked in the previous summer, had now shrunk to a "single, blind, insensate spot" inseparable from his crippling mental state, suggests that something to be
seen might lie beyond the frame of the photograph because it has clearly
been shot from a specific viewpoint. However the grid works against this
expectation by multiplying the sky's emptiness and making no conces-
sions to the imaginary priority of the reader as viewer. Narratively speaking, at the outset there is no reliable point of view with which the reader
can identify in order to interpret the tales of destruction that follow,
since the narrator has begun his tale with an account of his overwhelming by these very events. Thus we, too, become aware of inhabiting the
blind center of the narrative from the start.

One of *The Rings of Saturn*'s larger themes is the relation human beings have with nature. It is as though we plunder it in an attempt to make
up for our own humanness or lack of certainty, since humans are the
only species tormented by a consciousness of death. While it is a natural
principle that all things decay and die, nature is also characterized
by continuous renewal. But human beings are severed from nature—
in the sense of nature's being governed by laws that operate seasonally or
instinctually, from which renewal comes—by the irresolvable demands
of language and the culture it represents. As Judith Feher-Gurewich
describes the lack of natural cause that constitutes human being:

> The limited neurological ability to control movements, to
> reflexively avoid pain or seek comfort, and the extraordinary
> ability to be receptive to images and sounds, makes survival
> and adaptation [for the human infant] hardly an obvious
> proposition. Therefore, processes of maturation and social-
> ization cannot restore the biological connection that instinc-
> tively binds the animal to its caretaker and later to its mates.
> The disrupted instinctual life of the human being is therefore
> compensated—in the name of survival and adaptation—by
> the need to create order, whereas for the animal, order was
> created for it.[13]

This need to create order, however, never achieves its aim. And while nature makes sense of death for animals, it does not make it less enigmatic
for us.[14] We are entirely subject to nature in this one crucial respect that
cannot be imagined or fully expressed. It is the trouble wrought in
human beings by the absence within them of a biologically preoperative
nature and relation to death that is revealed by *The Rings of Saturn*. The
decline of the herring population in Lowestoft, of the peoples of the

African Congo colonized and exploited by the Belgians, of the dynasties of China, of the world's forests, all are in some respect the result of humanity, European in this case, endeavoring to extend its powers of life and dominion.

Humanity also imperils itself by this effort, however, for although human ambition and desire exceed our connection with nature, we continue to be dependent on the natural world. And our dependence is greater than we know, since the cycles of environmental and colonial destruction, once set in train, achieve their own momentum, making it increasingly unlikely that their connection with the absence of natural cause in humans will be recognized. With reference to nineteenth-century China, the narrator observes that the "ritualization of imperial power," which began as an attempt to placate the elements, "was at its most elaborate" at the point where "that power itself was . . . almost completely hollowed out."[15] The narrator's later overwhelming by the sensation that the world and its history have become a single blind spot is presaged by his getting lost several times in natural environments that are unnatural or have been altered: once in the man-made maze at Somerleyton Hall in Suffolk, where paradoxically the property's trees are at their "densest and greenest," another time while wandering on a "treeless heath," and another time within a dream made up of several *Rings of Saturn* elements—including a labyrinth that turns out, the narrator is convinced, to be a representation of his brain.[16]

The symptomatic excess of these instances indicates that human activity, conscious or not, demonstrates a structural lack of knowledge regarding power and the human place in nature, for only humans demonstrate power over others so strangely, through protective architectural structures. But this excess also demonstrates the impossibility of seeing things and seeing the field in which one sees them at the same time. Hence we dramatize our lostness retrospectively by making pedestrian tree-puzzles that turn on blindness, the same lostness that is signaled by the narrator's being unable to see the labyrinth in which he has been wandering until it is imaged in his dream.

And yet it is this functional blindness that is the point of connection—although operating negatively, as a specific lack of connection—between humans and nature. The void of causal explanation coming from the natural context, the condition of human life, means that at the heart of human being is a radical absence of meaning that is felt as a suffering, a trauma. How do we distinguish this absence of cause, this challenge to linear narratives, from the traumas of natural destruction? The answer—and on this answer turns much of the difficulty with accepting human responsibility for what we have made of nature—is that we can never be sure of doing so.

There is a related insight here about depression. The imaginary returns of acts of looking and the socially sanctioned competence they uphold depend upon a specific blindness embodied by each subject, normally relegated to the unconscious. The circular, repetitive structure of *The Rings of Saturn* suggests a connection between the cycles of human destruction of nature and the narrator's depressed state of mind—a connection which, within the narrative, is conspicuously lacking. In fact—and I will return to this—it is the reader who makes up for this lack of connection. But in the absence of causal explanation for the narrator's breakdown, the book suggests the possibility that depression may inhere in all acts of responsible looking, that is, looking that brings an awareness that there is no vision without an invisible, spectatorial involvement in each scene.

The price of this awareness in the early twentieth century for Roger Casement, whose story is told in section 5, was a death sentence, as he insisted on making known the effects of slave labor in the Congo (and later supported the Irish resistance to Home Rule), thereby confronting the British government directly with the effects of the blindness of its colonial vision. For the narrator at the close of that century, the sentence appears to be not death, but depression—indeed a twentieth-century illness—a seeming death of meaning that can be caused by the trauma of overwhelming sensations or events. The result of the narrator's growing knowledge of local and international history while walking is an acute overwhelming that shrinks the Suffolk geography and history to a "single . . . insensate spot," granting him a temporary release from feeling. Depression may, in this case, result from an inability to bear the knowledge of the connections that everyone, including the narrator himself, has disavowed in order to assume a competence supported by the imaginary dynamics of vision, the illusion that vision pertains only to what we see. It is perhaps in order to avoid this unsettling implication that we as readers— like the narrator before his breakdown—are compelled onward by our blind narrative positioning at the center of destructive events.

The psychoanalytic term for this aspect of the narrative is the death drive, which indicates the deadly, depressive possibility at the heart of what passes for normality, and is suggested by the narrator when he muses on what he calls "the ghosts of repetition," the sense that everything he experiences he has felt before. "Perhaps there is in this as yet unexplained phenomenon of apparent duplication some kind of anticipation of the end," he wonders, "a sort of disengagement, which, like a gramophone repeatedly playing the same sequence of notes, has less to do with damage to the machine itself than with an irreparable defect in its programme."[17]

This defect also lies at the heart of the western scientific worldview, which, driven by its efforts to improve on nature, is largely unable to take account of death. There is a visually defective instance early in the book where Sebald reproduces two images of Rembrandt's painting *The Anatomy Lesson*, in which, as Mark McCulloh notes, there is a "counterfeit detail . . . : the corpse has two right arms."[18] The narrator asserts that "there was a deliberate intent behind this flaw in the composition": the second right hand, which is being mutilated by the surgeon conducting the autopsy for the benefit of the watching doctors, "signifies the violence that has been done to Aris Kindt. It is with him . . . and not the Guild that gave Rembrandt his commission, that the painter identifies. . . . [H]e alone sees the shadow in the half-open mouth and over the dead man's eyes."[19]

In the painting, none of the men are looking at Kindt's body, instead looking past it at "the open anatomical atlas" that reduces the body to a diagram, "a schematic plan of the human being," and this kind of looking is connected clearly by the narrator with "the undaunted investigative zeal in the new sciences" of the time, 1632.[20] The second right hand, unseen by the scientists who are not looking at the physical body, is the sign, the narrator claims, of the gaze of the painter, as he pinpoints the blind spot of the diagrammatic view. The suggestion is that investigative science carried out on human bodies distorts their meaning, that it is not possible to follow the diagrammatic model while simultaneously acknowledging death: seeing the shadow over the dead man's eyes.

Medical science reappears obliquely later, when the narrator is convinced that his dream image of the labyrinth that depicts his earlier wandering represents a cross-section of his brain. A labyrinth, unlike a maze, is a single uninterrupted circuitous path leading to a center, not a series of dead ends. It is also the term for the membranous structures comprising the organs of hearing and balance that are housed in a similarly shaped bony cavity in the skull.[21] The labyrinth represents both the concealed fragility of the brain and the scientific ideal of following a circuitous path to a single center or definitive claim.

The fact that labyrinths lead their walkers to a single center is another instance of a man-made structure enclosing a blind spot, for one cannot be both at the center of the labyrinth and surveying its pattern from above simultaneously. Labyrinths dramatize this very lack of simultaneity and congruence between a planned, built structure—like the Dutch doctors' anatomical atlas in Rembrandt's painting—and the human experience of not knowing one's place, of being lost. But this is a distinction medical science, which presumes a single center whose operations are the same in all persons, tends to hide.

The rendering of the visual image as congruent with embodied vision in this way involves a blind spot that is reproduced in the scientific literature promising reduction in the global incidence of depression. I will provide two instances. Firstly, it is too seldom noted that humans' placement in nature as beings whose instinctual survival is far from given, and whose mortality is correspondingly more pressing, is erased in the application to human beings of observations made of animals, on which much neuroscientific research depends.[22] Secondly, in representing genes as carriers of information, molecular science posits significantly random cellular activity—something of a blind process, in fact—as predictable outcome, a reduction a number of biologists and science historians contest.[23] While cures developed by means of such understandings may certainly reduce symptoms, they remain powerless over cause; masking rather than attempting to incorporate the human lack of place in nature, the only cause they are able to identify is organic.

Sebald, in contrast, posits the relation of history to human suffering as an impasse that exerts a curious pressure on the human being. While the "rings" of the title refer to planetary cycles (notably those of Saturn, the planet associated with melancholy) and the cycles of history, they can also be read as the circuits of the drive that, Freud found, takes human beings repeatedly back to experiences in the past believed lost. But because human beings are not provided with a clear place in nature, the drive, which represents our liminal status between culture and nature and the need to find meaning, endlessly circuits around an empty place, producing a by-product of repetitive satisfaction that creates its own affective momentum and appears as its own reward.[24]

In *The Rings of Saturn*, the circular nature of the narrator's journeys and of the observations to which we are led about historical progress—that there is a deathly anticipation like a defect in the human program—is inseparable from our own readerly experience of the enjoyments of suspenseful repetition. We hope for an explanation of the narrator's opening state of mind, which we do not receive, but we do receive and participate in an accumulating sadness borne by the finely balanced combination of forward journeying and of continual news of destruction reaching far into the past. This in itself is satisfying; and through our registration of the pattern of repeating reach and losses, our initial question—why does the narrator fall into depression?—falls away.

Our uncertain but structurally compelled reading thus becomes a circling around our own historical lost cause or the singular impasse that gives rise to our subjectivity. For no human being's life can be explained with sole reference to historical conditions but must be lived as a narrative in which a void space is made bearable only by continual readerly interpretation of others and the world. The circular structures of the narrative and their imbrication with real, destructive historical events disable the reader from using history as a backdrop to the experience of reading. Instead history is at the repetitive and enigmatic heart of our reading of Sebald, where there is no way, apart from this experience, for us to see it.

This requirement that the reader support the form of vision made available by the text extends the fragility of the narrator's opening state of mind to that of the reader. Rather than enabling us to separate the narrator's position from our own in order to understand or diagnose it, like a doctor with a picture of the brain, *The Rings of Saturn* requires us to paradoxically inhabit and sustain it. In this way the narrative preserves the impasse of readerly subjectivity ethically in historical terms, for we are each responsible for this enjoyably sad, yet deathly, affect—as for many of the outcomes of history—as we read. If we register *The Rings of Saturn*'s observations together with their mode of address, then there is no outside such as that provided by scientific tricks of vision that might explain the defect in the human program. The defect is at the heart of the circular liminality, or topology, of reading and of the experience of desiring subjectivity itself.[25]

Sebald does not write depressing books, but he does shed light on the process whereby a deadly and depressive experience can be converted to narrative in such a way as to require readerly participation in its terms. Despite his exercising by the deadliness of the past, Sebald demonstrates an attachment to history that is not only deadly, but partakes of another kind of impasse—that of love—whose dynamism psychoanalysis uses to lever the subject away from attachment to his or her suffering. For while Sebald's narrators and characters may be driven by despair, life-threatening depression, or existential crisis, Sebald the author has placed these stories in the larger context of desiring engagement we call literature, where the reader is unavoidably caught up in looking for answers she must support with her compromised reading presence in the text. In the process of not finding these but instead undergoing an experience of unsettling satisfaction, the reader is granted a possible insight into her own normally invisible subjective workings, as well as the depressive or death-related possibility at the heart of all subjectivity and of all responsible thinking about the past.

Notes

1. Solomon, *The Noonday Demon*, 83–85.
2. In medical literature, the aim of which is to indicate clear causes of illness, the diagnostic understanding of depression and its companion anxiety is said to lag behind those of other areas by as much as fifty to sixty years. This is partly because mental suffering occurs in normally encountered situations such as those of loss and external threat; as well, the identification of clear syndromes and diseases is complicated in the case of depression by the high degree of variability between human responses to similar situations and between levels of articulateness. Unlike

physical illness, which may be obvious and for which there exist definitive tests obtaining objectively identifiable results, depressive diagnoses depend upon the sufferer's ability and readiness to speak of his or her symptoms. See Heninger, "Neuroscience, Molecular Medicine, and New Approaches to the Treatment of Depression and Anxiety."

3. *Austerlitz,* 16; *The Emigrants,* 62.

4. *Vertigo,* 33.

5. Ibid., 33–34.

6. Dyer, contribution to "A Symposium on W. G. Sebald."

7. Angier, "Who Is W. G. Sebald?" 29.

8. Ibid., 13.

9. Wood, "An Interview with W. G. Sebald," 29.

10. Gallagher, "Lacan's Summary of Seminar XI," 11.

11. *The Rings of Saturn,* 3–4.

12. Lacan, *The Four Fundamental Concepts of Psycho-Analysis,* 67–78.

13. Feher-Gurewich, "The New Moebius Strip," 153.

14. Death is further overdetermined for the human being because it is "radically unassimilable to the signifier," as Lacan puts it, which is to say language offers it no real further purchase. The full quotation reads: "There is . . . something radically unassimilable to the signifier. It's quite simply the subject's singular existence. Why is he here? Where has he come from? What is he doing here? Why is he going to disappear? The signifier is incapable of providing him with an answer, for the good reason that it places him beyond death. The signifier already considers him dead." *The Seminar of Jacques Lacan,* 179–80.

15. *The Rings of Saturn,* 139–40.

16. Ibid., 38, 171–72, 173.

17. Ibid., 187–88.

18. Ibid., 14–16; McCulloh, *Understanding W. G. Sebald,* 61.

19. *The Rings of Saturn,* 17.

20. Ibid., 12–13.

21. "Labyrinth," *Concise Medical Dictionary; A Dictionary of Biology.*

22. Rogers, *Sexing the Brain,* cited in Feher-Gurewich, "The New Moebius Strip," 149–54; Heninger, 199, 205, 211.

23. Heninger, 196; Kay, *The Molecular Vision of Life,* 1–3, 11, 326–31; Lewontin, "The Dream of the Human Genome"; Haraway, "A Gene Is Not a Thing."

24. Freud, "Beyond the Pleasure Principle"; Ragland, *Essays on the Pleasures of Death,* 84–114; Copjec, *Imagine There's No Woman,* 59–60.

25. Topology is the branch of mathematical science that concerns "the qualitative laws of relations of place." Pont, *La Topologie,* 110, quoted by Charraud in "Topology: The Möbius Strip between Torus and Cross-Cap," 204. Invoked by Lacan late in his teaching career, it was used to problematize the idea that the subject has an inside and an outside "like a bag or sphere. What characterizes the subject for Lacan," as Nathalie Charraud puts it, "is rather that what appears to be its most intimate or radically interior part, is at the same time that which is most radically foreign or exterior to it." Charraud, "Typology," 208.

Bibliography

A Dictionary of Biology, 5th ed. *Oxford Reference Online.* http://www.oxford reference.com/views/BOOK_SEARCH.html?book=t6&subject=s2 (accessed June 30, 2006).

Angier, Carole. "Who Is W. G. Sebald?" *The Jewish Quarterly* 164 (Winter 1996/97): 10–14.

Charraud, Nathalie. "Topology: The Möbius Strip between Torus and Cross-Cap." Translated by Dominique Hecq and Oliver Feltham. In *A Compendium of Lacanian Terms*, edited by Huguette Glowinski, Zita Marks, and Sara Murphy, 204–10. London: Free Association Books, 2001.

Concise Medical Dictionary. Oxford Reference Online. http://www.oxfordreference.com/ views/BOOK_SEARCH.html?book=t60&subject=s14 (accessed June 30, 2006).

Copjec, Joan, ed. *Supposing the Subject.* London: Verso, 1994.

_____. *Imagine There's No Woman: Ethics and Sublimation.* Cambridge, MA: MIT Press, 2002.

Dyer, Geoff. Contribution to "A Symposium on W. G. Sebald." *The Threepenny Review* (Spring 2002). http://www/threepennyreview.com/samples/sebaldsympos_ sp02.html (accessed December 11, 2002).

Feher-Gurewich, Judith. "The New Moebius Strip: Biology Starts in the Other." *Journal of European Psychoanalysis* 14 (Winter/Spring 2002): 147–54.

Freud, Sigmund. "Beyond the Pleasure Principle." In *The Standard Edition of the Complete Psychological Works of Sigmund Freud*, Volume 18, 1–64. Translated and edited by James Strachey. London: Hogarth Press, 1955.

Gallagher, Cormac. "Lacan's Summary of Seminar XI." *The Letter: Lacanian Perspectives on Psychoanalysis* 5 (1995): 1–17.

Haraway, Donna J. "A Gene Is Not a Thing." In *How Like a Leaf: An Interview with Thyrza Nichols Goodeve*, 89–95. New York: Routledge, 2000.

Heninger, George R., M.D. "Neuroscience, Molecular Medicine, and New Approaches to the Treatment of Depression and Anxiety." In *From Neuroscience to Neurology: Neuroscience, Molecular Medicine, and the Therapeutic Transformation of Neurology*, edited by Stephen Waxman, 193–214. Burlington, MA: Elsevier, 2005.

Kay, Lily E. *The Molecular Vision of Life: Caltech, the Rockefeller Foundation, and the Rise of the New Biology.* Oxford: Oxford University Press, 1993.

_____. *Who Wrote the Book of Life? A History of the Genetic Code.* Stanford: Stanford University Press, 2000.

Lacan, Jacques. *The Four Fundamental Concepts of Psycho-Analysis.* 1978. Translated by Alan Sheridan. Edited by Jacques-Alain Miller. London: Vintage, 1998.

_____. *The Seminar of Jacques Lacan, Book III, The Psychoses, 1955–1956.* Translated by Russell Grigg. Edited by Jacques-Alain Miller. New York: Norton, 1993.

Lewontin, R. C. "The Dream of the Human Genome." In *Culture on the Brink: Ideologies of Technology*, edited by Gretchen Bender and Timothy Druckrey, 107–28. Seattle: Bay Press, 1994.

McCulloh, Mark. *Understanding W. G. Sebald.* Columbia: University of South Carolina Press, 2003.

Pont, J.-C. *La Topologie algébrique des origines à Poincaré.* Paris: Presses Universitaires de France, 1974.

Ragland, Ellie. *Essays on the Pleasures of Death from Freud to Lacan.* New York: Routledge, 1995.

Rogers, Lesley. *Sexing the Brain.* New York: Columbia University Press, 2001.

Sebald, W. G. *Austerlitz.* Translated by Anthea Bell. Harmondsworth: Penguin, 2002.

_____. *The Emigrants.* Translated by Michael Hulse. London: Vintage, 2002.

_____. *The Rings of Saturn.* Translated by Michael Hulse. London: Harvill, 1998.

_____. *Vertigo.* Translated by Michael Hulse. London: Harvill, 1999.

Solomon, Andrew. *The Noonday Demon: An Atlas of Depression.* New York: Scribner, 2001.

Wood, James. "An Interview with W. G. Sebald." *Brick* 59 (Spring 1998): 23–29.

Contributors

Debra Beilke is a Professor of English at Concordia University, St. Paul, where she teaches American, African, and Classic literature. She has published numerous essays on Southern literature, including "'The Courage of Her Appetites': The Ambivalent Grotesque in Ellen Glasgow's *Romantic Comedians*" in *Scenes of the Apple: Food and the Female Body in Nineteenth- and Twentieth-Century Women's Writing* (State University of New York Press, 2003).

Kiki Benzon is Assistant Professor of English Literature at the University of Lethbridge, where she is also pursuing a BSc in Neuroscience. Her recent publications include "Thought Orders and Disorders in the Fiction of David Foster Wallace" in *Creativity, Madness and Civilization* (Cambridge Scholars Press, 2007), as well as interviews with authors Mark Z. Danielewski, Alan Lightman, and Michael Moorcock.

Sophie Blanch is a British Academy Postdoctoral Research Fellow in English at the University of Sussex. Her current book project is entitled *"Lively Words": Wit, Women and Writing 1905–39*. Her doctoral thesis explored the relationship between women modernists and feminist revisions of psychoanalysis in the 1920s and 1930s.

Hilary Clark is Professor of English at the University of Saskatchewan. She coedited *Scenes of Shame: Psychoanalysis, Shame, and Writing* (State University of New York Press, 1999), and has chapters on illness narrative in the volumes *Unfitting Stories* (Wilfrid Laurier University Press, 2007) and *Illness in the Academy* (Purdue University Press, 2007).

Mark A. Clark, PhD, is Assistant Professor of English at Saint Louis University, where he teaches courses in Medicine and Literature, Narrative and Health Care, and Nineteenth-Century British Literature, with particular emphases on the dramatic monologue and Victorian poetry. Dr. Clark is also an autobiographical ghostwriter.

Brenda Dyer is a doctoral student in Counseling Psychology at the University of British Columbia. Brenda has published in the areas of cross-cultural composition theory and English language and literature pedagogy. Her current research interests include narrative theory, depression, action theory and agency, and mechanisms of action in mindfulness.

Kimberly Emmons is Assistant Professor of English at Case Western Reserve University. She is the coeditor of *Studies in the History of the English Language II* (Mouton de Gruyter, 2004) and has work in *Composition Studies* and *The Rhetoric of Healthcare* (Hampton Press, 2007). She is currently completing a book on depression discourse.

Suzanne England is Dean and Professor of the School of Social Work at New York University. Her publications focus on the ways that social policy and the organization of health care affect families with ill or disabled members, and include the analysis of literary, biographical, and clinical narratives on illness, disability, and care-giving.

Carol Ganzer, PhD, is on the faculty of the Institute for Clinical Social Work. She is a past president of the Chicago Association for Psychoanalytic Psychology and serves on the editorial board of *Clinical Social Work Journal*. She maintains an independent practice of psychotherapy and consultation in Chicago.

Linda M. McMullen is Professor of Psychology at the University of Saskatchewan. Recent projects include how women account for their decision to stop taking antidepressants. Along with Janet Stoppard, she is editor of *Situating Sadness: Women and Depression in Social Context* (New York University Press, 2003).

Joanne Muzak defended her PhD dissertation, "High Lives/Low Lives: Women's Memoirs of Drug Addiction," in 2007 in the Department of English and Film Studies at the University of Alberta. She is currently a Postdoctoral Fellow in the Community Service-Learning Program at the university, working on a project on the discourses of individual and community health.

Jennifer Radden is Professor and Chair of the Philosophy Department at the University of Massachusetts, Boston. Her published works include *Madness and Reason* (1985), *Divided Minds and Successive Selves: Ethical Issues in Disorders of Identity and Personality* (1996), and as editor, *The Nature of Melancholy: From Aristotle to Kristeva* (2000) and *The Philosophy of Psychiatry: A Companion* (2004).

Andrew Schonebaum is Assistant Professor of English and Chinese at the State University of New York, New Paltz. He is editing *Approaches to Teaching "The Story of the Stone,"* forthcoming from MLA, and finishing a manuscript entitled *Fictional Medicine: Disease, Doctors and the Curative Properties of the Chinese Novel.*

Deborah Staines is a cultural theorist teaching at Monash University. Her principal research areas are genocide and war; textuality and visual media; trauma and cultural memory. She has edited *Interrogating the War on Terror: Interdisciplinary Perspectives* (Cambridge Scholars Publishing, 2007) and *The Chamberlain Case Reader: Nation, Law, Memory* (Australian Scholarly Publishing, 2008).

Eluned Summers-Bremner is Senior Lecturer in English at the University of Auckland, New Zealand. She has published *Insomnia: A Cultural History* (Reaktion Books, 2007) and numerous essays on literary and psychoanalytic topics.

Carol Tosone, PhD, is Associate Professor at New York University School of Social Work and holds the NYU Distinguished Teaching Award and the Postgraduate Memorial Award. She is a Distinguished Scholar in Social Work in the National Academies of Practice in Washington, D.C., and Editor-in-Chief of the *Clinical Social Work Journal.*

Frederick H. White is Associate Professor of Russian at Memorial University, Newfoundland. He is the author of *Memoirs and Madness: Leonid Andreev through the Prism of the Literary Portrait* (2006) and is currently working on a book on Andreev's narratives of mental illness.

Diane R. Wiener, MSW, PhD, is Assistant Professor of Social Work at the State University of New York, Binghamton. She has recently published on antipsychiatric activism and feminism in the *Journal of Public Mental Health* and on medical anthropology in relation to disability studies in *The Review of Disability Studies.*

Index

manic depression narrative, 29–38,
39n38, 195–206, 208n13, 208n17
Manning, Martha, 41, 47–48, 153n3;
Undercurrents, 41, 47–48
Marcus, Laura, 226n18
Markou, Athina, 106n5
Martin, Emily, 10n18
Maruna, Shadd, 64n24
Mattingly, Cheryl, 77n10
Mauthner, N.S., 139n18, 139n22,
139n24
Mays, John Bentley, 11n27
Mazure, C. M., 139n5
McCulloh, Mark, 237
McGhie, Andrew, 26n8
McMullen, Linda M., 7, 127–42,
139n19
Meadowlands (Glück), 88
medical profession, 9, 230; authority
of, 68, 99, 105, 160
medication: benefits of, 34, 36, 43,
46–47; critique of, 237–38; enforced,
32–33; and identity, 20, 83; rejection
of, 32–33, 36, 204; self-medication,
70, 75, 90, 101, 208n13; side-effects,
159; social authority of, 32–33, 83,
99, 160; as turning-point, 46
medications: Celexa, 115–16, 119;
Lithium, 32–33, 35, 149; Prozac, 20,
50, 92, 104, 149, 171–72; Ritalin, 97,
106n1; SSRIs, 175n38; Valium, 90
melancholy: construction of, 67–68;
glamour of, 23, 145; and mourning,
85; novel as medicine for, 8,
179, 181–85, 187–90, 191nn5–7,
192nn10–11; Saturn and, 238; suicidal, 55–57, 70–71, 73; woman's love
as cure for, 72–75. *See also* depression
memoir: of addiction, 7, 97–107;
author versus protagonist in, 58–61;
"boom" in and since 1990s, 1, 101,
107n17, 154n11; celebrity, 146,
154n7; as confession, 55–64; critique
of biomedicine in, 19–20; of depression, 1, 6, 9n5, 41, 45, 47–48, 84, 92,
98, 100; early modern, 16–17, 19;

on internet, 147–53, 154n11; of
madness and recovery, 6, 55–64; of
manic depression, 18, 29–38; of mental illness, 15–27; poetry as, 6, 88; of
postpartum depression, 8, 154n7. *See
also* autobiography; diary; life-writing
mental disorder. *See* disorder; mental
illness; mood disorder
mental health, 146, 148, 173; consumers' movement, 15; discourse of,
7, 145, 149; women's, 128, 135–38
mental illness: and celebrity, 154n7;
as contested term, 9n6, 30, 164n3;
as crime, 32–35, 37; and culture, 3,
33; as divine punishment, 55–64,
76n4; experience of, 9n6, 15–26,
30–31, 38, 58, 62, 67–77, 207n11,
225; as flaw of the self, 34–35; global
burden of, 9n2; and language,
29–38; medical / psychiatric understanding of, 19, 34, 207n11; and
narrative, 3, 5–6, 15–27, 38, 62,
67–77, 171; no such thing as, 33, 37;
problems in communicating, 23–25,
33; and self's relation to symptoms,
15–27; and shame, 62, 147; and
stigma, 9n2, 56, 62, 74–75; understanding at turn of twentieth century, 75, 76n1. *See also* depression;
disorder; manic depression
(bipolar disorder)
Messenger, Chris, 174nn10–11
metaphor: conveying depression as
experience, 83, 93, 100; and gender,
111, 127; and identity, 31–32, 37;
and illness framing, 21–22, 32, 37,
83; and the inexpressible, 88, 151;
resisting patriarchy, 85–87; resisting
psychiatric narrative, 83–84; shaping
depression as construct, 4, 100, 111.
See also myth
metaphors for depression: absence, 89,
102, 105; beast, 49, 90, 92; darkness,
18, 37, 46, 57, 100, 151; descent, 48,
50, 92, 100; dragon, 47–50; emptiness, 71, 92; enemy, 37, 42–44, 50;

metaphors for depression (*continued*),
entrapment, 49, 100, 102, 151;
hell, 46; military metaphors, 4, 37,
43, 90; seasonal metaphors, 89;
similarity to metaphors for addiction, 100
metaphors for recovery: ascent, 46,
48, 50, 92; journey, 47, 92, 116, 223;
light, 46
Michie, Helena, 107n24
Millett, Kate, 5–6, 29–38, 39n38;
The Loony-Bin Trip, 29–38, 39n38
Milton, John, 145
"Mirror Image" (Glück), 88
Mitchell, Margaret, 185
model. *See* framing
Montgomery, Kathryn, 3
mood (affective) disorders, 29–38;
interpreting, 30–31; medical model
of, 31; as represented in fiction,
146, 150, 152; and the self, 29–38
Mood Disorders Society of Canada,
139n5
moods: as always interpreted, 31;
contagiousness of, 204; cultural /
historical context of, 25, 31; and
depression, 22–23, 69–72, 74,
76n3, 98, 104, 112, 115–16, 145–46,
153n1, 229–30; and identity, 22–23,
29. *See also* emotions
Morahan-Martin, J. M., 139nn11–13
More, Now, Again (Wurtzel), 97–100,
102, 105–6
Morgan, Janice, 226n18
Morris, David, 10n18
Morris, John N., 63n10
Morris, Simon, 22
Morrison, Martha, 106nn9–10
"Most Precious Thread, A" (Champ),
21–22
mourning: and depression, 85–92,
159
Mrs. Dalloway (Woolf), 158–59, 161,
163, 164n7
Mudan Ting. See *Peony Pavilion, The*
Muzak, Joanne, 7, 97–109
Mystic River (film), 173

myth: "monomyth" of depression
recovery, 50; of St. Martha and the
Dragon, 47; shaping depression
narrative, 6, 43–50; *The Sopranos* as,
171. *See also* metaphor; metaphors
of depression

narcissism: and depression, 145; and
manic depression, 197, 203, 205;
Western, 171
Narcotics Anonymous, 106n8
narrative: archetypes, 6, 42, 47, 84,
111–12; chaos narrative, 41–43,
51n21; cinematic, 157–58, 161;
collective, 117–18, 122, 146, 149; as
compulsion, 154n11, 231; conversion
narrative, 6, 55–62, 62n3; counter-
narrative, 26n16, 120–21; emplotment, 68, 157, 163n1; endings, 6,
42–43, 45–46, 150, 231; as escape,
153, 225; ethics of, 4, 9, 239; expert,
99, 106, 129–35, 138; and gender,
6–7, 111–122, 123n2, 127–28, 138,
173, 190, 214; and healing, 4, 8–9,
26n16, 93, 179–91; heredity as, 230;
and illness, 3–6, 31, 38, 41, 48, 67–68,
74–75, 100, 120, 150, 214, 225; imperialism, 2, 10n12; and insight, 43–44,
48–49, 159, 163, 205–6, 229, 239;
life as, 2–3, 83, 157, 238; limits of, 4,
8–9; master narratives, 6, 26n16,
41, 83–84, 112; and memory, 117,
123n2, 145, 162–63, 224; networked,
146–50; oral, 3, 41, 44, 48–49, 111,
117–22, 137–38, 180; as peregrination, 157–63; personal, 3–4, 7, 73, 75,
99, 106, 117, 122, 136–38, 146–48,
162, 219–20; quest narrative, 42–44,
47–50; as recon-figuring events, 4, 19,
23, 30, 55–56, 58, 68, 74–75, 87, 93,
145, 214, 216; redemption narrative,
2, 45, 55–62, 99; regeneration
(resurrection) narrative, 41, 43, 47;
restitution narrative, 41–42, 47,
49–50, 225; television, 166, 168–69,
173; and temporality, 8, 157–63,
163n1,164n7; as therapy, 75, 90–92,